MUSIC THROUGH MIDI

MUSIC THROUGH MIDI

USING MIDI TO CREATE YOUR OWN ELECTRONIC MUSIC SYSTEM

MICHAEL BOOM

PUBLISHED BY

Microsoft Press
A Division of Microsoft Corporation
16011 NE 36th Way, Box 97017, Redmond, Washington 98073-9717
Copyright © 1987 by Michael Boom

Library of Congress Cataloging in Publication Data

Boom, Michael.
Music through MIDI.
Includes index.
1. MIDI (Standard). 2. Musical instruments, Electronic.
3. Electronic music. 4. Computer sound processing.
I. Title.
MT723.B66   1987   789.9′9   87-7831
ISBN 1-55615-026-1

Printed and bound in the United States of America

1 2 3 4 5 6 7 8 9   MLML   8 9 0 9 8 7

Distributed to the book trade in the
United States by Harper & Row.

Distributed to the book trade in
Canada by General Publishing Company, Ltd.

Distributed to the book trade outside the
United States and Canada by Penguin Books Ltd.

Penguin Books Ltd., Harmondsworth, Middlesex, England
Penguin Books Australia Ltd., Ringwood, Victoria, Australia
Penguin Books N.Z. Ltd., 182-190 Wairau Road, Auckland 10, New Zealand

British Cataloging in Publication Data available

This book is dedicated to all the musicians I've made music with over the years; they've taught me that music is never found in instruments or notes, but only in the souls of those who play them.

CONTENTS

FOREWORD

MIDI, the Musical Instrument Digital Interface, has revolutionized the world of professional music. Now it's poised to do the same for all the potential musicians in the world—people who would love to actively participate in *making* music instead of merely listening. What makes this magical opportunity possible is the computer, which, when connected to electronic music devices via MIDI, can be anything from a patient teacher to a compositional tool to a high-tech toy. In all these guises, the computer provides a gateway to the fun inherent in the music-making process.

If you already own a computer—anything from a humble Commodore 64 to a brand-new Macintosh II—you already have most of what you need to enjoy music to a greater degree than you ever thought possible, regardless of whether you're an amateur or a professional. But you need more than a computer to make the most of MIDI, and that's where this book comes in.

Unlike MIDI books written for musicians who are already familiar with concepts such as sound synthesis, *Music Through MIDI* is written for those who know little about the technology behind today's music. You'll find background information about sound. You'll learn how music synthesizers (the workhorses behind most MIDI systems) operate and how non-keyboard players (guitarists, drummers, singers, woodwind players, and so forth) can hook up to MIDI. And you'll see some typical computer systems, some examples of "real-world" devices, and of course, an explanation of the MIDI "language" itself.

Is getting involved with MIDI worth the effort? If you like music, my answer would be an unqualified yes. I've watched children who couldn't be expected to hold a cello (much less play it) successfully push buttons on synthesizers and create not only cello sounds, but their own string quartet orchestrations. People whose musical knowledge consisted solely of flipping on the stereo are now hooking up a MIDI interface to the computers they've been using for word processing or spreadsheets, loading in a program, and composing their own tunes. And what if you're starting with zero compositional sense? No problem. Either check out some of the educational and music-training software, or if that seems too much like work, look into MIDI programs with "artificial intelligence" that can come up with a basic melodic framework for you to modify as you want—you can't get much easier than that.

Of course, this isn't to say that your MIDI experiments will put the London Philharmonic out of business. But music need not be the province solely of the virtuoso; the more the merrier, I say. Music should include large amounts of fun as part of the learning process. You don't have to be a race-car driver to enjoy taking your car out for a spin, nor do you have to be a wine expert to appreciate a good Cabernet. So too you don't have to be a virtuoso to enjoy yourself musically. Composing a simple tune yourself can give you more satisfaction than listening to someone else playing something far more sophisticated.

MIDI has helped me save tens of thousands of dollars on album pre-production. MIDI has allowed me to salvage studio sessions and has made it easier to share music with others. But perhaps the most important contribution MIDI has made for me was the least expected: Even though I've been playing professionally for longer than I'd care to think, when MIDI came along, music suddenly became new again.

Craig Anderton
Editor, *Electronic Musician*

ACKNOWLEDGMENTS

The world of MIDI is a large one, and any writer who tries to cover much of its territory needs some guidance along the way. I've been fortunate to receive help from people with a great knowledge of the terrain. Jim Smerdel of Yamaha, Dave Kusek of Passport Designs, and Dave Smith of Sequential Circuits all helped with valuable information about the origins of MIDI, and I'd like to thank them for it. I'd also like to thank the people who helped me line up interviews for the later chapters of this book: Bob Wehrman of Ensoniq, Jeannie Ditter of Passport Designs, and Michael Raskovsky of Bananas At Large all cheerfully pointed me in different directions until I found the right people to interview for each chapter.

The four people whose musical lives are laid open to the public eye in those last four chapters deserve special thanks for allowing me to invade their privacy, ask too many questions about their equipment, and go around pulling at cables and drawing diagrams. Thank you Tim Gorman, Tom Scott, Larry Polansky, and David Ocker.

It would have been impossible to write this book without using more MIDI equipment and software than I could possibly afford to buy. Many companies graciously lent me their products to use while I was writing, and I'd like to thank them for providing high-budget productions for a low-budget writer. They are, in no particular order: IVL Technologies, Ltd.; Mark of the Unicorn, Inc.; Ensoniq Corporation; Atari, Inc.; Casio, Inc.; Yamaha International Corporation; RolandCorp US; Blank Software; Dr. T's Music Software; Passport Designs; and Austin Development. I'd also like to thank Computers and Music in Daly City, and Leo's Audio in Oakland, two MIDI-knowledgeable stores that let me play with equipment, ask questions, and run off with armloads of brochures.

Turning a manuscript into a finished book is no easy task. I've been very fortunate to work with the talented staff of Microsoft Press, who made the job much easier. I'd like to thank them all, especially my ever-patient editor, Eric Stroo. And finally, I'd like to thank Lynn Morton, who had the really tough job of dealing with me while I worked on this book. Thanks, honey, this is the last book I'll write. You can depend on it, just like last time.

INTRODUCTION TO MIDI

MIDI seems to be on everyone's tongue these days, an unusual position for a technical computer acronym. The difference between MIDI and its fellow acronyms is that MIDI seems to be making the rounds of guitar players, music teachers, keyboard ticklers, and many other people who could care less about the details of computer bit twiddling and who quite frankly hope they never have to find out.

What draws people to MIDI's world of synthesizers, sequencers, sound samplers, speakers, and synchronization signals (not to mention cables, computers, controllers, clocks, cords, and chords) is the chance to sound good while making music on electronic instruments and to have a lot of fun doing it. MIDI lets you build your own electronic music system using components together that had no practical means of communicating prior to MIDI. A good MIDI system significantly expands both sound possibilities and playing capabilities. Using a computer in a MIDI system, non-players (or timid players) can uncork flashy passages that even the most nimble-fingered performers can't duplicate.

Although the promise of MIDI is alluring, its realization can be frustrating if you don't know what you're doing. Ideally, building a system of MIDI components should be as simple as putting together a stereo system using separate audio components; you make the right cable connections, plug everything into the right power source, and away you go. Unfortunately, MIDI doesn't always work that way. The MIDI components in a system have to "talk" to each other, and if you don't know how to accommodate them, the only talking that will take place will be you mumbling to yourself in frustration.

This book will help you understand and use MIDI. It covers all aspects of MIDI, from fundamental facts to advanced uses. If you're a rank beginner and have never pressed a key on a synthesizer or put on a disk in a computer's disk drive, *Music Through MIDI* explains the fundamentals of electronic music and shows you some typical electronic musical instruments. It shows you how these instruments work together in a system and how MIDI works to control and synchronize. A special section on MIDI and computers shows you how to control MIDI components with a computer and introduces software to run your computer. With the information in these pages, you'll be able to put together and use your own MIDI system. If you're a jaded synthesizer or computer techie, you'll also find quite a bit that's of interest: a full explanation of the way MIDI sends data back and forth between components, with a bit-by-bit and byte-by-byte look at channels and messages, and a pin-by-pin description of MIDI connection requirements. You'll also appreciate Appendix A, which provides a complete description of all the MIDI messages and their formats.

Many people take an interest in MIDI for reasons that are quite specific. A music instructor, for example, might want to use it to teach Bach études; a composer might want to use it to hear a complex passage for the first time. Chapters at the end of the book cover four special uses of MIDI: live performance, studio recording, music education, and home hobby use. These chapters feature interviews with prominent MIDI users who explain how they get the results they do. The chapters also provide full diagrams of the MIDI systems they use to get those results. You'll find tips and hints here that will help you customize your own MIDI system to do the job you want it to do.

HOW TO USE THIS BOOK

This book starts with fundamental facts and progresses to more advanced topics. If you're a MIDI novice, start at the beginning and work toward the end. If you already know something about synthesizers and MIDI, you might want to skip early chapters and go straight to more advanced topics. The following chapter descriptions give you an idea of what each chapter contains.

Chapter 1 provides a brief explanation of MIDI, including a look at its history and its capabilities. Chapter 2 introduces the basic attributes of sound, which are manipulated to produce music. It includes an overview of the system of musical notation.

Chapter 3 shows you the fundamentals of music and sound synthesis and gives you a look inside a typical synthesizer. It also acquaints you with the different types of synthesizers and synthesizer controllers in use today.

Chapter 4 goes on to explain MIDI connections and shows you how to use MIDI cables to connect synthesizers and other MIDI devices in useful configurations. You should definitely read these chapters if you aren't up on the world of electronic synthesizers.

Chapter 5 peeks into the heart of MIDI; it shows how MIDI carries information from one component to another using special messages and channels. This chapter is essential to understanding how MIDI works.

In Chapter 6, you'll see how a computer in a MIDI system can control all the other MIDI components. It introduces different types of MIDI computer software and tells you what you can expect to do with each type.

Chapters 7 and 8 take the leap from the world of MIDI theory to the MIDI marketplace. They show you the typical MIDI components you can buy today and describe equipment by brand name. In Chapter 8, you'll also read about a sample MIDI system. You'll acquaint yourself with the MIDI components used in the system and see what's involved in making them work together. Get the practical lowdown in these two chapters before you head down to the music or computer store to buy a system.

Chapters 9 through 12 reveal MIDI in actual applications. Chapter 9 covers live performance, using keyboard player Tim Gorman's MIDI system as an example. In Chapter 10, you'll learn about MIDI in the recording studio, the way Tom Scott employs it. Chapter 11 finds MIDI at work in music education, with a detailed look at the Mills College electronic music laboratory. On the practical side, Chapter 12 shows how composer David Ocker, a dedicated home MIDI user, gets the most out of his system, on a limited budget.

At the end of the book are some useful appendices. Appendix A is for people who like to take a screwdriver to new equipment to see what's inside. It introduces the binary number system and the fundamentals of serial communication. The appendix then undertakes a detailed description of the MIDI specifications, with full explanations of status and data bytes, channel flags, and bit specifications of MIDI messages. This appendix is for those readers willing to tackle advanced topics. Beginners and the faint of heart can skip it altogether without ill effect.

Appendix B gives the name, address, and phone number of each manufacturer and publisher mentioned in this book. To help you continue your exploration of MIDI, Appendix C lists books and magazines you can read and MIDI users' groups you can contact. To identify words in the text that might mystify you, a complete glossary appears in the back of the book. Last, but certainly not least, this book has a full index to help you find information pertaining to specific topics.

Reading this book is an excellent way to begin learning about MIDI. Master the concepts and examples here, and you'll soon be at home in the world of synthesizers and computers. Then, you can enjoy making your own *Music Through MIDI!*

1 | MIDI: AN OVERTURE

MIDI is a new phenomenon. It's been around for only a few years, and many people have never heard of it. Others have encountered the word, but they haven't the slightest idea what MIDI does. If you're new to MIDI and want to know what you're getting into before you continue with the rest of this book, this chapter is for you.

The first half of the chapter deals with the first questions people often ask about MIDI: What is MIDI? What does it do? With what kinds of equipment does it work? The answers aren't detailed explanations—you'll find those later in the book—but they'll clear up some of MIDI's mysteries and give you a feel for the subject.

To put MIDI in perspective, the second half of the chapter is a necessarily brief history of MIDI's few short years of existence. You'll see how MIDI was created to fill a need in the electronic music world, and you'll see why MIDI is what it is today. Armed with the facts in this chapter, you can march boldly ahead into the rest of this book.

FIVE FAVORITE QUESTIONS ABOUT MIDI

When you first encounter the word MIDI (which rhymes with *giddy*), you have a right to some bewilderment. The natural response is to ask questions, starting with everyone's favorite...

What Is MIDI?

MIDI is an acronym for "Musical Instrument Digital Interface." MIDI is not a physical object that you can see and touch; it's also not a piece of software that runs a computer. It is a standard that manufacturers of electronic musical instruments have agreed on, a set of specifications that they can use in building their instruments so that instruments of one manufacturer can, without difficulty, communicate musical information with instruments of another manufacturer.

The word "interface" in MIDI is a technical term that refers to a connection between two separate pieces of equipment. An interface has two different aspects: the hardware that actually connects the equipment and the *data format,* the form of the information that travels through the hardware. The hardware portion of the MIDI standard specifies the physical connection between musical instruments. It stipulates that a certain type of socket, called a *MIDI port,* be built into an instrument. It also specifies that a *MIDI cable,* a special kind of cable that can plug into a MIDI port, be used to connect two instruments. You can see in Figure 1-1 what typical MIDI ports and a MIDI cable look like.

Figure 1-1.
MIDI ports with an unattached MIDI cable lying alongside.

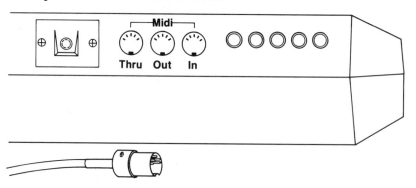

Another part of MIDI's hardware specifications deals with the electronic signals that are sent over the cable: MIDI signals must be sent using a standard voltage at a standard rate. If the voltage or transmission rate of one instrument's signals is different from those of a second instrument, the two instruments will be unable to read each other's signals.

MIDI's data format is digital (as the third word of MIDI indicates). This means that two instruments communicating using the MIDI standard send information (data) as a series of numbers over the connecting MIDI cables. This is the same method that computers use to send and receive data. The MIDI standard specifies that the numbers sent as data be sent in groups called *MIDI messages.* Each MIDI message communicates one *musical event* between machines. These musical events are usually actions that a performer makes while playing a musical instrument—actions such as pressing keys, moving slider controls, setting switches, and adjusting foot pedals.

MIDI uses MIDI messages as a sort of "musical code." Each set of numbers in a message helps define the musical event. For example, one series of numbers in a MIDI message transmits the beginning of a note at a certain pitch and loudness, and a different series transmits the end of a note. By setting up a full musical language of code numbers, MIDI allows all the elements of a musical performance to be transmitted digitally over a MIDI cable from one instrument to another.

If a musical instrument satisfies both parts of the MIDI standard— that is, it has MIDI ports and can send and receive MIDI codes—then the instrument is a *MIDI device,* capable of communicating with other MIDI devices. MIDI devices are available in a wide range of forms, prices, and degrees of usefulness.

What Can Be a MIDI Device?

First, almost any musical instrument can be a MIDI device, either by being manufactured as such or by being altered to fit MIDI specifications. All MIDI devices have one common requirement, though: They must have a *microprocessor,* a small computer chip that can read, send, and react to MIDI messages.

The most common MIDI device made today is a synthesizer. Because almost all synthesizers use a microprocessor internally to control sound generation and to read activity on the synthesizer's keyboard, it's not very difficult for a manufacturer to add MIDI ports and to program the microprocessor to understand MIDI code. Drum machines (instruments that synthesize percussion sounds and play them back using stored rhythms) also use microprocessors and are easy to manufacture as MIDI instruments.

Many electronic musical instruments are normally constructed without microprocessors. One of these is an electric guitar, which often uses electromagnetic pickups directly under the guitar strings to sense string vibrations. Another method employs audio pickups, small microphones located over the guitar strings. The pickups convert the string vibrations to voltages that the guitar then sends directly to an amplifier to make sound on a loudspeaker. These pickups don't need a microprocessor to sense what the string is doing, so there's usually no microprocessor built into an electric guitar. To turn an electric guitar into a MIDI instrument, a manufacturer adds a microprocessor that can read the voltages coming from the pickups and that can send and receive MIDI messages through MIDI ports.

Acoustic instruments present a different challenge. They don't rely on electricity and so can't use microprocessors. To turn an acoustic instrument such as a saxophone, a flute, or even a voice into a MIDI instrument, the player or singer uses a microphone (or similar device) to pick up the notes and send them to a box with a microprocessor. The microprocessor reads the notes and sends corresponding messages over MIDI ports.

Musical instruments aren't the only devices that can speak MIDI. Computers can also be fluent in MIDI. Because all computers have microprocessors (or the not-so-micro equivalent in big computers), all you need to turn a computer into a MIDI device is a MIDI adaptor (a device that adds MIDI ports to the computer) and some software to tell the computer how to send and receive MIDI messages. Although many computers are unable to make sounds and play notes, they can easily send messages to attached synthesizers that play notes for them.

The list of MIDI devices includes equipment you normally wouldn't associate directly with musical instruments. For example, a lighting panel with MIDI ports and a microprocessor can respond to incoming MIDI information by changing light colors and intensities. A simple amplifier can also be a MIDI device if it has a microprocessor to control volume and special effects, such as chorusing and equalization.

What Information Can MIDI Devices Send and Receive?

The most fundamental type of musical event that MIDI can transmit is the presence of a note. For example, when a performer presses a key on a synthesizer, MIDI sends a Note On message. When the performer releases the key, MIDI sends another message, a Note Off message. These MIDI messages can describe the pitch, length, and volume of the notes. Other MIDI messages transmit the nuances of the notes played on the keyboard, such as the amount of *vibrato* the player can add to a note by pressing a key more or less forcefully.

If a performer uses synthesizer controls other than the keyboard— buttons that change the synthesizer's sound, or controls such as foot pedals, modulation wheels, or pitch bend wheels—MIDI sends messages when each button is pressed, each wheel turned, or each pedal adjusted. In the case of a controller that can be turned over a wide range of settings, such as a modulation wheel, MIDI sends a continuous stream of information while the controller is moving to show where and at what speed the controller moves. When the controller stops, MIDI stops sending information about its current setting.

MIDI can also transmit information about prerecorded songs, called *scores,* that MIDI devices can play together in synchronization. To be able to play scores, a MIDI device must be controlled by a *sequencer,* a device that can store and play back a series of notes. Some MIDI devices have built-in sequencers; others are controlled by attached sequencers.

Several different MIDI devices can play together as a combo if each has its own part to a score stored in its sequencer. For example, one device might have the bass line stored in its sequencer, another could have the rhythm line, and still another the lead line. MIDI can start the sequencers at exactly the same time by sending a Start message simultaneously to all of them. To conclude the score, simultaneous MIDI Stop messages can stop all the sequencers at the same spot.

Other MIDI messages control score playback. One kind of message can start a score at any point in the sequence of notes. Another kind can change the tempo of the sequencers, speeding them up and slowing them down simultaneously. If the sequencers can store more than one score in their memories, MIDI can tell them to select a particular score before they start playing.

There are many other miscellaneous pieces of information that the MIDI code can send over the cables. One type of MIDI message asks all the synthesizers to tune to a standard pitch, and another helps one MIDI device check the connection to a second MIDI device.

In addition, MIDI provides *system exclusive* code that enables devices made by the same manufacturer to exchange information. Using this code, a device can send certain information using the manufacturer's own messages to only those devices that need and can use it. For example, you can create a desired sound quality, called a *patch,* on a synthesizer by setting controls and entering numbers. This patch can be stored in the synthesizer, to be called up at a press of a button during performance when you want to use the sound. If you use MIDI to connect two synthesizers made by the same manufacturer, one synthesizer can send the data for a patch to the second synthesizer using system exclusive messages. Other devices connected by means of MIDI won't receive the system exclusive data because it isn't coded for them. As a result, they won't be confused by patch data that they can't use.

How Many MIDI Devices Can Be Connected in a Single System?

In theory, MIDI can connect an infinite number of MIDI devices so that they can communicate with each other. In practice, there are limitations. One of the first is financial: Hooking up seven or eight MIDI devices at $1,000 a pop can rapidly deplete a musician's budget. Another is message capacity: If many MIDI devices connected on one system are sending long messages simultaneously, the messages can overload MIDI's capacity. This is called *MIDI clog,* a condition that can limit the number of devices in a given MIDI system if they're all trying to communicate at once. Among serious MIDI users, a system might have five or six MIDI devices without overtaxing the budget or MIDI's data transmission capacity. Figure 1-2 shows a typical MIDI system.

Figure 1-2.
A typical MIDI system: a computer, a drum machine, and three synthesizers connected using MIDI cables.

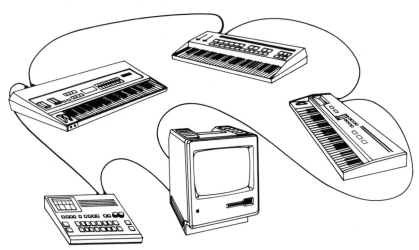

What Can I Do with MIDI?

Perhaps the simplest and most common use of MIDI is to synchronize the notes produced by synthesizers. By connecting one synthesizer to another with MIDI cables, you can play at the keyboard of the first synthesizer and have both the first and second synthesizers play your notes in unison. If the two synthesizers use different yet complementary sounds, they "fatten up" the resulting notes. You can take this to a ridiculous extreme if you want—MIDI makes it possible to gang together 20, 30, or even more synthesizers to play in unison.

If you have more than two synthesizers connected via MIDI, you can use one of the synthesizers as a master keyboard to play any one of the other synthesizers, as shown in Figure 1-3. With a push of a button or two, you can select the attached synthesizer you want to sound as you play the master keyboard. This is very convenient if you're a performer who normally has to jump from keyboard to keyboard to play the synthesizer that has just the right sound. With MIDI, you can stay at one keyboard and play the other synthesizers by "remote control."

Figure 1-3.
A master keyboard
can control many
different devices.

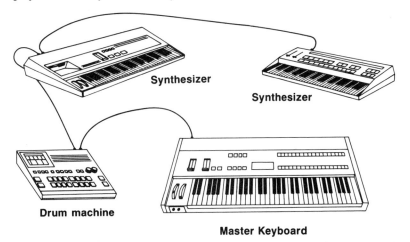

The concept of the master keyboard extends beyond controlling other synthesizers. By adding MIDI-controlled amplifiers, mixing panels, lighting controls, and other accessories, you can turn lights on and off, rearrange the balance between instruments on stage, and change the volume, all by working with buttons at the master keyboard.

Recording and
Editing with MIDI

Adding a computer with some good software to a MIDI system opens up an entirely new range of possibilities. Because the computer can store in its memory all the MIDI messages it receives, you can use it as a MIDI recording device. When you play something on a MIDI instrument, all the notes you play and controls you set are stored by the computer. By playing back all the MIDI messages later and sending them to the synthesizer you played on, the computer can recreate your original performance.

The computer records performance events, such as keystrokes, button pushes, control settings, and the like, instead of actual sounds (as with a tape recorder). As a consequence, it is much easier to edit a MIDI-recorded performance than it is to edit a tape-recorded performance. The computer can display all the MIDI messages it recorded. If you played some wrong notes, you can remove them from the MIDI recording by removing the messages that play them. If your rhythm wasn't quite right, you can change the timing of the messages in the computer to tighten up the rhythm in playback.

Another advantage of using a computer as a MIDI recorder instead of using a tape recorder to record a performance is that you can easily alter the speed of the playback without also changing the pitch of the playback. This is very convenient if you want to record a performance of your own at half speed so that you can play all the notes without mistakes. Then, you can speed up the playback to normal speed. You can also change keys easily in playback. For example, if you record a performance in the key of D major and would rather have it play back in B major, the computer can quickly transpose the playback to the new key.

Computer MIDI-recording can get quite fancy. A good piece of software can turn the computer into a multi-track recording studio, where you can lay down performances in separate tracks—perhaps one track for the bass line, another for a tenor line, a third for an alto line, and a fourth for a soprano line. You can record these tracks one at a time and then have the computer play them back at the same time, so that the recorded result sounds like many musicians performing at once.

If you connect the computer to a number of MIDI devices, it can act as a master controller, much as a master keyboard controls other devices. By recording music on separate tracks in the computer, you can assign a different device to each track. The computer can then play back a song using an orchestra of instruments, each with its own part. Additional tracks can control lighting, mixing, and other effects.

Making Sheet Music

Some computer software can take performances recorded as MIDI messages and turn them into printed music. Although a lot of the variables of musical notation must still be entered by the musician (because a computer can't tell whether you're playing in $3/4$ time or $6/8$ time, for example), the software is able to represent pitches and durations of notes on the staff for further editing. Once the musician touches up the notes in the score, it can be printed on paper. The computer can also print individual parts from the score to be handed out to individual musicians. Chapter 8 spotlights some of the current entries in this exciting arena of software development.

Setting Up Patch Libraries

A computer can store much more information than the simple MIDI messages that are sent during music performance. It can also store the system exclusive messages that MIDI devices use to transmit patch data. By storing this data, the computer can serve as a "patch librarian." A musician can design new and unique sound qualities on the synthesizer, store them as patches in the computer, and then recall them as they are called for. Because a computer usually has a much larger memory for patch storage than a synthesizer (capable of storing thousands of patches instead of 20 or 30), a computer patch library substantially increases the number of patches you can work with on a synthesizer.

Inventing the Future of MIDI

Obviously, the music you can produce using MIDI depends on the equipment available to you. MIDI connections by themselves won't enable you to put on a full rock concert with lighting effects; you need the MIDI devices capable of making the sounds and controlling the effects as you conceive them. With the price of electronic instruments dropping and their capabilities rising, there are constantly new possibilities for great MIDI systems. The only real limitation will be your imaginative use of the devices in the system.

THE ORIGINS OF MIDI

The MIDI standard wasn't handed down on tablets of stone to the musical instrument manufacturers of the world. Nor did MIDI magically appear one day on synthesizers and other equipment. It resulted from the hard work of many people and from agreement and compromise among the world's major musical instrument manufacturers. To understand how MIDI came about, you need to know a little bit about the history of synthesizers and of electronic instruments in general.

A Short History of Synthesizers

Synthesizers have been around almost as long as electronic loudspeakers have existed. The first instruments to create music over loudspeakers, without merely playing back prerecorded sound, appeared as early as 1906. By the 1920s, advances in technology yielded two popular synthesizers, the Theremin and the Ondes Martenot, as well as numerous other experimental instruments. Composers of the time, people such as Edgard Varese, Darius Milhaud, Henry Cowell, and Olivier Messiaen, began to use these instruments in their music. Many film composers, intrigued by the haunting and unearthly quality of synthesized music, used the Theremin and Ondes Martenot in movie scores.

From the thirties to the fifties, synthesizers continued to emerge. Most of them were esoteric instruments occupying rooms in universities or sound studios. Many were experimental devices, developed by companies such as RCA and Bell Labs. For the most part, the instruments were in the hands of classically trained avant-garde composers, teachers, or students at universities or conservatories. The general public was largely ignorant of synthesizers, hearing them only occasionally in a movie score or at a world's fair. In 1968, a young composer named Walter Carlos (now Wendy Carlos) recorded an album that changed all that.

Switched On Bach, an album of Johann Sebastian Bach's music played on a Moog synthesizer, was a tremendous success. S.O.B. (as it was affectionately called) got air time on radio stations around the country and opened the ears of the public to the sounds of a synthesizer. To many, the Moog became synonymous with synthesizers and initiated a flood of interest in the instrument itself. No longer was the synthesizer an avant-garde oddity or a background effect in a movie; it had a voice of its own, and the public wanted to hear more.

By the early seventies, synthesizers had made their way into rock bands. Keyboard players sat in front of banks of switches and jacks, all wired together with tangles of patch cables intertwined like black spaghetti. With rock musicians as potential customers, new manufacturers started to appear, prices began to drop, and synthesizers began their move from college music studios to rehearsal garages throughout the world.

The first commercial synthesizers weren't especially reliable. The internal electronic components were highly susceptible to bumps and changes in temperature. The pitch of the synthesizer was usually unstable and hard to control; as the instrument warmed up, it would change its tuning unpredictably. When microchips appeared in the late seventies, synthesizers (and their users!) were ready for them.

By substituting digital components on microchips for analog circuits, manufacturers made their synthesizers much more reliable and cut costs at the same time. Adding a microprocessor to the synthesizer gave it features not previously possible. The computing power of the microprocessor enabled it to read the keyboard, to control the sound-generating chips, and to help the musician design synthesized sounds without using clumsy cables and switches.

As synthesizers dropped in price to an affordable level, many musicians started to accumulate them. Generally, each synthesizer was a self-contained unit, with its own keyboard, its own control panel, and its own range of sounds. A musician might like the sound of one synthesizer for loud, rocking music, and the sound of another for slow, lyrical music. Still another might have just the right sound quality for a "country" effect. To get all these sounds during a single concert, the keyboard player would cart all the synthesizers on stage and then jump from keyboard to keyboard to create each new sound.

The holy grail for synthesizer players, then and now, is the "fat" sound. For despite the complex appearance of many synthesizers, synthesized sound is inherently simple and somewhat bland when compared to sounds made by an acoustic instrument, such as a guitar or a piano. Musicians used every trick possible to beef up the sound. Some enterprising synthesizer owners found that playing two synthesizers in unison caused their sounds to blend together, creating a fatter sound. And if two synthesizers were good, wouldn't three or four or even more synthesizers be better? Synthesizers were soon stacked in banks to create fat, juicy, layered sounds.

The problem with playing several synthesizers in unison is that a human being doesn't have enough hands to play that many keyboards at once. The obvious solution was to set up one master keyboard that played all the other synthesizers. However, this wasn't a particularly easy solution to implement. Each synthesizer manufacturer had its own keyboard system, so the keyboard on one synthesizer controlled its own sound-generating circuitry just fine, but produced only gibberish when connected to the sound generators of an "alien" synthesizer.

A wealthy keyboard player could find and afford to hire a knowledgeable technician to rewire the keyboard and the other synthesizers to work together. Other keyboard players either learned to be their own technicians or were stuck playing their synthesizers as separate instruments. As more people tried to gang their synthesizers together, the customer service departments of synthesizer manufacturers got many calls asking for technical help. But most of these callers needed information for a second synthesizer that was made by another manufacturer, and they rarely got the help they needed. Tying synthesizers together was a mess.

MIDI Steps In

In 1981, three men working with synthesizer companies—Dave Smith of Sequential Circuits, I. Kakehashi of Roland Corporation, and Tom Oberheim of Oberheim Electronics—met at the June show of the National Association of Music Merchants (NAMM). They discussed the possibility of creating a standard for synthesizer control so that synthesizers from different companies could talk to each other without difficulty. After the show, Dave Smith took time to write a proposal for the standard, called at this time Universal Synthesizer Interface (USI, for short). In November, he made the proposal public at a meeting of the Audio Engineers Society.

By the beginning of 1982, there was enough interest in USI to call a meeting of manufacturers at the January NAMM show. Among the principal companies represented at the meeting were Sequential Circuits, Roland, Oberheim, Yamaha, Korg, and Kawai. Because most of these companies had their own standards for communication between instruments in their product lines, compromises had to be made. Equipment standards specified by USI had to be simpler and less expensive than some of the standards already in use so that USI would work with synthesizers having differing capabilities and would be affordable to implement.

With some of the specifics of USI hammered out, the companies left NAMM to refine the interface further. The original idea for USI had two simple objectives: to allow the keyboard of one synthesizer to play notes using the sound generators of another synthesizer, and to synchronize the playback of equipment that used sequencers. The Japanese synthesizer engineers, in communication with the engineers at Sequential Circuits, took USI a step further and included codes that allowed other controllers such as pitch wheels, foot pedals, and modulation wheels to control remote sound generators.

When the companies met a second time, at the June 1982 NAMM show, the efforts of the different companies were combined, and the result was the framework of what is now MIDI. In time, the term USI was dropped because the word "universal" could conjure up antitrust suits against the group of companies proposing it. The new name that emerged for the standard reflected the wider range of equipment that could use the standard: the Musical Instrument Digital Interface.

With the standard proposed, the companies began to incorporate the necessary equipment and microprocessor programming into their new synthesizers, enabling the new instruments to communicate with other MIDI equipment. By the NAMM show of January 1983, there were enough new synthesizers built with MIDI to put it to the test. In one of the first trials, a Sequential Circuits Prophet 600 synthesizer was connected to a Roland JP-6 synthesizer. To the jubilation of spectators, playing the keyboard of one synthesizer produced notes on the other. MIDI was up and running!

MIDI was not without its problems. Many sections of the MIDI standard were loosely defined and open to interpretation. The different manufacturers often used entirely different internal standards for features such as pitch bend, resulting in confusion for MIDI. Synthesizers could not always talk to each other about everything they could do. To clear up the confusion, the full MIDI specifications were released to the public as MIDI 1.0 in August of 1983. The International MIDI Users' Group (IMUG) was formed to help distribute the specifications to manufacturers and musicians alike and soon evolved into the International MIDI Association (IMA). In Japan, the synthesizer companies formed their own MIDI group, called the JMSC (Japanese MIDI Standard Committee), to solidify the MIDI standard there.

Some discord resulting from the limitations of MIDI led to attempts by parties within the IMA to change the MIDI standard. Some people were unhappy with the slow rate at which MIDI sent data between machines; others didn't care for MIDI's bandwidth (its data-carrying capacity). With these pressures threatening to destroy the MIDI standard or to change it to a point where manufacturers would no longer support it, Jim Smerdel of Yamaha, along with representatives of other synthesizer manufacturers, started the MIDI Manufacturers Association (MMA) to keep MIDI's definition in the hands of the manufacturers. In the fall of 1984, they printed full MIDI specifications with detailed explanations of features to help eliminate confusion.

Together with the JMSC, the MMA now controls the definition of MIDI. If any changes or further definitions of the specifications are to take place, both the JMSC and the MMA must agree to them. Although they recognize the limitations of MIDI, most members also accept the need for compromise if MIDI is to work with all machines. They realize as well that it must remain simple if it is to be inexpensive enough to include on synthesizers and other devices in all price ranges.

Since 1984, MIDI has been stable enough to make its mark on the music industry. The Yamaha DX7, one of the most popular synthesizers ever sold, was also one of the first to include MIDI. As users found out how convenient MIDI was, they began to demand it on other instruments, as well. Manufacturers who didn't initially support MIDI began to include it in their machines when they saw that a failure to include MIDI ports on their instruments was costing them sales. MIDI became a magical marketing buzzword.

Computer users quickly recognized the opportunity that MIDI presented: a digital interface sending data in a form perfect for use with a home computer. And software companies, notably Passport Designs, led the way with MIDI software to control synthesizers from a computer and to help synthesizer owners do things not possible with their own two hands. MIDI also spread beyond the computer industry; as MIDI proliferated, manufacturers of synthesizer accessories began to include MIDI in equipment such as signal processors and amplifiers. More MIDI peripherals are on the way today.

The direct beneficiaries of MIDI are the musicians who use MIDI-equipped musical instruments. They can now build their own music systems, picking and choosing components from the manufacturers that offer the best quality and value. Computer control of musical instruments is extending the possibilities of electronic music in exciting, new directions. In growing numbers, musicians and interested non-musicians are buying equipment, and business is booming for the manufacturers. All this creative activity evolved from a simple agreement to use a communications standard for synthesizers—proof that harmony is not the exclusive property of music itself.

2 | SOUND AND MUSIC

Any MIDI system, no matter how complex it is and how much hardware it uses, has one main purpose: to create sound, an ethereal set of vibrations traveling through the air. To understand what MIDI does, you need to know the language of sound, such terms as pitch and duration, or the terms that fill the pages of synthesizer manuals—timbre, amplitude, and oscillation.

In this chapter, you'll learn how sound is created and how you hear it. You'll also learn the characteristics of sound and how those characteristics are altered to produce different sounds. The chapter even describes the way that a loudspeaker turns an electric signal into sounds you can hear, a critical step in electronic music production.

Sound becomes music when it's set at definite pitches and used in durations that have meaning to us as listeners. In the last part of this chapter, you can read about the way music treats sound, with sections about traditional musical notation. Although you won't learn to be an accomplished sheet-music reader (an attainment which requires far more reading and quite a bit of practice), you will learn enough to understand MIDI messages that describe pitches and that use durations such as quarter notes, half notes, and other traditional note lengths.

THE
FUNDAMENTALS
OF SOUND

Sound is the result of three different agents: a vibrating object, a medium such as air, and your ears. The sound starts with the vibrating object—any object. Some common examples of vibrating objects are gongs, vocal cords, and plucked strings. As an object vibrates forward, it pushes and slightly compresses the air ahead of it. As the object vibrates back, it pulls back and rarefies (creates a slight vacuum in) the air. This vibration is called *oscillation*. As the object continues to oscillate, it creates more compressions and rarefactions of the air. These pressure variations travel away from the object as sound waves, shown in Figure 2-1. They spread through the air much as ripples spread from a rock thrown into a still pond.

Figure 2-1.
In the drawing at left, a vibrating object oscillates out, compressing the air beside it. In the middle drawing, the same object oscillates back in, rarefying the air beside it. The drawing at right shows these compressions and rarefactions as sound waves spreading out from the object.

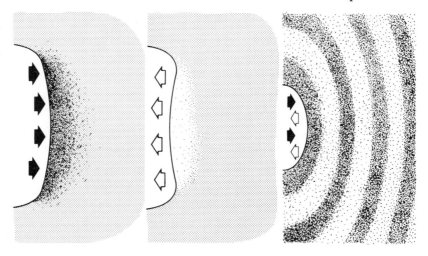

How the Ear Hears
Sound

There are three parts to a human ear that receive sound waves: the outer ear, which you can see sticking out from either side of your head; the middle ear; and the inner ear, tucked deep inside your skull. Figure 2-2 shows these three parts. The flesh and folds of the outer ear gather and concentrate sound waves and pass them on to the middle ear. Here, the sound waves meet the eardrum, a small membrane that transmits vibrations to three small bones (called the hammer, anvil, and stirrup), which amplify the sound waves and pass them on to the cochlea, a part of the inner ear.

The cochlea is a cavity in the bony part of the skull. Coiled like a snail shell, it is filled with a liquid called perilymph and is divided along its coiled length by a very sensitive membrane, the basilar membrane. The amplified vibrations pass from the eardrum to the perilymph and make the basilar membrane vibrate. Nerve endings on the basilar membrane detect the vibrations and transmit these sensations to the brain, which interprets them as sounds.

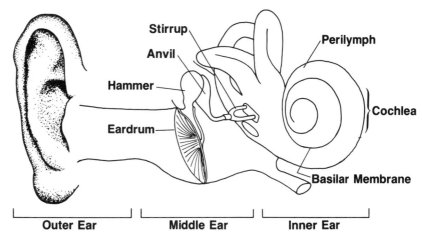

Figure 2-2.
The parts of the ear.

Outer Ear   Middle Ear   Inner Ear

Characteristics of Sound

When your brain analyzes sounds, it discerns four main characteristics of vibration: *frequency, amplitude, timbre,* and *duration.* Using these four characteristics, you can describe any sound you hear or provide the specifications for creating any new sound.

Frequency

Frequency is the speed of vibration. When an object vibrates slowly, it creates a low-frequency sound; when it vibrates rapidly, it creates a high-frequency sound. The frequency of a sound determines its pitch—the higher the frequency, the higher the pitch.

As an example of the role frequency plays in shaping sound, think of plucking the strings on a guitar. The strings are arranged in graduated thicknesses and tuned to different pitches. Because the thicker strings are heavier than the thin strings, they vibrate more slowly and therefore sound lower in pitch than the thin strings.

Frequency is measured in *hertz,* abbreviated Hz, a unit that stands for cycles (vibrations) per second. The average range of human hearing stretches from 20 Hz to 20,000 Hz.

Amplitude

Amplitude is the strength of vibration. When an object vibrates with strong vibrations (that is, it vibrates back and forth over a relatively large distance), it creates a sound of high amplitude. When it vibrates with weaker vibrations (vibrating back and forth over a relatively small distance), it creates a sound of lower amplitude. The amplitude of a sound determines its volume—the higher the amplitude, the louder the sound.

As an example of amplitude, think of the guitar strings in the previous example. If you pluck them hard, they vibrate forcefully, creating a sound of great amplitude. If you pluck them gently, they vibrate so little that you barely see them move, making sounds of low amplitude.

The amplitude of a sound is measured in *decibels.* A decibel is the smallest change in loudness that a human ear can detect. Increasing a sound's amplitude by 10 decibels doubles the loudness of the sound as perceived by the human ear. Human hearing ranges from 1 decibel (the threshold of hearing) to more than 120 decibels (the threshold of pain).

Timbre

Timbre (pronounced tam´ burr) is a little more complicated than frequency and amplitude. It is a mixture of frequencies within a single sound. Most vibrating objects don't vibrate at a single frequency; they vibrate at several frequencies simultaneously. The lowest frequency is called the *fundamental,* and it's the fundamental that you hear as the main frequency, or pitch, of the sound. The higher frequencies are called *overtones*; they blend in with the fundamental frequency to change the tonal quality of the sound.

The timbre of a sound determines its tone color. The more overtones present in the sound, the richer its timbre; the fewer the overtones, the thinner the timbre. Timbre doesn't have a unit of measurement. Through a process called *Fourier analysis,* however, it is possible to analyze the overtones in a sound to see how many are present and how strong each is. Most people don't analyze timbre this way; instead, they use descriptive words such as "rich," "thin," "fat," and "buzzy."

To understand the importance of timbre, consider the difference between a violin and a flute playing exactly the same note. Each instrument produces sounds with an entirely different overtone series; each has a distinct timbre, and the two instruments are not easily confused.

Although Fourier analysis can show the individual overtones of a sound, a more common way to represent the timbre of a sound is to use a waveform. A waveform is a visual record of the air pressure of a sound wave over time, showing the summation of the sound's overtones. By looking at the shape of the cycles in the waveform, you can see differences in timbre. In Figure 2-3, you can see three basic wave shapes: the sine wave, the square wave, and the sawtooth wave. All have the same frequency and thus the same pitch. But the sine wave sounds gentle and smooth, the square wave sounds rich and full, and the sawtooth wave sounds piercing and colorful.

Figure 2-3.
Three waveforms:
a sine wave,
a square wave, and
a sawtooth wave.

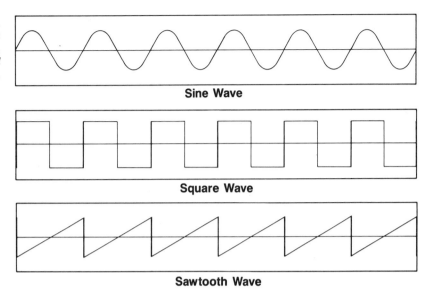

Sine Wave

Square Wave

Sawtooth Wave

Duration

Duration is used to measure the first three sound attributes: frequency, amplitude, and timbre. In its simplest use, duration measures all three together and so measures the length of the entire sound from its inception to its last fadeout. In other cases, duration measures the attributes individually, recording how each one changes over time. For example, a singer can hold a note at one pitch but increase the volume of the note before allowing it to fade. Duration can measure the period over which the amplitude increased and the period over which it decreased. In another example, a trumpet player plays a long note at a constant pitch but sticks a mute in halfway through the note. Duration could be used in this case to measure the length of the initial timbre before it was replaced by the muted timbre. If a saxophone player squeaked at the beginning of a note, duration could measure the time it took the frequency of the squeak to drop back down to the frequency of the final note.

The graph of any of these three sound attributes over time defines the *envelope* of that attribute. Envelopes are very important in describing the quality of a sound. For example, a plucked harp string has a sharp twang that dies away as the note lingers. The amplitude envelope of that note, shown in Figure 2-4 on the next page, reveals that the note jumps immediately to a high amplitude (gets loud fast), then slowly decreases its amplitude over time (gradually gets softer and fades away).

Figure 2-4.
*The amplitude
envelope of a
harp note.*

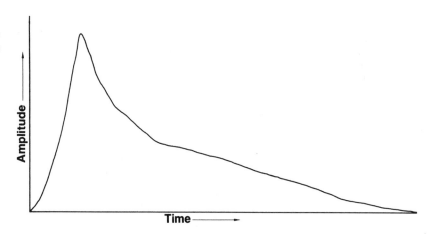

Envelopes tell us a great deal about the sounds we hear. And because any sound is a result of the way its pitch, loudness, and timbre are shaped over time, changing the envelope of any one attribute makes a distinct change in the character of the sound.

PRODUCING ELECTRONIC SOUNDS

To understand how electronic sounds are generated, you need to distinguish two general categories of musical instruments: *acoustic instruments* and *electronic instruments.* Acoustic instruments produce sound by vibrating to create sound waves in the air. Electronic instruments, such as synthesizers, don't create sound directly by vibrating as do acoustic instruments; instead, they create an electric signal, called an *audio signal,* which must be fed to a sound system before it becomes sound. The sound system has two essential parts: an amplifier and a speaker. The amplifier takes the weak audio signal from an electronic instrument, strengthens it, and then sends the "amplified" signal to the speaker. The speaker does the physical work of converting the amplified audio signal into sound waves. In doing so, it has the difficult task of creating a huge variety of sounds—sounds with many different timbres, sounds occurring within a wide range of pitch and loudness.

The Speaker

In Figure 2-5, you see a cutaway drawing of a speaker. The vibrating part of the speaker, the part that produces sound waves, is the *speaker cone.* A speaker cone is a conical piece of stiff paper or plastic mounted in a circular metal frame. The outer edge of the cone is suspended in the frame by very flexible folds of rubber or rubber-like material so that the cone can move in and out easily within the metal frame.

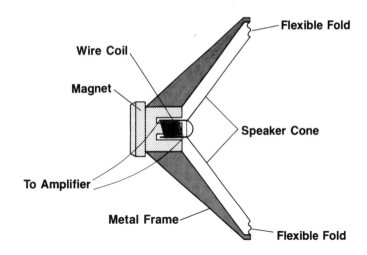

Figure 2-5.
*A cutaway view
of a speaker.*

In a typical speaker, the center of the speaker cone is attached to a coil of wire. The coil is suspended in the magnetic field of a very powerful magnet, which is attached to the rear of the metal frame. Both ends of the coil of wire lead out of the speaker to the amplifier. When the amplifier sends an audio signal through the coil, it creates a magnetic field in the coil that either attracts or repels the field created by the fixed magnet. These forces push the coil forward or backward, moving the speaker cone with it. The direction and amount of the cone movement depend on the strength of the magnetic field created by the audio signal going through the coil. The stronger the field, the more the cone moves.

The audio signal coming from the amplifier changes the strength of the field very quickly, vibrating the speaker cone rapidly enough to create sounds. As the audio signal changes in frequency, amplitude, and tonality, the sound produced by the speaker changes with it. A good speaker cone accurately interprets every minute variation in the audio signal as a nuance in the sound it creates.

Most speakers are considerably more complex than the one in the last figure. For example, in a high-fidelity speaker, there are usually at least three specialized speaker cones. One speaker cone, appropriately called the woofer, produces low sounds. The mid-range speaker cone produces mid-range frequencies, and the tweeter is a specialized speaker cone that produces high pitches. A system of filters, called the *crossover network,* separates the audio signal from the amplifier into three separate frequency ranges, so that the original signal emerges as three signals, one for each speaker cone. The result, if the speaker components are of good quality, is excellent reproduction of all the frequencies in the human hearing range.

MUSICAL CONCEPTS OF SOUND

The principles of sound and electronic sound production reviewed in the preceding sections can be used to describe and produce any sound, from the crash of a dish on the floor to the delicate crooning of a soprano. The art of music confines itself to a small set of these possible sounds, strictly controlling frequency, called *pitch* in music; amplitude, called *dynamics* or sometimes *volume*; timbre; and duration. As musicians over the centuries have used sound, they have arrived at their own set of words to describe their activities and have created a system of written notation to record music so that other musicians can play it.

Although musical terms and notation can vary greatly from culture to culture, Western classical musical notation is the prevalent standard for writing down and describing music. Look at any sheet of music in a music store, and you can see this system of notation in print: five-line staves covered with notes, sprinkled throughout with Italian words. If you don't know how to read sheet music, it looks like a formidable spattering of ink. After a little exposure to its workings, however, you'll find that the notation is really not difficult to decipher. It systematically describes the attributes of sound discussed earlier.

Pitch in Music

The human ear can hear a range of pitches from approximately 20 Hz to 20,000 Hz. As the frequency of a sound increases, you hear the sound going up in pitch, becoming higher or *sharper,* in musical terms. As the frequency of a sound decreases, you hear the sound going down in pitch, referred to as going lower or *flatter.* When the human ear listens to two sounds with different pitches, the difference it detects between the pitches is called an *interval.*

Half-Steps

The smallest standard interval that traditional music uses is called the *half-step.* If the frequency of one pitch is approximately 1.059 times the frequency of a second pitch, the pitches are a half-step apart. The half-step is the smallest interval that we can hear as separate pitches. If two pitches are less than a half-step apart, you are likely to hear one as a slightly sharp version of the other rather than two separate pitches. If you play a black key on a piano keyboard along with the white key just next to it, the two pitches you play will be one half-step apart. (Not surprisingly, two pitches that are two half-steps apart are said to be a *whole step* apart. On a piano keyboard, this is the interval between two white keys separated by a black key.)

Octaves

Another important interval in music is the *octave*. If one pitch is twice the frequency of a second pitch, the two pitches are one octave apart. Because the higher pitch is a simple multiple of the second, two pitches an octave apart seem, to our ear, to have almost the same pitch. For example, if a man and a woman sing the same melody together, they're likely to sing each note an octave apart from each other because women's voices are usually higher than men's. Because the notes in the melody are an octave apart, the two voices blend together and sound as though they're singing the same note.

There are twelve half-steps within an octave. You can see this on a music keyboard, as shown in Figure 2-6. The two keys marked on the keyboard play pitches an octave apart. Between these two keys are 11 intermediate keys. With a half-step between each key, there are 12 half-steps from the bottom pitch of the octave to the top pitch.

Figure 2-6.
The interval of an
octave is marked
on the keyboard.
Within the octave
are 12 half-step
intervals.

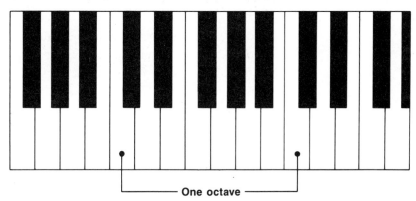

Pitch Names

Standard musical notation gives letter names (shown in Figure 2-7 on the next page) to the pitches in an octave. The first pitch labeled on the keyboard is called A. The next pitch to the right is called A sharp (written A♯). The pitches that follow are, in order, B, C, C♯, D, D♯, E, F, F♯, G, and G♯. Once the pitches reach the end of the octave, they repeat again: A, A♯, B, and so on, because each of these new pitches is exactly an octave above the corresponding pitch in the last octave, and we hear each as a higher version of the same pitch.

Notice that the pitch names coincide with the types of keys on the keyboard. The straight letter names—A, B, C, D, E, F, and G—all fall on the white keys. Pitch names accompanied by a sharp—A♯, C♯, D♯, F♯, and G♯ —all fall on black keys. Any time a sharp is used with a pitch name, it means the pitch is one half-step sharper than the pitch name without the sharp, called a *natural* pitch. This is the case in Figure 2-7: The

Figure 2-7.
*Pitch names for
pitches of keys on a
music keyboard.*

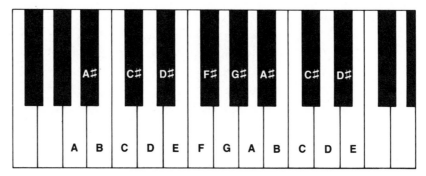

sharp pitches are always one half-step higher than the natural pitches just below them. For example, the pitch F♯ is one half-step higher than the pitch F.

Another symbol, the *flat* symbol, shown as a ♭, means the pitch is one half-step lower than the pitch name without the flat. For example, a G♭ is one half-step flatter than a G. To show that a pitch is neither sharped nor flatted, you can use a third symbol, the natural symbol, marked ♮. As an example, A♮ means the pitch is neither sharped nor flatted a half-step. If a pitch name is spelled (written) without any symbol, the pitch is always assumed to be a natural.

Because sharps and flats let you raise or lower any pitch by a half-step, you can use them to create several different names for the same pitch. For example, the black keys in the last figure were spelled with sharps, but you can also spell these same pitches with flats, as shown in Figure 2-9 on the facing page. Each is a half-step above the white key below it and also a half-step below the white key above it. This gives each pitch two names: A♯ can also be B♭, C♯ can also be D♭, D♯ can also be E♭, and so forth.

These alternate names for the same pitch are called *enharmonic* pitch spellings. The white keys on the keyboard can have enharmonic spellings, too. For example, the C♮ can also be spelled B♯ because the C is one half-step above the B♮. Likewise, the B♮ can also be spelled C♭.

Figure 2-8.
*Octave numbering
on a standard
piano keyboard.*

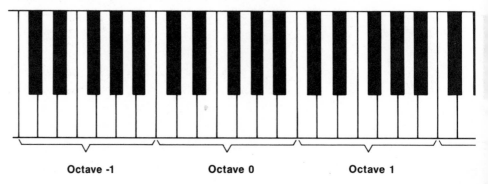

Octave -1   Octave 0   Octave 1

Figure 2-9.
*The pitches on a
keyboard spelled
using flatted pitch
names.*

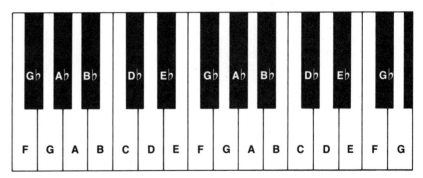

Numbering Octaves

A pitch name by itself can specify a pitch in any octave. If you ask some-one to play an A♭ on a piano keyboard, the result can be any of seven A♭'s. To specify an octave when you spell a pitch, you can number the octaves.

When pitches are split into octave ranges for numbering, the split comes between B♮ and C♮. The pitches ascend from a C♮ at the bottom of the octave to a B♮ at the top. Unfortunately, there is no standard way to number octaves in traditional pitch spelling. Some systems start numbering the lowest octave we can hear at 0; others start at 1.

Many synthesizer manufacturers use an octave-numbering system that starts at -1 for the lowest audible octave and goes up to 9 for the highest audible octave; this book adopts the same system. Figure 2-8 shows you the locations of these octaves within the range of a standard piano key-board. The lowest C♮ on a standard piano keyboard is the first pitch of octave number 0, and the octave below that (only partially represented on a piano keyboard) is octave number -1. The octave that starts on middle C (the C♮ in the middle of a piano keyboard at the frequency 261.63 Hz) is octave number 3, while the highest octave on the keyboard is octave num-ber 6. The octaves can continue all the way to octave number 10, higher than most keyboards go.

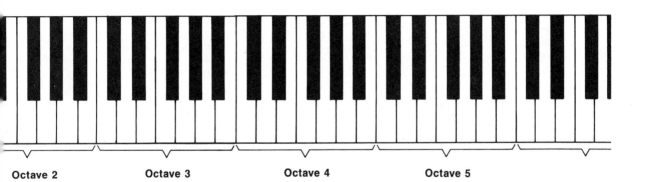

Octave 2   Octave 3   Octave 4   Octave 5

Spelling a pitch within any octave is a simple matter of adding the octave number to the pitch name. For example, if you want to spell the B♭ above middle C, you'd spell B♭₃ to specify the B♭ in octave number 3. To spell the A♮ at the bottom of the piano keyboard, you'd spell A₋₁.

Writing Pitches on a Music Staff

Spelling pitches is handy for talking about one pitch at a time, but if you want to write down a series of pitches, as you would to write a melody, it gets pretty cumbersome. That's why most musicians use a music staff to write pitches.

The most commonly used music staff is the *grand staff,* illustrated in Figure 2-10. It's made up of two five-line staves, one on the top that shows high pitches, and one on the bottom that shows low pitches. The top staff is marked by the *treble clef* to show that it's meant for high pitches, and the bottom staff is marked with a *bass clef* to show that it's meant for low pitches.

Figure 2-10.
The parts of the grand staff.

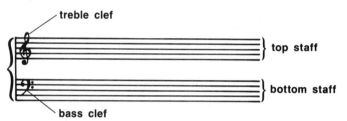

Pitch on the grand staff is shown vertically: The higher a note is placed, the higher the pitch. The spaces and lines of the staff correspond to the white keys of a music keyboard; that is, they're all natural pitches. In Figure 2-11, you see a series of notes on the staff, each spelled to show you where the pitch names fall and where the different octaves are located.

Figure 2-11.
Different pitches located on the grand staff.

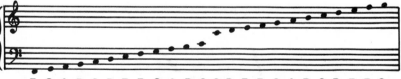

F₁ G₁ A₁ B₁ C₂ D₂ E₂ F₂ G₂ A₂ B₂ C₃ C₃ D₃ E₃ F₃ G₃ A₃ B₃ C₄ D₄ E₄ F₄ G₄

Notice that the middle C (C_3) is located on its own small line. This line is called a *leger line* (pronounced "ledger") and is used to show pitches between or beyond the range of the two five-line staffs in the grand staff. Middle C is the only pitch between the two staffs that needs a leger line, but they are used extensively above the treble staff and below the bass staff. Figure 2-12 shows some examples of leger lines used for different pitches. These lines can be added indefinitely above or below the grand staff to show very high and very low pitches. (Admittedly, leger lines look very confusing beyond the first four or five. It becomes difficult to count them to figure out what pitch you're looking at.)

Figure 2-12.
Leger lines used in the grand staff to denote high and low pitches.

F_0 G_0 A_0 B_0 C_1 D_1 E_1 A_4 B_4 C_5 D_5 E_5 F_5 G_5

Because the lines and spaces of the staff show only natural pitches, you indicate flat and sharp pitches by adding flat and sharp symbols immediately before a note. These added symbols are called *accidentals,* and they apply to all subsequent pitches on the same staff line or space until the appearance of a *bar line,* a vertical bar used to divide music on a staff. Figure 2-13 shows accidentals in use; the ♭ sign on the B at the beginning of the staff makes that B and all the B's that follow become B♭'s. This flat sign applies until the bar line appears, halfway across the staff. At the bar line, all accidentals lose effect. Notice that the B after the bar line is a B♮. To stop the effect of an accidental before a bar line, you can use a natural sign before a note. The natural sign, like other accidentals, remains in effect as far as the bar line.

Figure 2-13.
Using accidentals on a staff.

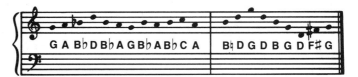

G A B♭ D B♭ A G B♭ A B♭ C A   B♮ D G D B G D F♯ G

Some music uses sharps or flats on certain pitches throughout the entire piece. To avoid writing accidentals throughout the entire score, a *key signature* at the front of the staff shows which pitches are affected. For example, the key signature shown in Figure 2-14 specifies that B's and E's are always played as B♭'s and E♭'s. To specify a B♮ or an E♮ in the music, you can use the natural sign as an accidental.

Figure 2-14.
*The key signature
sets two flats for
the piece of music.
Natural signs
cancel the flats
temporarily.*

B♭ F D B♭ FE♭ D E♭ F D B♭ F   B♭B♭ C D E♮ F G F B♭

Miscellaneous Pitch Notation

Some pitch changes don't fall neatly on the half-steps used in traditional musical notation. For instance, one effect used quite often with synthesizers is called *portamento.* If you play two consecutive notes using *portamento,* you slide the pitch from the first pitch to the second pitch in one smooth slide, like playing a note on a trombone while moving the trombone slide from its farthest extension to its closest position. (Don't confuse *portamento* with *glissando,* an effect that involves playing all the half-steps between two pitches, like running your finger up or down a piano keyboard. A *glissando* hits only half-note pitches, whereas a *portamento* slides through all the frequencies between the half-steps, as well.) To write a *portamento* on a staff, draw a line between two pitches and write the word *portamento* or the abbreviation *port.* above or below the staff, as shown in Figure 2-15.

Figure 2-15.
*A portamento
between two notes
shown on the
grand staff.*

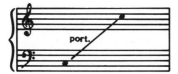

Dynamics in Music

Indicating dynamics on a staff is a simple process compared to denoting pitch. Traditional notation simply describes the volume at which the music should be played using the Italian terms shown in the table that follows.

Italian term:	Literal translation:	Abbreviation:
pianissimo	very soft	*pp*
piano	soft	*p*
mezzo piano	moderately soft	*mp*
mezzo forte	moderately strong	*mf*
forte	strong	*f*
fortissimo	very strong	*ff*

The terms in the table, as their literal translations imply, range from a very low volume (*pianissimo*) to a very high volume (*fortissimo*). When these terms, called *dynamic markings,* appear in printed music above or below the staff, they are usually abbreviated as shown in the table. You can make the range of volume even more extreme if you add extra *f*'s to the *fortissimo* or *p*'s to the *pianissimo,* so that *ppp* is quieter than *pp,* and *pppp* is quieter yet. Each letter you add to the abbreviation adds an "iss" in the full Italian dynamic name. Thus, *pppp* is actually named *pianississississimo.*

Whenever a dynamic marking appears in a musical score, its dynamic lasts until a new dynamic marking appears. A new dynamic takes effect at the position of the first letter in the dynamic marking. For example, if you enter *fff* as a dynamic marking under three notes, the *fortississimo* takes effect at the first note.

Dynamic markings are all relative; they don't specify a given volume in decibels. Instead, they're meant to give a general impression of volume. The performer decides how soft to play a *pp* and how loud to play an *fff.*

Dynamic Markings: **Crescendos** *and* **Diminuendos**

Using dynamic markings in a score creates volume changes in sudden increments: For example, going from an *mp* section of music to an *ff* section results in a sudden increase in loudness. To indicate a gradual increase or decrease in volume, you can use a *crescendo* or a *diminuendo.* A *crescendo* asks for the volume to increase gradually; a *diminuendo* asks for the volume to decrease gradually.

A *crescendo* in a score usually has a dynamic marking at the beginning of the *crescendo* to show the initial volume level, and a louder dynamic marking at the end of the *crescendo* to show the concluding volume level. If the *crescendo* is short, the music might use a *crescendo* sign (shown in the left half of Figure 2-16 on the next page) between the two dynamic markings. If the *crescendo* occurs over a long stretch of music, you might see the abbreviation *cresc.* immediately after the first marking. It denotes a continuous *crescendo* up to the second dynamic marking.

Figure 2-16.
A crescendo
followed by a
diminuendo.

A *diminuendo* (also called a *decrescendo*) looks almost exactly like a *crescendo*: It is written with one dynamic marking at its beginning, and a second, softer dynamic marking at its end. Between the two markings, there is either a *diminuendo* sign or the abbreviation *dim*. The right half of Figure 2-16 shows a *diminuendo* marked with a *diminuendo* sign.

Timbre in Music

There is no formal system for marking changes of timbre in traditional musical notation. The most common way of choosing a particular timbre for music is to specify that it be played by a certain instrument, usually by putting the name of the instrument just above the staff at the beginning of the score. A different instrument name above the staff specifies that a new instrument starts playing at that point, replacing the previous instrument and resulting in a timbre change.

There are also timbre changes that can occur in a section of music for a single instrument. For example, violinists get a different tone color by playing close to the bridge of the instrument than they do by playing near the fingerboard. Instructions in the music written above or below the staff (traditionally in Italian) tell the player to change bow locations, altering the timbre of the notes: The instruction *sul ponticello* specifies that the performer play close to the bridge; *sul tasto* specifies close to the fingerboard. Other performers can change the timbre of their instruments. Brass players, for example, can insert or exchange mutes. Instructions in the score for mute changes can specify different timbres.

Duration in Music

Time, as measured by duration, is arguably the most important element of music. When you dance to music or tap your toe to a beat, you are responding to the music's structure in time. It's no surprise then that a major part of traditional musical notation has to do with capturing time on a sheet of paper as a series of note durations.

To specify different durations, musical notation offers a wide variety of notes that you can write on a staff. The most commonly used notes appear in the chart in Figure 2-17.

Figure 2-17.
The notes commonly used in traditional music.

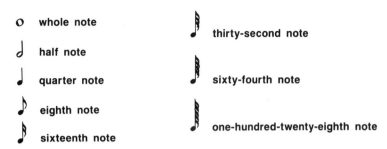

Each note in the chart is exactly half as long as the note that precedes it. For example, the eighth note is half as long as the quarter note, and the sixteenth note is half as long as the eighth note. This relationship determines the relative duration of the notes. For example, a sixteenth note is one fourth as long as the quarter note, which means that you would have to play four sixteenth notes in succession to get the full duration of a quarter note. Figure 2-18 shows a whole note broken into half notes, which are in turn broken into quarter notes, which are broken into eighth notes, and so on. You can see how the lengths of the notes are related to each other.

Figure 2-18.
A whole note is broken down into shorter notes that add up to an equivalent duration.

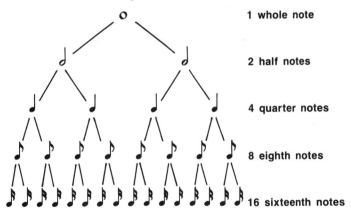

The lengths of these notes are all relative. Their durations depend on the speed at which the musician wants to play them. For example, if a musician holds each quarter note exactly 1 second, then an eighth note will require ¹/₂ second, while a half note will require 2 seconds, and a whole note, 4 seconds. Using the same reasoning, if a musician plays each quarter note for exactly ¹/₂ second, then an eighth note will require ¹/₄ second, a half note will require 1 second, and a whole note, 2 seconds. The speed at which a musician chooses to play music is called the *tempo*.

Rests

Notes aren't the only element of music that uses duration; periods of silence between notes also need duration. Musical notation uses *rests* to denote periods of silence. There is a series of rests that correspond directly to the durations of the notes you learned. Figure 2-19 shows these rests along with their names.

Figure 2-19.
The rests used in
traditional music.

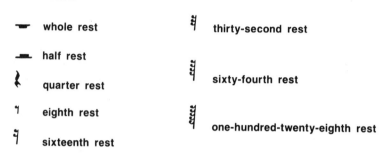

Musical notation allows you to make ever shorter notes by adding more flags to the note or rest. Each flag you add halves the duration of the note or rest. For example, adding a flag to a thirty-second note creates a sixty-fourth note—half the length of the thirty-second note. By adding still another flag, you can create a one-hundred-twenty-eighth note, half as long as the sixty-fourth note. In theory, you can add an infinite number of flags to a note or rest. In practice, it's very rare to see anything shorter than a sixty-fourth note or rest, because the flags become very hard to read after that point and because the relative length of such a note is so small that it becomes almost insignificant.

Ties and Dots

If you're writing a rhythm on paper, you might need to indicate note lengths other than those already mentioned. To do so, you can combine notes of different lengths (all on the same pitch) by using *ties*. A tie is a curved line placed between two notes. To tie more than two notes together, you add ties between the subsequent notes to be connected. A musician who encounters tied notes plays them as one note with the length of all the notes combined. You can see ties used in Figure 2-20.

A very common note length combines the length of one note with another note exactly half as long as the first note. Instead of taking the time to write a second note and tie it to the first, musical notation uses an abbreviation. It simply adds a dot after the first note. Any note written this way is called a *dotted note,* and its duration is exactly half again that of the same note without the dot. Some examples of dotted notes, along with their equivalents in tied notes, appear in Figure 2-20.

Figure 2-20.
*The dotted notes
in the figure are
equal in length to
the tied notes
as shown.*

Triplets

One restriction of standard note lengths, even with dots and ties, is that the length increments are restricted to multiples of two of each other or multiples of one half of each other; it's very hard to write notes that use different length increments. For example, writing a note length that is exactly one third as long as a half note can be a very tricky proposition. Fortunately, there is a simple solution—*triplets.*

To create triplet notes, group three notes of the same value and put a brace over or under them labeled with the number 3. This shortens the length of the notes so that three of them are exactly as long as the next higher note value. For example, two quarter notes are usually as long as one half note. Three quarter notes are as long as one-and-a-half half notes (a dotted half note). But by putting a triplet bracket over three quarter notes, they become equal in length to one half note, so that each triplet quarter note is exactly one third the length of a half note. Figure 2-21 shows triplets that are commonly used.

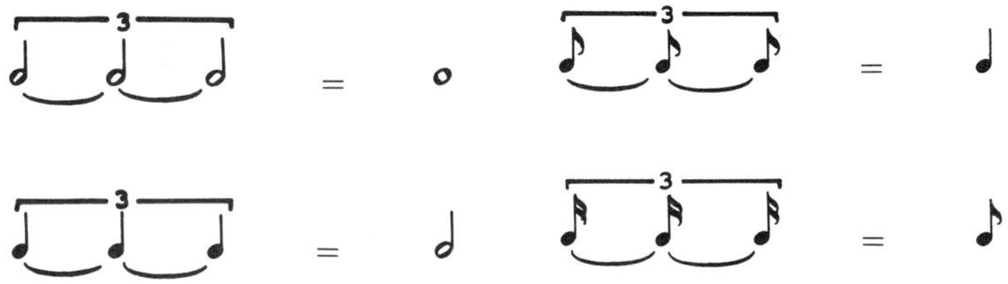

Figure 2-21.
*Different kinds of
triplets.*

Although triplets might seem an esoteric note length, they are, in fact, what gives music a "swing" feel. They take the "corners" off the rhythms and make the music feel more free and easy.

Writing Notes on a Staff

With conventions for writing durations and pitches, you can use notes on a staff to write out music. Every note, except the whole note, has two parts: the *head* and the *stem*. The head of the note is the round part, and it goes on the space or line of the staff that corresponds to the pitch of the note. The stem of the note is the vertical line attached to the head; it can go either up or down, whichever way looks clearer in the score. (The rule of thumb is to point the stem toward the center of whichever five-line staff the note head occupies.)

You write the notes in the order they're to be played, from left to right, exactly as you write sentences. When the staff reaches the end of the page, begin a new staff below it, again writing from left to right. If you want several notes to start at exactly the same time, you write them at the same vertical location on the staff. Figure 2-22 shows a melody written on the staff, with *chords* (the vertical stacks of notes) sprinkled throughout. All the notes in a chord are to be played at exactly the same time.

Figure 2-22.
A melody with chords.

Time Signatures and Measures

Long melodies on a staff become hard to follow as you play them; it's easy to lose your place in a long line of similar-looking notes. To help you keep your place, musical notation breaks the music into small sections called *measures*. A *time signature* at the beginning of the piece tells you how long the measures will be.

The principle behind measures and time signatures is fundamental to music: Most music has a steady beat that lends itself to grouping. For example, a waltz has a steady beat that falls into groups of three. The first beat of the three is stronger than the others and is called the *downbeat*. March music often has beats in groups of two, with a strong downbeat on the first beat. Bar lines on a music staff divide the notes on the staff into regular groups of beats, each group called a measure. Each bar line falls between the last note of one group of beats and the first note (the downbeat) of the next group of beats.

The time signature, two numbers at the beginning of the first staff that look like a fraction, tells you how long the measures are. The upper number in the time signature tells you how many beats there are in a measure. For example, a 3 at the top of the signature means there are three beats per measure, while a 4 in that position means there are four beats per measure. The lower number tells you what note length is equivalent to a beat. For example, a 4 means that each quarter note is a beat, an 8 means each eighth note is a beat, and a 16 means each sixteenth note is a beat.

Together, the two numbers in the time signature determine the length of a measure. For example, a signature of $^3/_2$ means that each measure has three beats and that each half note in the music is the equivalent of a beat. That means that each measure is exactly as long as three half notes. In Figure 2-23, you see a short section of music in $^3/_2$ time. Notice that the notes in each measure total exactly three half notes in duration. The only exception to this rule is the first measure. Because music doesn't always start exactly on the downbeat, the first measure is often a partial measure filled with leading notes.

Figure 2-23.
Music in $^3/_2$ time.

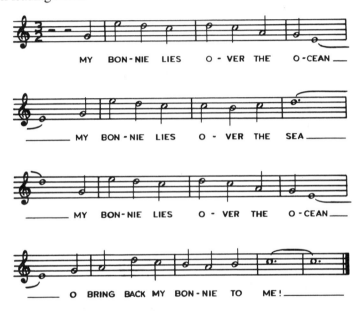

This chapter has introduced the basic elements of sound, electronic sound production, and the musical concepts of sound. By learning the elements of sound and the way music uses and describes them, you've equipped yourself with the conceptual tools you need to create your own sounds and music. In the next chapter, you can read about the physical tools you can use with MIDI to create sound and music: synthesizers.

3 | SYNTHESIZING SOUND

The heart of any MIDI system is the synthesizer, a very powerful and flexible instrument. You can play music at its keyboard, design your own sounds on the control panel, and run the synthesizer from another source using MIDI messages. Because MIDI was originally designed to work with synthesizers, it comes as no surprise that MIDI is structured to exploit the capabilities and features of synthesizers. There are MIDI messages devoted to reading synthesizer keyboard strokes, conveying button pushes on the control panel, and transmitting all types of controller movement. Other MIDI messages pass on important information used by the internal circuitry of the synthesizer for sound generation. To understand how these MIDI messages relay information, you need to understand how a typical synthesizer works and what features it offers.

This chapter is an introduction to the world of the synthesizer. It gives you a quick tour of the parts of the synthesizer, starting with its array of controls, then opening the synthesizer for a look at its interior. It shows you in detail how these parts work: There is a description of the sound generators and the principles of sound synthesis, a discussion of the keyboard and how it works, a look at the control panel, and a survey of auxiliary controls often used with synthesizers. At the end of the chapter, you'll learn about other MIDI devices typically used in MIDI systems.

A TYPICAL SYNTHESIZER

On the surface, a typical synthesizer (shown in Figure 3-1) looks like a simple piano keyboard with a panel full of buttons. It is far more than that. Under its cover, a synthesizer contains chips and circuitry that respond to activity on the keyboard and on the control panel, store information used to create patches, and create the audio signals sent to the loudspeaker.

Figure 3-1.
A typical synthesizer.

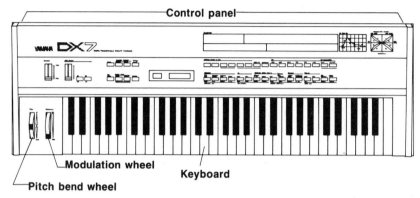

Although they have different features and use different methods to create sound, most synthesizers have these common components:

◆ Sound generators

◆ A microprocessor

◆ A keyboard

◆ A control panel

◆ Auxiliary controllers

◆ Memory

Each of these synthesizer components has its own function and works with the other components to create music.

Sound Generators

The sound generators are the heart of the synthesizer. They do the actual work of synthesizing the sound; the purpose of the rest of the synthesizer is to control the sound generators. Sound generators differ greatly from synthesizer to synthesizer, but their principal purpose is to produce an audio signal that becomes sound when it is fed into a loudspeaker. By varying the voltage oscillation of the audio signal, a sound generator changes the quality of the sound—its pitch, its loudness, and its tone color—to create a wide variety of sounds and notes.

Microprocessor   The microprocessor is the brain of the synthesizer. It looks at the keyboard to see what notes the musician is playing and at the control panel to see what orders the musician wants to give the microprocessor; it gives orders to the sound generators to tell them what notes and sounds to emit; it sends and receives MIDI messages. Altogether, the microprocessor performs thousands of chores, coordinating the actions of all the synthesizer's components with the wishes of the musician playing the synthesizer.

Keyboard   The keyboard is the musician's direct performance control of the synthesizer. Pressing keys on the keyboard tells the microprocessor what notes to play and how long to play them. Some synthesizer keyboards can also tell the microprocessor how loud to play the notes and whether to add *vibrato* or other effects to the notes. Not all synthesizers have keyboards. Those that don't can receive notes from another keyboard or from a sequencer by means of MIDI. The microprocessor passes the information it receives to the sound generators.

Control Panel   The control panel of a synthesizer controls those functions not directly concerned with notes and durations (which are controlled by the keyboard). Some of the controls in the panel are simple and straightforward: a slider that sets the overall volume of the synthesizer, a button that turns the synthesizer on and off. Other controls can be used to design and call up different patches for the sound generators to play, to turn different synthesizer features on and off, or to perform any number of other tasks.

Auxiliary Controllers   Auxiliary controllers are available to give you even more control over the notes you play on the keyboard. Two very common variables on synthesizers are *pitch bend* and *modulation*. Pitch bend controllers can bend pitch up and down, adding *portamento* to notes; modulation controllers can increase or decrease effects such as *vibrato*.

Memory   Memory is an invisible internal component of a synthesizer that the microprocessor uses to store important information. Most synthesizer memory is used to store patches for the sound generators, but it can also store settings on the control panel. Many synthesizers also have a slot in which you can plug *external memory cartridges*. The microprocessor can store information on one of these cartridges, enabling you to use the information at a later time. By using several memory cartridges, you can plug in a different cartridge each time you want a set of new sounds for the synthesizer.

HOW SOUND GENERATORS WORK

To understand how a sound generator works, consider once again the material you read in Chapter 2 about the process by which a loudspeaker converts an audio signal into sound waves. When the loudspeaker receives a positive voltage from the audio signal, it pushes its speaker cone forward; when it receives a negative voltage, it pulls its speaker cone back. Each thrust forward creates pressure in the air, each pull back creates rarefaction, and the rapid alternation between the two positions vibrates the speaker cone, creating sound waves in the air.

The voltage in an audio signal directly controls the motion of the speaker cone and so controls the quality of the sound the speaker creates. If the audio signal has a high frequency (that is, the voltage oscillates rapidly between negative and positive), it vibrates the speaker cone at a high frequency and creates a high-pitched sound. And if the audio signal has a low frequency, it vibrates the speaker cone at a low frequency and creates a low-pitched sound.

The amplitude, timbre, and duration of the audio signal also have a direct effect on the sound the speaker produces. Stronger and weaker audio signals create louder and softer sounds, while audio signals with more overtones create sounds with richer timbres. When an audio signal stops oscillating, the speaker cone stops vibrating, and the sound ceases. In fact, the correlation between the voltage oscillations of an audio signal and the sound it creates is so direct that by describing the audio signal, you describe the sound. The waveform for the voltage of an audio signal should be exactly the same as the waveform for the sound it creates (except for the inevitable distortion that creeps in due to amplification and speaker imperfections).

The job of a sound generator is to manipulate the voltage of an audio signal to synthesize new sounds. It directly controls the frequency, amplitude, timbre, and duration of voltage changes to control those same properties in the sounds it creates. Although there is a wide assortment of sound generators and sound synthesis techniques on the market today, the current approaches to sound synthesis fall into two categories: *analog synthesis* and *digital synthesis*.

Analog Sound Synthesis

Analog synthesis creates sounds by generating an oscillating voltage in an audio signal and then running the signal through different electronic components that enrich, shape, and otherwise modify the original signal to create complex and pleasing sounds. An analog sound generator in a synthesizer is rarely a single electronic component; it's usually a chain of components, controlled by the synthesizer's control panel, that work together to produce the final audio signal that is fed into the loudspeaker.

Controlling Frequency   The source of the audio signal in a typical analog synthesizer is the *voltage-controlled oscillator*, or *VCO* for short. The VCO creates an oscillating voltage by resonating electronically when current is applied to it. The VCO can oscillate through a full range of audible frequencies (20 Hz to 20,000 Hz) and beyond to inaudible frequencies.

A *control voltage* sets the frequency of the VCO. The control voltage is fed into the VCO, but it does not get mixed into the audio signal; its sole purpose is to control the frequency generated in the VCO. As the control voltage gets higher, the frequency (and therefore the pitch) of the VCO gets higher; as the control voltage gets lower, the frequency also gets lower.

The control voltage usually comes from a keyboard. Pressing a high key on the keyboard sends a high control voltage to the VCO to create a high pitch; pressing a low key on the keyboard sends a low control voltage to create a low pitch. The control voltage can also come from a secondary oscillator called a *low-frequency oscillator,* or *LFO.* An LFO usually oscillates at a low frequency, below the range of hearing (less than 20 Hz). This slow oscillation in the control voltage makes the pitch of the VCO rise and fall with the oscillations of the LFO. This is an effective way to add *vibrato* to a synthesized sound.

Controlling Amplitude   The audio signal goes from the VCO to a *voltage-controlled amplifier,* or *VCA* for short, that controls the amplitude of the signal. Like the VCO, the VCA has a control voltage that controls the amplification of the audio signal. If the control voltage is not present, there is no amplification; the sound is turned off. As the control voltage increases, the amplification increases, and the resulting sound gets louder.

The control voltage for the VCA usually comes from the keyboard. Pressing a key sends a full control voltage to the VCA to start a note, and releasing a key drops the control voltage to zero to end the note. The VCA control voltage can also come from another source, such as an LFO, which gives the audio signal a sort of "amplitude *vibrato*"—the sound grows louder and softer with the slow oscillations of the LFO.

Controlling Timbre   The timbre of an audio signal can be set at the source by altering the waveform the VCO uses to produce oscillating voltage. Most VCOs offer a
choice of at least three or four different waveforms. Typically, they include
a sine wave, a square wave, a sawtooth wave, and a notch wave. You can
further alter the timbre by passing the audio signal through *filters* that subtract low or high frequencies from the signal. A *low-pass filter* passes low
frequencies unaltered and filters out high frequencies. A *high-pass filter*
passes high frequencies and filters out low frequencies, and a *band-pass
filter* passes middle frequencies and filters out both low and high frequencies. A *notch filter* passes both low and high frequencies and filters out a
section of middle frequencies. Figure 3-2 shows how these four filters pass
frequencies.

Figure 3-2.
*(a) A low-pass
filter passes low
frequencies. (b) A
high-pass filter
passes high
frequencies. (c) A
band-pass filter
passes a band of
frequencies. (d) A
notch filter passes
both high and low
frequencies.*

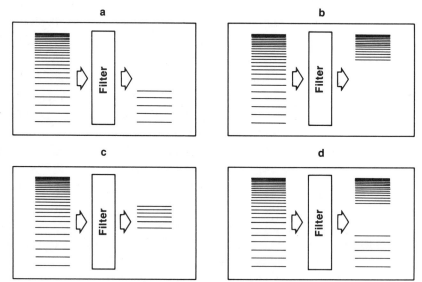

Filters, like amplifiers and oscillators, can be regulated by a control
voltage. The control voltage determines the *cutoff frequency* for the filter,
the level at which a filter starts to filter out sound. Raising the cutoff frequency of a low-pass filter allows more high frequencies to pass through;
lowering it reduces the number of frequencies that pass through. Although
the control voltage for filters can come from a keyboard or an LFO, it usually comes from an envelope generator (described in the next section).

There are other components of an analog synthesizer that affect timbre. Ring modulators and white noise generators can add tone color to the

audio signal as well. Each of these acts in a different way and is usually regulated by a control voltage. The tone color of the audio signal that finally passes through is the result of all these timbre-controlling devices.

Controlling Duration   The simplest type of sound duration—the duration of a note from its beginning to its end—can be controlled easily by connecting the keyboard with a control voltage to the VCA and pressing keys to start and stop notes. To change the duration of individual sound characteristics—pitch, amplitude, and timbre—the synthesizer uses an *envelope generator.*

An envelope generator, referred to as an *EG* for short, is a synthesizer component that creates a control voltage. Unlike a keyboard or an LFO, which usually creates constant or steadily oscillating control voltages, an EG creates a control voltage that can change quite irregularly over the length of a note. As the control voltage from the EG changes, it adds the shape of an envelope to the frequency if it controls a VCO, to the amplitude if it controls a VCA, or to the timbre if it controls the cutoff frequency of a filter or affects other components that alter timbre.

The standard shape of an EG's envelope is described in four stages by the initials ADSR, which stand for attack, decay, sustain, and release (all shown in Figure 3-3). When you press a key to begin a note, the envelope generates a voltage that rises from zero to the "attack" voltage, then drops down to the "decay" voltage, and moves to the "sustain" voltage. As long as you hold the note, the control voltage from the envelope stays at the level of the sustain voltage. When you release the key, the voltage of the envelope drops down to the "release" voltage, which is usually zero.

Figure 3-3.
An envelope shown
using attack,
decay, sustain, and
release stages. The
figures under the
envelope show how
the envelope is tied
to the beginning
and ending of a
note played on a
keyboard.

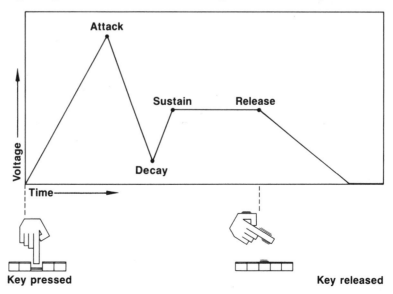

Using the synthesizer's control panel, you can adjust the shape of the envelope. Various controls enable you to determine the levels for the attack, decay, sustain, and release voltages, as well as the rate at which the EG moves from one voltage level to the next. Once the shape of the envelope is set, you can connect the control voltage coming from the EG to any of the other components to create a frequency, amplitude, or timbre envelope. Some synthesizers have more than one EG, allowing you to use different envelopes for different components.

Creating a Patch

Creating a particular sound quality on an analog synthesizer is a matter of setting envelopes, waveforms, filters, and other components. On some older synthesizers you use knobs to set individual components and patch cords to connect the components and pass the signal to the loudspeaker. The sound that is ultimately produced is called a *patch* because of all the patch cords used in its creation. The term is used today even with synthesizers that don't need patch cords between components.

Digital Sound Synthesis

Digital sound synthesis differs from analog sound synthesis in that it doesn't create an audio signal using a chain of electronic components that tickle and tease the signal into the shape you want. Instead, the digital process creates the final audio signal in a single step by constructing voltage waveforms mathematically.

Describing a Sound Digitally

To understand how digital synthesis works, it's important to understand that the final audio signal that enters a loudspeaker can be shown as one waveform. That final waveform can be as simple as a sine wave, or it can be a very complex waveform that is the sum of many different waveforms emanating from different sources. Think, for example, of the audio signal coming from a tape recorder that is playing a Mahler symphony. That audio signal can contain a combination of sounds coming from a hundred different orchestral instruments, yet it is a single signal with a very complex waveform (like the waveform in Figure 3-4) that drives the loudspeaker and enables you to hear the symphony. Your ears and brain interpret the sound from the speaker as the product of a hundred different instruments.

A digital synthesizer uses numbers to create complex waveforms such as the one shown in Figure 3-4. These waveforms are very hard to describe using frequency, amplitude, timbre, and duration because they are

Figure 3-4.
*A very short
section of a
complex waveform.
A waveform like
this can be the sum
of many other
waveforms with
different timbres.*

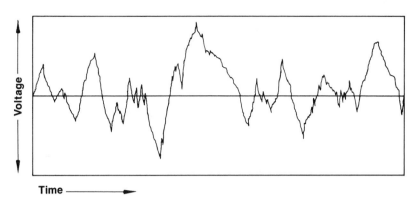

a combination of so many different component waveforms, each with its own attributes. It's easier simply to describe the complex shape of the waveform, showing it as a series of numbers. To see how that's done, consider the following example.

The complex waveform on the left in Figure 3-5 creates a sound typical of a digital synthesizer. The fluctuations of the waveform up and down represent the fluctuations of the voltage in the audio signal (and the resulting vibration of the loudspeaker's speaker cone). The length of the waveform from left to right represents the time that it takes for the voltage fluctuations to occur. If you place the waveform on a graph, as on the right in Figure 3-5, you can read its ups and downs as numbers at regular time intervals, and you can develop a table of these values, as shown below the figure.

Figure 3-5.
*The waveform at
left is positioned on
a graph at right
where it is
segmented into a
sequence of
numerical
readings.*

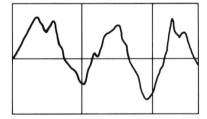 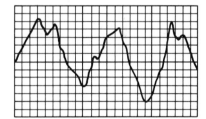

By storing the numbers in the order they occur from left to right, you can create a *waveform table* that describes the waveform in numbers. Reading back the numbers in the waveform table enables you to recreate the waveform, as in Figure 3-6 on the next page. If you make the time intervals

Figure 3-6.
A waveform table
might produce the
graph at left in this
figure. Shortening
the interval lets
you reproduce the
original waveform
more faithfully
(at right).

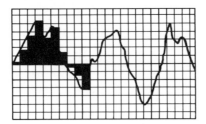 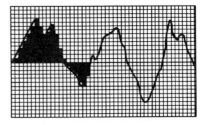

between waveform readings very small, you can so closely reproduce the original waveform that distinguishing the reproduction from the original becomes increasingly difficult.

Digitally Generating an Audio Signal

To synthesize sound, a sound generator in a digital synthesizer calculates the numbers necessary to create a given waveform and sends them to a device called a *digital-to-analog converter*, or *DAC*. The DAC turns the numbers into the fluctuating voltages of an audio signal. To make the audio signal sound convincing, the sound generator must send numbers to the DAC at a very high rate of speed, typically over 40,000 times per second.

Digital sound synthesis is all a matter of mathematics. Complex timbres and envelopes are created using equations either programmed into the synthesizer's memory or built into its integrated circuits. Creating a new patch on the control panel alters the values in the equations. Because many players are already familiar with the concept of analog synthesis, most digital synthesizers are designed to work like analog synthesizers, with controls that set envelopes, change filter cutoff frequencies, change the waveforms of oscillators, and perform other similar functions. In reality, many of the "components" exist only as parts of an equation.

After you create a new patch by setting the controls on the synthesizer's control panel, you can save the values that define the patch in the synthesizer's memory. A digital synthesizer usually has enough memory to store 16, 32, or even more of these patches. Because the digital synthesizer is actually a computer that calculates waveforms, creating a patch is equivalent to programming the synthesizer to create sound. Therefore, patches on digital synthesizers are often called *programs*. In this book, however, such programs are referred to as patches to avoid confusing them with the software used to run a computer in a MIDI system.

Sampling Synthesis   In theory, it is possible to express any sound with the right calculations, but in practice it is quite hard to digitally synthesize sounds as complex as acoustic sounds from traditional instruments. The synthesized result can sound thin when compared to an acoustic performance. An approach to digital synthesis that tries to combat this problem is *sampling synthesis.* A sampling synthesizer doesn't generate waveforms by calculating them. Instead, it records a waveform created by an acoustic source and plays it back at different pitches to create notes.

To record an acoustic waveform, the sampling synthesizer uses a microphone, an *analog-to-digital converter,* and memory. The microphone converts sound waves into an audio signal of fluctuating voltage. The audio signal goes to the analog-to-digital converter, or *ADC*, which turns the signal into a series of numbers (performing the exact opposite function of a DAC). The synthesizer stores these numbers in its memory as a waveform table. This whole process is called *sampling,* and the recording it creates is called a *sampled sound.*

When the sampling synthesizer plays back the waveform table stored in its memory, it can alter the sample to create different sounds and notes. By sending the numbers of the waveform table back to the DAC at a different speed, the synthesizer can change the pitch of the sound it creates. By increasing or reducing the numerical values of the waveform table, it can raise or lower the volume of the sound. By other complex manipulations of the values in the waveform table, the synthesizer can change the envelope of a sampled sound, filter it, or add other effects.

To better understand sampling synthesis, consider an example. You have recorded the sound of a drop of water falling into a bathtub. You have stored the sampled sound in the format of a waveform table in the memory of your synthesizer. The original sound was a C♮. You can play back the sound of the drop at a G♮ above the C by sending the values in the waveform table back to the DAC one-and-a-half times faster than they were recorded. To make the drop sound louder, you can increase the value of all the numbers in the waveform table; to make the sound softer, you can decrease all the values. By setting other controls that change the sound envelope, you can make the water drop sound more like honey or more like falling crystals. Of course, the keyboard can control the synthesizer's sound generator, enabling you to play scales and chords using the sound of a drop of water.

**Using Multiple
Sound Generators**

Most sound generators, whether they're analog or digital, produce only one note at a time. This is fine for playing a solo melody line but falls short of the mark if you want to add chords or use harmony. To compensate, synthesizers usually employ multiple sound generators. Some have as few as 4 sound generators; others, as many as 16, 32, or more than 100.

Synthesizers usually offer two ways of playing the sound generators: *monophonically,* where all the sound generators play just one note at a time, and *polyphonically,* where each sound generator can play a different note (letting the synthesizer play more than one note at a time).

Many polyphonic synthesizers let you select only one patch for all the sound generators, so that all the notes you play have the same sound quality. These synthesizers are called *monotimbral* synthesizers. Others, called *polytimbral* synthesizers, let you use a different patch for each sound generator, enabling you to play different patches simultaneously.

**HOW A
KEYBOARD
WORKS**

The traditional music keyboard on pianos and synthesizers has been around for almost 400 years. It evolved as a very flexible control mechanism for performing musicians, one that almost everybody has had some experience playing, even if it's only plunking on a key in a piano store.

A good piano keyboard is a miracle of nuance and control. Each key controls a complex system that uses a felt hammer, a damper, springs, levers, and other minute mechanisms to strike several strings tuned to the same pitch. Pressing a key softly yields a quiet note; attacking it with great force yields a loud note. Slight differences in the attack (the first part of the key press) change the character of the resulting note and produce a range of tones from sharp and brittle to gentle and singing. If you release a key slowly, the instrument produces a lingering note; if you release it quickly, the note ends abruptly.

A good synthesizer keyboard attempts to provide the nuances of a piano keyboard and adds some extras, as well. Of course, the synthesizer doesn't use hammered strings to produce its sounds; instead, its keyboard depends on electronic sensors to detect the nuances of a player's keystrokes. The sensors send signals to the microprocessor, which adds nuances to the sound from the sound generators.

The subtlety of the sounds that emerge from your synthesizer is limited by the ability of the sensors to detect and transmit changing conditions on the keyboard (information that MIDI can convey, as well).

**Note On and
Note Off**

Note On and *Note Off* are two very simple conditions that occur every time you press and release a key on a keyboard. At the moment you press a key, a Note On condition occurs that lasts until you release the key, at which point Note Off occurs. Every synthesizer keyboard must be able to read Note On and Note Off conditions for each of its keys. When you press a key, the keyboard sends the microprocessor a Note On message along with the pitch of the key that you pressed. In turn, the microprocessor asks the sound generators to start playing that pitch. As soon as you release the key, the keyboard sends a Note Off message (again, with the pitch of the released key) to the sound generators, so that they stop playing that pitch.

Velocity Sense

Many inexpensive synthesizer keyboards send only Note On and Note Off messages when you press a key. It doesn't matter how forcefully or how softly you press the key; the volume of the note you play is preset by the synthesizer. A *velocity sensitive* keyboard, however, has extra sensors that detect how quickly the key moves when it's pressed and pass that information to the microprocessor. The microprocessor can then ask the sound generators to play softer or louder notes, depending on the velocity it senses.

Most synthesizer keyboards sense only the *attack velocity,* the velocity of a key when it's first pressed. This is enough information to set the volume of the note. A few synthesizer keyboards also sense the *release velocity,* the velocity of a key as it is released. The microprocessor can use the release velocity to set esoteric nuances in a note that affect the way a note dies out.

Aftertouch

If you press a piano key and continue to hold it down, there is no further way to affect the note it plays: The string has already been struck, and there's no way to get the hammer to strike again unless you release the key and press it again. Synthesizer keyboards go beyond this limitation by adding a feature called *aftertouch.*

A keyboard with aftertouch senses pressure on a key while you hold it down. If you put a lot of pressure on the key as you hold it down, the keyboard sends this information to the microprocessor. If you change pressure on a key by letting up on the key or by adding yet more pressure, the keyboard sends this information to the microprocessor. The microprocessor can use aftertouch information from the keyboard in different ways, affecting *vibrato* or amplitude. By increasing pressure on a key, you can add *vibrato* or make a note swell in volume. Relaxing pressure on the key has the opposite effect.

There are two types of aftertouch used with keyboards. The most common is *monophonic aftertouch.* A keyboard with monophonic aftertouch senses the overall pressure on all the keys on the keyboard, usually by a pressure-sensitive ribbon under all the keys. The ribbon reports the heaviest pressure anywhere on the keyboard to the microprocessor. This means that if you press four keys simultaneously, adding very firm pressure to one key while lightly holding down the other three, the keyboard reports heavy pressure for all four keys.

Some synthesizer keyboards have *polyphonic aftertouch,* using individual pressure sensors under each key. The keyboard reports the individual pressure for each key to the microprocessor, so that the microprocessor can respond to different pressures for the notes it plays. This means that you can play several different notes at once with different volumes, *vibratos,* or other qualities by applying different pressures to the keys you press. The expense of adding a sensor to every key restricts polyphonic aftertouch to top-of-the-line synthesizers.

Keyboard Splits   Most synthesizer playing uses the entire synthesizer keyboard to play a single patch. All the notes you play from the top to the bottom of the keyboard play different pitches using the same sound quality. If you have a poly-timbral synthesizer (one that can use several different patches at once), or if you are using one keyboard with MIDI connections to play several different synthesizers at once, it is convenient to have a separate keyboard for each patch you're playing. Then, you can play one patch with one hand and a second patch with the other. Some synthesizer keyboards offer *keyboard splits* to give you this ability without requiring a second keyboard.

A keyboard with splits gives you the option of splitting the keyboard into smaller sections, each of which acts as a separate keyboard. Most keyboards split into only two sections (as shown in Figure 3-7): the upper half of the keyboard and the lower half. On such a keyboard, you can assign a different patch to each section. When you play keys in a particular keyboard section, you hear the patch for that section. This feature is very handy for playing a bass line with your left hand using a bass patch and playing a lead line with your right hand using a solo patch.

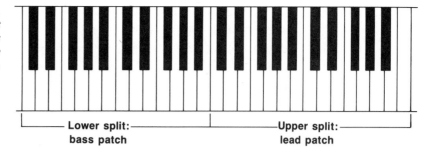

Lower split:—————————|Upper split:————————
bass patch   lead patch

There are variations in the way keyboard splits work. Some synthesizer keyboards allow you to set the point where the split occurs. For
example, if your bass line, played with the left hand, covers only an octave
and a half, you might want the split to occur only an octave and a half from
the bottom of the keyboard so that the rest of the keyboard is dedicated to a
wide-ranging lead line. Or you might want to move the split toward the top
of the keyboard to give you more room for the bass line.

A few keyboards allow you to set more than one split, so that you can
play more than two patches at once. By splitting the keyboard into three
or more sections, you can play different patches immediately, merely by
jumping from one keyboard section to another. You can also set the octaves
of the notes in different sections of the keyboard. This is useful if you split
a keyboard and want to play two different lead lines, one with the left hand
and the other with the right hand. By changing the notes in the left section
so that they play one or two octaves higher than they would normally, you
can be sure that the patch you play in that section sounds high enough to be
a lead line, even though you're playing a section of the keyboard that usually plays low pitches.

**WORKING
WITH A
CONTROL
PANEL**

As you might expect, control panels vary greatly from one brand of synthesizer to the next. After all, they control synthesizer features that also
vary greatly from one brand to the next. Unfortunately, this variety makes
it difficult to switch from one synthesizer to another without learning a
whole new set of controls and functions. The lack of consistency in controls and functions has also made it difficult to evolve standard MIDI messages to convey control panel information.

Some controls in the control panel are common to most synthesizers. These controls are shown in Figure 3-8. An on/off switch turns the synthesizer on and off (sometimes located on the back of the synthesizer so you don't hit it accidentally); a volume knob or slider changes the amplitude of the synthesizer's audio signal. Other common controls have more complex functions. For example, you use one set of buttons to call up different patches for the sound generators. These are called *patch buttons,* usually labeled with numbers and arranged in a row so that you can find them easily. Most synthesizers have the equivalent of a typewriter's Shift key so that you can use the patch buttons to select more than one set of patches.

Figure 3-8.
Common controls
found in a
synthesizer control
panel.

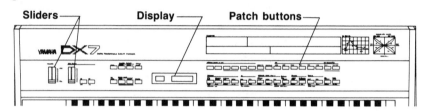

Other controls that differ from synthesizer to synthesizer are those that control different synthesizer features such as keyboard splits, *portamento,* and *vibrato.* The buttons, sliders, and other controls used to program patches are perhaps the most unique to each synthesizer, because each synthesizer has its own method of creating patches. Some of these controls set envelopes; others choose basic waveforms and set other qualities of the patch.

**The Control Panel
Display**

The control panel display (usually a liquid-crystal display) takes on special importance when you program a new patch. As you change the control settings, it shows the current status of each variable quality of the patch. Unfortunately, most synthesizer displays are quite small and show only a small part of the patch definition at one time. Usually, the display changes each time you use a new control so that it shows the patch quality with which you're currently working.

**AUXILIARY
CONTROLS**

A synthesizer's auxiliary controls supplement the keyboard during performance, giving you more control over the notes you play. Like the keyboard, auxiliary controls can send MIDI messages as you use them. The two most common auxiliary controls are the *pitch bend wheel* and the *modulation wheel.* (Joysticks or sliders are sometimes used instead of adjustment wheels.) These controls are usually located immediately to the left of the keyboard, as depicted in Figure 3-9.

The pitch bend wheel bends the pitch of any notes being played up or down in a smooth *portamento.* Most pitch bend wheels can be set to bend the pitch anywhere from a single half-step to an octave, a subtle difference or a dramatic one. The pitch bend wheel is usually connected to springs that return it to its center position when you release it. At its center position, the control does not modify the pitch at all.

The modulation wheel sets the amount of modulation in synthesized sound, which usually means it sets the amount of added *vibrato.* When the wheel is set all the way toward the front of the synthesizer, it adds no modulation to the sound. Moving it toward the back adds more modulation. Unlike the pitch bend wheel, the modulation wheel doesn't return to a central position when you release it—it stays wherever you leave it.

Some auxiliary controls aren't located on the synthesizer itself but are attached to it by a cord. A *foot control,* for instance, sits on the floor beneath the synthesizer. It is typically a flat pad you can push up or down with your foot. (See Figure 3-9.) A foot control usually controls volume— the more you push down, the louder the sound gets—but you can also use one (with some synthesizers) to control some other characteristic, such as *vibrato* or the amount of *portamento.*

Figure 3-9.
*Common
synthesizer
controls.*

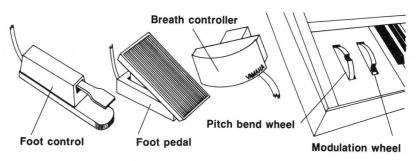

Breath controller

Foot control   Foot pedal   Pitch bend wheel

Modulation wheel

A *foot pedal* (shown in Figure 3-9), like a foot control, sits on the floor. You use it with your foot, but instead of offering a wide range of settings like the foot control, it offers only two settings: off and on. When you press a foot pedal, it turns on, and when you let it go, it turns off. Foot pedals are usually used to turn *sustain* on and off. Sustain is an effect that keeps notes playing on a synthesizer even after you release the keyboard keys that started the notes.

A *breath controller* (shown in Figure 3-9 on the previous page) is an auxiliary controller that comes out from the synthesizer on a cable. You put it into your mouth and blow to control it. Like a foot control, a breath controller offers a range of settings, depending on how hard you blow. Typically, it is used to control volume or *vibrato*. Using a breath controller, you can change the volume or *vibrato* without taking your fingers away from the keyboard.

OTHER TYPICAL MIDI DEVICES

There are many other MIDI devices that commonly augment the standard synthesizer in a MIDI system. Some are specialized synthesizers or parts of synthesizers that offer greater quality or power than a standard synthesizer; others are specialized controllers that enable non-keyboard players to control synthesizers. These devices add versatility and convenience to a MIDI system.

Drum Machines

The drum machine (shown in Figure 3-10) specializes in percussion sounds and rhythms. Often less formally referred to as a drum box, it is the most common auxiliary MIDI device. Like a synthesizer, it uses sound generators to create sounds. Unlike synthesizers, most drum boxes don't let you create your own sounds: The sounds are usually preset at the factory and are percussion sounds such as those produced by a bass drum, a hand clap, different types of snare drums, congas, toms, and other percussion instruments.

Figure 3-10.
A typical drum machine.

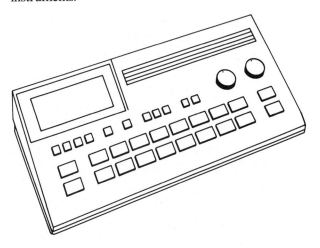

A drum machine doesn't have a keyboard. Instead, it has a collection of buttons on the front panel, one for each percussion sound. Each time you press a button, the drum machine plays the sound corresponding to the button. Although you can play rhythms on the buttons, the buttons are usually small, hard to play, and not really meant for live performance. To play complex rhythms, you'll have better results with a drum machine that has a built-in sequencer.

You'll recall that a sequencer is a bank of memory that holds a sequence of notes. The sequencer in a drum machine holds sequences called *rhythm tracks*, each of which is a "song" that uses the percussion sounds that the sound generators make. A drum machine playing a rhythm track can be used as a rhythm section backup to music you play on a synthesizer.

Drum machines usually have built-in rhythm tracks in memory that you can select by pushing a button. They also let you create and store your own rhythm tracks in the sequencer. During performance, you can load any one of the tracks in memory and start it playing.

Expansion Modules

There are many times when you might want more than one synthesizer in a MIDI system—perhaps to increase the number of notes available at one time or to add a completely new range of sounds. But if you're using a single keyboard to control all the synthesizers, you don't need another keyboard with every additional synthesizer you acquire. Extra keyboards are unnecessary and expensive.

An *expansion module* is a less expensive way to add a synthesizer to a MIDI system. Some instrument manufacturers offer two versions of their synthesizers, one with a keyboard and one without. The version without the keyboard is an expansion module, an instrument with the microprocessor, the control panel, the memory, and all the sound generators contained in the keyboard version. To produce music, however, it depends on an external keyboard or source of notes.

Master Keyboards

The keyboards of most standard synthesizers are limited to four or five octaves and don't always have velocity sensitivity or aftertouch. If the quality of your keyboard is extremely important to you, you might consider using a *master keyboard* in a MIDI system. The opposite of an expansion module, a master keyboard does not have its own sound generators and patch-programming controls. It looks almost exactly like a synthesizer, but looks can be deceiving. In fact, you can't produce a single note with a master keyboard until you connect it to a synthesizer.

Because a master keyboard offers only keyboard functions, it's usually a better keyboard than you'll find on a standard synthesizer. Some master keyboards stretch out over a full seven and a half octaves, with the 88-key range of a piano keyboard and weighted keys that have the feel of a true piano keyboard. Most master keyboards are velocity sensitive and have aftertouch. They also include a full set of auxiliary controls such as pitch and modulation wheels, foot controls, foot pedals, and breath controllers.

A master keyboard has a built-in microprocessor, enabling it to send MIDI signals to attached synthesizers. Unlike the buttons in a synthesizer control panel, those on the master keyboard control panel don't design patches. Instead, they control the operation of the keyboard and the auxiliary controls. You can use them to assign the MIDI messages sent by the devices on the control panel, and so tailor its MIDI output to work with whatever synthesizers you're controlling. You can also assign keyboard splits, set the volume, and select patches (using MIDI) on attached synthesizers.

Using a master keyboard with expansion modules is an economical way to create a powerful MIDI system. Because a master keyboard is usually much more flexible than a built-in synthesizer keyboard, you're likely to have much greater success controlling the varied features of synthesizers of different makes.

Guitar Controllers and Guitar Synthesizers

Most synthesizer players are keyboard players, simply because most synthesizers are played with a keyboard. To open up the world of synthesized sounds to the many guitar players in the world, synthesizer manufacturers now make *guitar synthesizers*. You can play a guitar synthesizer using a *guitar controller* that works like a standard six-string guitar. You can see both a guitar synthesizer and a guitar controller in Figure 3-11.

A guitar controller has electronic sensors that detect the instant at which a string is plucked, how hard it is plucked, and whether or not the string is bent to alter the pitch. The controller sends this information to the microprocessor of a guitar synthesizer, which uses it to play notes on the synthesizer's sound generators. Like a standard synthesizer, a guitar synthesizer allows you to create your own patches on its control panel and has a series of patch buttons that you can use to call up a patch. Because guitar players usually have their hands full playing, most guitar synthesizers lie on the floor and have big, rubberized patch buttons that the musicians press with their feet while playing.

Figure 3-11.
*A guitar
synthesizer with a
guitar controller.*

A bass guitar player can use a *bass guitar synthesizer*, an instrument that works almost exactly the same way a guitar synthesizer works, but the musician uses a four-string bass guitar controller instead of a regular guitar controller.

**Drum Pad
Controllers**

Drummers can also play synthesizers by using a *drum pad controller,* shown in Figure 3-12. A drum pad controller usually has six or more separate pads, rubberized areas that a drummer can hit with drum sticks. These

Figure 3-12.
*A drum pad
controller.*

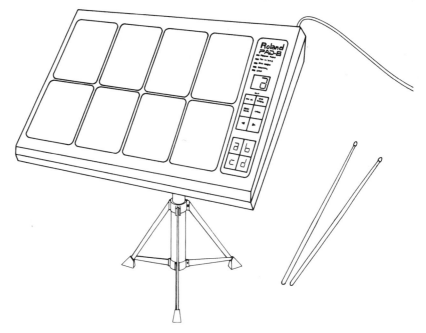

pads are sensitive to the degree of force with which the drummer hits them and can send that information to an attached synthesizer to make it play louder or softer notes.

Drum pad controllers are most commonly attached via MIDI to a drum machine, where each controller pad plays a different percussion sound. With a drum pad controller, a good drum machine, and an amplifier, a drummer can have a good-sounding trap set without lugging around a lot of heavy equipment.

Pitch Followers

Singers, wind instrument players, and musicians of any other kind can play synthesizers using a *pitch follower*. This device takes an audio signal from a source such as a microphone and converts the signal into MIDI messages that control a synthesizer. A good pitch follower can detect pitch, volume, and the overall duration of notes in the audio signal, not always an easy task if the audio signal is complex. Pitch followers are monophonic; that is, they detect only one note at a time and don't respond to a chord being played. They work best with monophonic instruments, such as saxophones, flutes, and voices.

In this chapter, you've seen some of the instruments in a typical MIDI system and have learned the fundamentals of sound synthesis and keyboard control. Now that you know something about synthesizers, drum boxes, and their kin, you can read in the next chapter how all these devices are connected via MIDI.

4 | MIDI CONNECTIONS

Connecting MIDI devices is the simplest part of using MIDI. Standardized cables and ports make it very easy to plug one MIDI device into another. However, there is more to making a MIDI connection than running a cable between two devices. You need to know the direction that MIDI messages take as they flow through ports and cables and which ports to connect so that messages flow between the devices in your system the way you want them to flow.

This short chapter shows you how to make MIDI connections. The first part of the chapter discusses MIDI cables and how they're built, and the second part describes the different kinds of MIDI ports. The last section shows different configurations you can use to connect devices in a MIDI system and the path the messages follow between devices in each configuration.

MIDI CABLES   A MIDI cable is a *shielded, twisted-pair cable* with a *5-pin male DIN plug*
on each end. A shielded, twisted-pair cable (shown in Figure 4-1) is a cable
with a pair of wires inside that are twisted around each other. To serve as
shielding, a fine wire mesh runs along the entire cable, wrapped around the
twisted pair of wires. It is this pair of wires that transmits the signals that
MIDI uses to send messages.

Figure 4-1.
A shielded,
twisted-pair
cable.

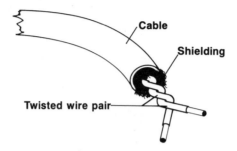

A 5-pin DIN plug (shown in Figure 4-2) is a standard plug used quite
commonly in European audio equipment. As its name implies, it contains
five small pins; each is numbered and can be connected to a wire in a cable.
Figure 4-2 shows how the pins are numbered.

Figure 4-2.
A 5-pin DIN
connector with the
pins numbered.

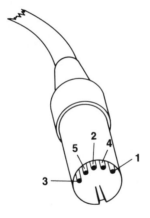

A MIDI cable uses only three of the DIN pins: Pins 4 and 5 carry the
MIDI signal and are connected to the twisted pair of wires in the cable;
pin 2 is a grounded pin (when it's plugged into a MIDI port) that is connected to the shielding of the cable. Pins 1 and 3 of the DIN plug aren't used
for MIDI but are available to carry more signals if the MIDI specifications
ever change. (As you'll see in Chapter 8, the Atari 520ST makes an interesting use of pins 1 and 3.)

Radio Frequency Interference

The shielding in a MIDI cable helps protect the signals carried by the twisted pair of wires from *radio frequency interference* (*RFI* for short), interference from television, radio, or other broadcast signals. If you have ever heard a CB radio come in over your stereo system or heard the hum of your refrigerator motor come in on your television speakers, you have experienced RFI.

Anytime you connect a long cable to a device, the cable acts as an antenna and picks up RFI. MIDI cables are no exception. RFI can disrupt MIDI signals by changing messages sent over the cable or by adding spurious (and unwanted) messages. This is the reason that MIDI cables are shielded. The wire mesh shield protects the MIDI signal sent over the twisted pair from RFI.

Making Your Own MIDI Cables

You can buy high-quality MIDI cables at most stores that sell synthesizers or other MIDI devices, but if you're on a limited budget and are handy with a soldering iron, you can easily make your own for a much lower price. All you need are 5-pin DIN plugs (such as Switchcraft 05GM5M plugs) and a piece of twisted-pair cable, all parts you can buy at a local electronics store. Don't make any cable longer than 50 feet. The MIDI specifications limit MIDI cables to that length because even shielded cable becomes more susceptible to RFI as its length increases. The diagram in Figure 4-3 shows how to solder the wires of the cable to each of the DIN plugs.

Figure 4-3.
Connections between DIN plugs and shielded cable.

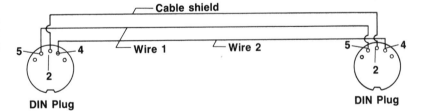

MIDI PORTS

MIDI ports pass MIDI information in and out of a MIDI device and provide a 5-pin DIN socket (the female equivalent of the DIN plug) as a place to plug in a MIDI cable. There are three different kinds of MIDI ports: *MIDI In, MIDI Out,* and *MIDI Thru.* Although these ports look the same, each passes MIDI messages in a different way. The MIDI ports are usually located on the back or sides of a MIDI device and labeled as shown in Figure 4-4 on the next page.

Figure 4-4.
*Three different
kinds of MIDI
ports on the back
of a synthesizer:
MIDI In,
MIDI Out, and
MIDI Thru.*

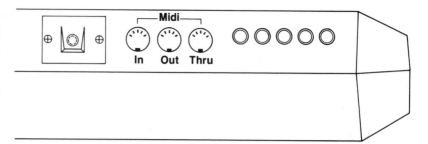

MIDI In

The MIDI In port receives messages from an attached MIDI cable and passes them to the device's microprocessor, as shown in Figure 4-5. The MIDI In port can't send any messages through the cable, which means that a device with only a MIDI In port can't send messages to other devices. Most devices have a single MIDI In port. A few devices (those that control other devices without receiving information in return) have no MIDI In ports at all.

Figure 4-5.
*MIDI In, MIDI
Out, and MIDI
Thru ports each
pass MIDI
messages in
different ways.*

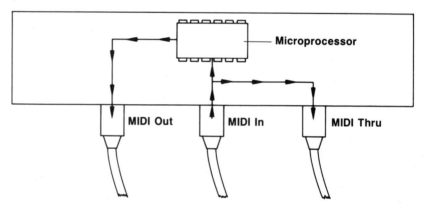

MIDI Out

The MIDI Out port sends messages from the device's microprocessor over an attached MIDI cable, as shown previously in Figure 4-5. This port can't receive any messages from the cable. Most devices have only one MIDI Out port. Some have more than one MIDI Out port, and in rare cases, a device might lack a MIDI Out port, restricting it to receiving messages.

MIDI Thru

The MIDI Thru port takes the messages coming in through the MIDI In port and sends an exact copy of them over an attached MIDI cable, as shown above in Figure 4-5. Normally, MIDI Thru merely copies the MIDI In messages; it doesn't send those messages to the device's microprocessor or receive any messages from the microprocessor to mix in with the messages it sends out over the cable.

MIDI Thru is used to create daisy-chain MIDI systems, as you'll find in the next section. Because a MIDI Thru port is not essential for sending and receiving MIDI messages, many MIDI devices don't include one, although those that do are more versatile.

ROUTING MIDI MESSAGES

Once you understand MIDI ports and cables, you can connect MIDI devices so that they can exchange information. As you connect them, keep two important facts in mind:

♦ MIDI messages travel in only one direction over a MIDI cable.

♦ A single MIDI port can either send or receive messages; it can't do both.

In order to let MIDI devices exchange information freely among themselves, you must connect the cables to the correct ports. The following sections illustrate some standard configurations for connecting devices in a MIDI system.

Connecting Two MIDI Devices

The simplest MIDI connection merely carries messages from one MIDI device to another. The left half of Figure 4-6 shows you the easiest way to connect two devices: a single cable connecting the MIDI Out port of one device to the MIDI In port of the second device. This lets the first device send messages through its MIDI Out port to the MIDI In port of the second device. With a single cable like this, the only flow of information is from the first device to the second device. The second device can't send information back to the first device.

Figure 4-6.
At left, a single MIDI cable permits data to flow in only one direction. At right, two MIDI cables permit both devices to send and receive messages.

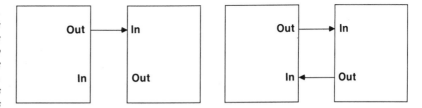

By adding cable from the MIDI In port of the first device to the MIDI Out port of the second device, as shown in the right half of Figure 4-6, you enable the second device to send information back to the first device. With this configuration, the devices can both send information to and receive information from each other.

This simple connection illustrates the most important rule of MIDI connections: You must always connect a MIDI port that sends messages to a MIDI port that receives messages. If you connect two sending ports (such as two MIDI Out ports, or a MIDI Out port and a MIDI Thru port) or two receiving ports (two MIDI In ports), no MIDI messages will be transferred.

Daisy Chaining

Because most MIDI systems use more than two devices, it's important to be able to connect them all together so that a message from one device can travel to all the other devices. If each device has a MIDI Thru port, then you can hook them up in a *daisy chain,* shown in Figure 4-7.

Figure 4-7.
A daisy chain of
MIDI devices uses
the MIDI Thru port
to pass messages.

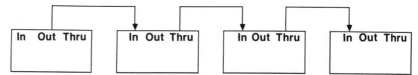

In a daisy chain, the first MIDI device sends messages through its MIDI Out port to the MIDI In port of the second device. The second device sends an exact copy of its incoming messages from its Thru port to the MIDI In port of the third device. The third device sends a copy of these messages from its Thru port to the MIDI In port of the fourth device. This chain can extend to include any number of MIDI devices by connecting the MIDI Thru port of one device to the MIDI In port of the next device.

MIDI Thru connections pass messages unaltered from the first device in the chain to all the other devices in the chain. The other devices can't add any messages to pass down the line. This makes daisy chaining very effective for one master device with a series of other devices connected to it. (Synthesizer players commonly term the subordinate devices "slave devices.") Because the master device usually has no need to receive information and the other devices don't need to send information between themselves, it doesn't matter that the slave devices can't transmit their own information. Of course, it is possible to connect the MIDI In port of the master device to the MIDI Out port of one of the other devices if you want the master device to receive messages from it.

MIDI Lag

It is, in theory, possible to create as long a daisy chain as you want if all the MIDI devices you use have Thru ports. In practice though, it's not always possible. Some MIDI Thru ports delay very slightly the MIDI messages they pass along. Most of these delays are caused when a MIDI device passes incoming messages to the microprocessor instead of sending them directly from the MIDI In port to the MIDI Thru port. The microprocessor reads the messages and then sends them to the Thru port, sometimes adding its own MIDI messages. This process can slow the transmission of the messages. Once MIDI messages pass through more than three or four Thru ports with small delays, the messages are slow enough to create a clearly audible delay. This delay is called *MIDI lag.*

MIDI lag causes timing problems in music performance. If you're playing notes on the keyboard of a master synthesizer at the head of a long MIDI chain with MIDI lag, the notes coming from the synthesizer at the end of the chain will sound later than the master synthesizer's notes. You'll hear scattered attacks at the beginning of each note. Fortunately, most MIDI devices today don't use a delaying Thru port (a feature that conflicts with MIDI specifications anyway). As a result, MIDI lag isn't a problem, and you can create long MIDI daisy chains.

Creating a Star Network

You can't always use a daisy chain to create a MIDI system because not all MIDI devices have Thru ports, and those that do may introduce the delays that create MIDI lag. Another way to connect a series of slave devices to a master device is to create a *star network,* shown in Figure 4-8. The star network avoids using MIDI Thru ports on a chain of devices by adding a device called a *MIDI Thru box.*

Figure 4-8.
A star network uses a MIDI Thru box to send incoming messages from a master device to all the other devices.

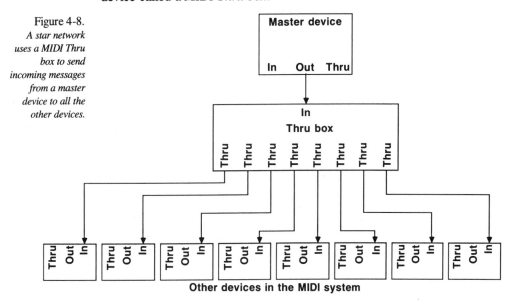

A MIDI Thru box has at least one MIDI In port and a whole row of Thru ports (typically about four). MIDI messages that enter the MIDI In port are copied and passed simultaneously through all the MIDI Thru ports on the Thru box. By connecting the MIDI Out port of the master device to the MIDI In port of the Thru box and then connecting the MIDI In port of each slave device to a MIDI Thru port of the Thru box, you transmit messages from the master device simultaneously to each of the other devices.

Creating a Ring Network

Any daisy chain or star network has a distinct limitation: MIDI messages flow mostly in one direction, from the master device to the slave devices. It's not possible for every device in the chain or network to talk to every other device in the chain or network. For example, consider the third device in the daisy chain illustrated in Figure 4-7 on page 64. It can receive messages only from the master device and can't send any messages. Even if you connect its MIDI Out port to another device, it can send messages only to that device and no others. To connect five devices so that each device can send and receive messages from any other device, you would need four MIDI In and four MIDI Out ports on each device and 20 MIDI cables to make all the connections, a prohibitively expensive and unwieldy solution even if you could find five MIDI devices with all the necessary ports.

A *ring network,* shown in Figure 4-9, allows MIDI devices to send and receive messages from any other device in the network without requiring many cables and ports. The MIDI Out port of each device in the ring is connected to the MIDI In port of the next device in the ring.

Figure 4-9.
A MIDI ring network lets each device send messages to all the other devices on the network.

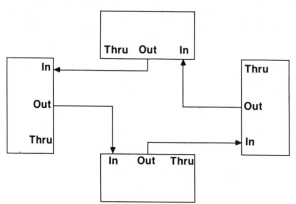

A ring network won't work with most MIDI devices, however, because the MIDI Out port sends messages from the device's own microprocessor and doesn't pass on messages received from the MIDI In port. But some devices (chiefly computers) have a microprocessor that is fast and powerful enough and uses the right programming to receive messages from the MIDI In port, mix them with the device's own originating messages, and then send the mixture through the MIDI Out port. If each device in a ring network has this kind of message pass-through in its MIDI Out port, any message sent by one device in the ring will be received and passed on by the other devices all the way around the ring.

There are problems to overcome with ring networks. For example, any device that sends a message over the network receives that same message on its own MIDI In port once the message has been passed around the ring by the other devices. If the original device isn't smart enough to recognize its own message, it will pass the message on again to the next device, and the message will go on looping through the ring network without stopping. Enough of these looping messages can create "message feedback" that overloads the network and stops any useful message exchange. Each device in the network must be programmed to recognize its own messages when they come back to it so that it won't send them again. MIDI lag can also be a problem, for reasons discussed previously.

At this writing, ring networks aren't always practical for MIDI devices because most synthesizers and other MIDI devices lack sufficiently powerful microprocessors and the right programming to work in a ring. With appropriate software, many personal computers can work in a ring network, but few people would use a MIDI system composed solely of computers. As new generations of synthesizers come out with more powerful microprocessors and programming capabilities, you may one day be able to use a MIDI ring network to set up a very flexible MIDI system.

With the information in this chapter, you've learned how MIDI devices are connected to create MIDI systems. Chapters 7 and 8 take this discussion a step further; they discuss actual MIDI devices and systems. But with your present grasp of MIDI systems, you can already get down to the really interesting business of sending MIDI messages through the system, the subject of the next chapter.

5 | MIDI MESSAGES

MIDI messages are the most important part of MIDI. They transmit information between MIDI devices and determine what kinds of musical events can be passed from device to device. To truly understand MIDI, you must get to know all the different kinds of MIDI messages and learn how MIDI devices respond to these messages.

This chapter takes you to the core of MIDI: It shows you how MIDI devices send messages over MIDI cables and what format they use to send the messages. The central section of the chapter introduces you to the MIDI messages; it tells you how each is used and what information it carries. In the final part of the chapter, you'll see what happens when MIDI messages are actually put to work. You'll also get a chance to examine a stream of messages that instruct a hypothetical MIDI system to play a short piece of music.

HOW MIDI DEVICES SEND AND RECEIVE INFORMATION

MIDI devices send information back and forth using a technique similar to that once used by telegraphers to send a telegram over a telegraph line. The telegrapher on one end of the line used Morse code to send each character in the telegram as a group of dots and dashes. The telegrapher at the other end of the line received a whole series of dots and dashes and broke it into groups of dots and dashes. To re-create the original telegram, a telegrapher translated each group as a different character and wrote the characters down in the order they arrived.

Like a telegrapher, the microprocessor in a MIDI device sends MIDI information through a MIDI cable using a series of short signals. Instead of dots and dashes, it sends a series of voltages that represent 1s and 0s. These 1s and 0s are called *bits* and are used together in groups of eight to represent different pieces of MIDI information, as shown in Figure 5-1. Each group of eight bits is called a *byte*. Because there are 256 different arrangements of 1 and 0 possible in each byte, a byte can represent any number from 0 to 255. (See Appendix A for a full explanation of bits and bytes in MIDI messages.)

Figure 5-1.
MIDI devices send information using bytes, each of which comprises eight bits.

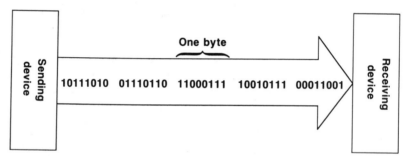

MIDI's method of sending each byte over a cable one bit at a time, as a series of bits, is called *serial data transmission*. It is somewhat slower than *parallel data transmission,* a method that sends each byte as eight simultaneous bits (requiring at least eight lines in a connecting cable, one for each bit in a byte), but it has an advantage: Cables used for serial transmission are much cheaper than cables used for parallel transmission, and they can be longer than parallel cables without picking up RFI. To keep data transmission speed respectable, MIDI sends 31,250 bits per second over the cables, a very high serial data transmission rate that allows MIDI to send about 3125 bytes per second. (If the arithmetic seems faulty, it's because MIDI uses two extra bits, one on each end of a byte, to separate one byte from another. This means it actually takes ten bits to send one byte of information through a MIDI cable.)

MIDI Messages

In the Morse code example, each group of dots and dashes in a signal coming over a telegraph wire stands for one character in a telegram. Groups of those transmitted characters make up words in the telegram. MIDI messages are like the words in a telegram—it usually takes two or three bytes to send a MIDI message.

The first byte of any MIDI message is called the *status byte*. It tells what kind of message it is. The status byte might identify the message as a Note On message (one that tells about a note that just started), a Pitch Bend Change message (one that tells that the pitch bend wheel controller on a synthesizer has been moved), or any number of other possible types.

The bytes that follow the status byte are called *data bytes*. Each data byte elaborates on the information given by the status byte. For example, the first data byte in a Note On message tells the pitch of the note, and the second data byte tells the attack velocity of the note so that a MIDI device can tell how loud to play it. Many types of MIDI messages use two data bytes to carry additional information; some need only one data byte; still others use no data bytes at all. Figure 5-2 shows a typical stream of data messages with status bytes and data bytes.

Figure 5-2.
*MIDI messages use
status bytes and
data bytes.*

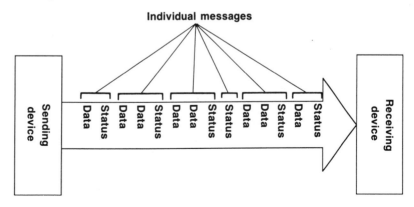

To distinguish data bytes from status bytes, MIDI uses only bytes that range from 0 to 127 as data bytes and only bytes that range from 128 to 255 as status bytes. (Remember that each byte can stand for a number from 0 to 255.) When a MIDI device receives a status byte over a MIDI cable, it knows what kind of message it is receiving and how to interpret any data bytes that follow. For example, if a device receives a Note On status byte, it interprets the next two data bytes as pitch and velocity data. If a device receives a Pitch Bend Change status byte, it interprets the next two data bytes as pitch bend data.

MIDI Channels   Consider the Morse code analogy once again. Suppose there are many different telegraphers all connected to the same telegraph line. When any one telegrapher sends a telegram, all the other telegraphers receive it. This might not be practical. For example, if you want to send a telegram to telegrapher A without telegraphers B, C, and D also receiving it, you'll find it isn't possible.

The same situation exists in MIDI systems. Consider a master device connected to many subordinate devices through a daisy chain. When the master device sends a message, all the other devices in the system receive that message. The master device can't run one device without running all the other devices at the same time. This situation is satisfactory if you want to use a master keyboard to play all the other devices in unison, but it won't work if you want to use the master device to tell each device to do something different.

MIDI uses *MIDI channels* to allow communication between individual devices in a MIDI system. To understand how they work, consider the telegraph line again. The owners of the telegraph line set some rules: There will be two kinds of telegrams—public telegrams that everyone can receive and read and private telegrams that only authorized telegraphers can receive and read. The telegraph company gives each telegrapher a number, and tells the telegrapher to read private telegrams only if they start with that number. When a private telegram arrives that begins with someone else's identification number, the telegrapher promptly ignores the rest of the telegram. (Of course, all these hypothetical telegraphers are scrupulously honest!)

MIDI uses the same technique. It divides all messages into two different types: *system messages* that go to all devices in a MIDI system, and *channel messages* that go only to specified devices. Each channel message has a channel number from 1 to 16 included in the status byte. When a MIDI device receives the status byte of a channel message, it looks at the channel number. Then, it checks to see if it's allowed to receive messages on that channel. If so, it acts on the message. If not, it ignores the message. Because system messages have no channel number in the status byte, all devices that receive them pay attention to them.

Although this technique sounds tedious, it all takes place at great speed. The practical effect is that MIDI channels act more like television channels than a telegraph line, as shown in Figure 5-3. The sending device can send messages on any of 16 channels. Only the receiving devices tuned to that channel receive the messages. Devices not set to receive that channel ignore the messages.

Figure 5-3.
MIDI devices set to
receive messages
on a particular
MIDI channel
receive only
messages sent for
that channel.

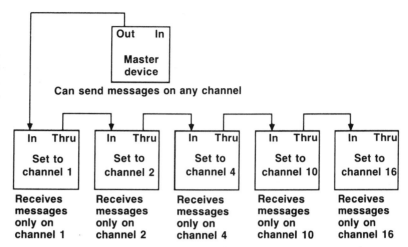

MIDI Channel Reception Modes

To tune a MIDI device to one or more channels, first use the control panel to set the device in one of its MIDI *reception modes*. The reception mode you choose determines how the MIDI device listens to different channels. The four modes are:

♦ Mode 1: Omni On/Poly

♦ Mode 2: Omni On/Mono

♦ Mode 3: Omni Off/Poly

♦ Mode 4: Omni Off/Mono

The first half of the mode name tells how the MIDI device monitors the incoming MIDI channels. If Omni is turned on, then it monitors all the MIDI channels and responds to all channel messages, no matter what channel they're transmitted on. If Omni is turned off, then the MIDI device responds only to channel messages sent on the channel or channels that the device is set to receive.

The second half of the mode name tells the MIDI device how to play notes coming in over the MIDI cable. If you set the mode to Poly, the device can play several notes at a time, like a polyphonic synthesizer. When a MIDI message comes in telling it to start a note, the MIDI device will keep playing that note even when it receives a message to start a second note. The first note stops playing only when the device receives a message that ends it or when the number of concurrent notes exceeds the synthesizer's voice count. If the mode is set to Mono, the device plays notes like a monophonic synthesizer—one note at a time. Whenever a MIDI message starts a new note, the device stops playing any previous note whether there was a MIDI message to end the note or not.

By combining the two different aspects of a mode in every possible way, you end up with the four modes described in the sections that follow. Each has its own unique way of responding to MIDI channel messages.

Mode 1

Mode 1 is Omni On/Poly. A device set to this mode receives channel messages sent on any channel and plays notes polyphonically. This is the mode that most MIDI devices are set to use when they're first turned on. It's a "safe" mode because the device responds to messages sent on any channel. You won't be stymied by a machine that sits idle because it's not set to receive messages on the correct channel.

Mode 2

Mode 2 is Omni On/Mono. When set to this mode, a device receives channel messages sent on any channel and plays the notes monophonically. Because most people prefer to have a device play notes polyphonically whenever possible, Mode 2 is rarely used.

Mode 3

Mode 3 is Omni Off/Poly. A device set to this mode receives channel messages on discrete channels and plays the notes polyphonically. You can specify the receiving channels to be any of the 16 MIDI channels. Most MIDI devices receive messages on a single channel when they're set to Mode 3. Some polytimbral synthesizers, however, can receive messages on several channels at once and can play the notes for each channel using a different synthesizer patch. This mode effectively breaks the synthesizer into several smaller polyphonic synthesizers, each responding to a different MIDI channel.

As an example, consider a polytimbral eight-voice synthesizer, shown in Figure 5-4, set to Mode 3. You can set three of its voices playing an electric piano patch to respond to MIDI channel 1, two of its voices playing a flute patch to respond to channel 2, and the three remaining voices playing a vibes patch to respond to channel 3. The synthesizer now acts like three small synthesizers, each with a different patch, each receiving messages on its own MIDI channel.

Mode 4

Mode 4 is Omni Off/Mono, which enables a device to receive messages on discrete channels and play the notes monophonically. This mode is used almost exclusively by polytimbral synthesizers. A synthesizer in this mode sets a different patch for each of its voices and then assigns a different MIDI channel to each voice. The channels are consecutive; you can assign the first synthesizer voice to any MIDI channel, but all the other voices are assigned to consecutive channels following that first channel. The effective

Figure 5-4.
*A polytimbral
synthesizer set to
Mode 3 can receive
channel messages
on discrete
channels and
play them
polyphonically.*

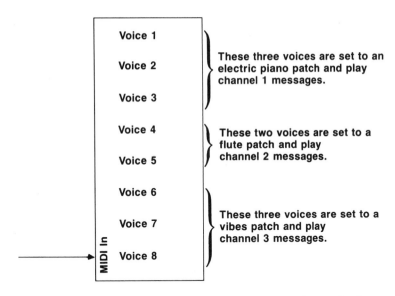

result is to divide the synthesizer into many monophonic synthesizers, each receiving messages on its own MIDI channel.

As an example, set a four-voice polytimbral synthesizer to Mode 4, as shown in Figure 5-5. Then set each of the four voices to a different patch and assign a MIDI channel number for the first voice. The channels for the remaining voices are determined automatically, based on the channel you assign to the first voice. If you choose channel 5 as the channel for the first voice, then the second voice uses channel 6, the third voice channel 7, and the fourth voice channel 8.

Figure 5-5.
*A polytimbral
synthesizer set to
Mode 4 can receive
channel messages
on discrete
channels and
play them
monophonically.*

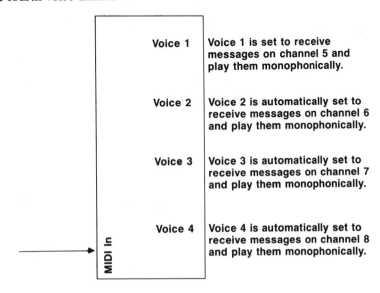

Like Mode 2, Mode 4 is usually less desirable than its polyphonic counterpart, but the technical limitations of some synthesizers create a need for it.

CHANNEL MESSAGES

Now that you know how MIDI devices use serial data transmission, bytes, and MIDI channels to send messages back and forth, you are ready to examine the messages themselves (shown in Figure 5-6) to find out exactly what the devices are saying to each other. This section on channel messages and the section that follows on system messages list all the different kinds of messages specified by MIDI and tell you what kind of data each message can carry.

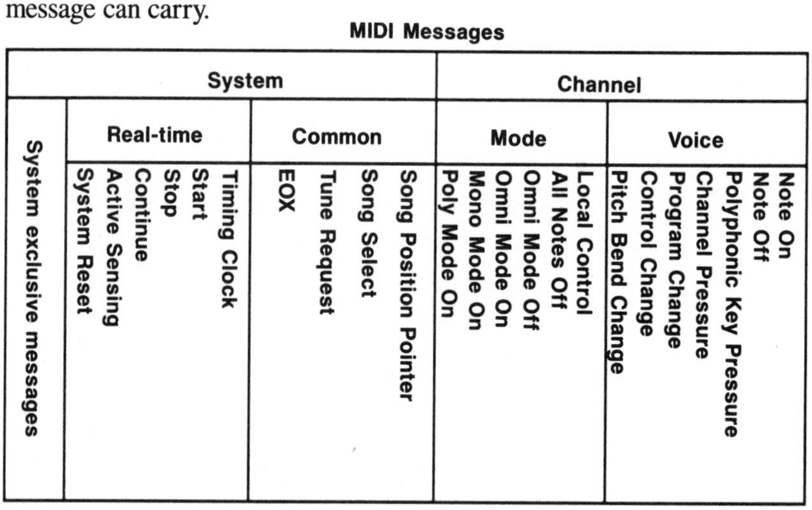

Figure 5-6.
The different MIDI messages, arranged by message type.

MIDI Messages

System			Channel	
	Real-time	Common	Mode	Voice
System exclusive messages	System Reset / Active Sensing / Continue / Stop / Start / Timing Clock	EOX / Tune Request / Song Select / Song Position Pointer	Poly Mode On / Mono Mode On / Omni Mode On / Omni Mode Off / All Notes Off / Local Control	Pitch Bend Change / Control Change / Program Change / Channel Pressure / Polyphonic Key Pressure / Note Off / Note On

There are two different types of channel messages: *channel voice messages* and *channel mode messages*. Channel voice messages send actual performance data between MIDI devices, describing keyboard action, controller motion, and button presses on control panels. Channel mode messages determine the way that the receiving MIDI device responds to channel voice messages. All these messages are sent with a specific channel number so that they will be received only by devices that are set to respond to that channel.

Channel Voice Messages

Most channel voice messages describe music by defining pitch, amplitude, timbre, duration, and other sound qualities. Each message has at least one and usually two data bytes that accompany the status byte to describe these sound qualities.

Note On

The Note On message signals the beginning of a note. It is usually sent by a MIDI-equipped keyboard when a player first presses a key. Note On tells a receiving device to start playing a note. A Note On message transmits three pieces of information: the channel the message is being sent over, the pitch of the note (a number from 0 to 127), and the attack velocity of the note (also a number from 0 to 127).

The pitch value (0-127) represents the number of half-steps the note lies above the C♮ that is five octaves below middle C (two octaves below the bottom C♮ on a piano keyboard). The lowest pitch value, 0, represents that low C♮, 60 represents middle C, and the highest pitch, 127, represents a G♮ five and a half octaves above middle C (one and a half octaves above the top note of a piano keyboard). To see how these pitch values work, look at the series of numbers in Figure 5-7. It represents a C major scale starting at middle C.

Figure 5-7.
The C major scale depicted on a keyboard with corresponding pitch values.

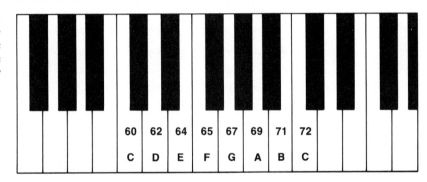

The velocity value ranges from 0, which represents no velocity, to 127, which represents maximum velocity. Because synthesizers usually use note velocity to set the loudness of the note, a velocity value of 0 means that the note doesn't sound at all. A velocity value of 1 is very soft (a *pianissississimo*), while a velocity value of 127 is very loud (a *fortissississimo*). A value of 64, midway between the two extremes, is moderately loud, somewhere between a *mezzo piano* and a *mezzo forte*. MIDI devices that can't handle variations in attack velocity usually send a 64 as the velocity value of every Note On message they send.

Note Off

The Note Off message signals the end of a note. It occurs when a player releases a key on a MIDI-equipped keyboard. A device receiving a Note Off message stops a note it started playing previously in response to a Note On message. Note Off conveys three pieces of information: the channel the message is being sent over, the pitch of the note (a number from 0 to 127), and the release velocity of the note (also a number from 0 to 127).

The pitch values for Note Off represent the same notes as they do for a Note On message, and release velocity also works much the same as attack velocity: A value of 0 means that the note isn't released at all, and 127 means that the note is released very quickly. Because release velocity often controls the way notes die out, a low release velocity value usually means a note dies away slowly, while a high value usually means that a note dies away quickly. MIDI devices that don't handle release velocities use a value of 64 with every Note Off they send.

Polyphonic Key Pressure

The Polyphonic Key Pressure message reports on pressure for any individual note being played. It is usually sent by a keyboard that's capable of detecting the pressure put on individual keys. A device receiving a Polyphonic Key Pressure message can act on it in any number of ways, although most devices add more *vibrato* to a note when they receive information indicating more pressure for the note. Polyphonic Key Pressure conveys three pieces of information: the channel the message is being sent over, the pitch of the note the pressure affects (a number from 0 to 127), and the pressure of the note (a number from 0 to 127).

Pitch values are expressed precisely as they are for Note On. The pressure value ranges from no pressure at 0 to the highest possible pressure at 127. Because pressure often determines *vibrato,* a low pressure value usually sets a narrow (small amount of) *vibrato* for the note it affects, and a high pressure value usually sets a wide (large amount of) *vibrato.*

Channel Pressure

The Channel Pressure message reports on overall pressure for any notes being played. It is usually sent by a keyboard that can detect overall pressure on its keys but not pressure on each individual key. A device receiving a Channel Pressure message can react in many different ways, but most devices use the information to set the *vibrato* for all the notes the device is playing. Channel Pressure conveys two pieces of information: the channel the message is being sent over, and what the overall pressure is (a number from 0 to 127).

As with Polyphonic Key Pressure, the pressure value for the Channel Pressure message ranges from no pressure at 0 to maximum pressure at 127, and it usually affects the amount of *vibrato* that is used to play notes. The main difference is that the pressure expressed in a Channel Pressure message affects all the notes currently being played on a single MIDI channel, while pressure in a Polyphonic Key Pressure message affects only a single note on a specified pitch.

Program Change

The Program Change message signals a patch change in a synthesizer, which usually occurs when a player presses a patch button on the control panel of a synthesizer. A device receiving a Program Change message changes the patch it's using to play notes. A Program Change message conveys two things: the channel it's being sent over and the number of the new patch selected (a number from 0 to 127).

Because a Program Change message selects a new patch on a receiving MIDI device, the patch number it sends affects the characteristic sound of all the notes played on the receiving device. Patch numbers do not produce standard results on all synthesizers, however. The specific patch stored for each number varies from synthesizer to synthesizer, and this can lead to problems. For example, if you press patch button number 4 on a synthesizer to select an electric kazoo patch, the synthesizer sends a Program Change message with patch number 4 to an attached synthesizer. When the attached synthesizer receives the message, it changes to its own patch number 4, which might be a bass piccolo patch, or whatever other kind of patch the synthesizer stores as patch number 4.

Control Change

The Control Change message sends information about a new setting for a control on a MIDI device. It can be sent whenever you move a controller or push a switch on a synthesizer or other MIDI device. Many synthesizers have controls that do not send Control Change messages, however. The volume control on some synthesizers, for example, does not send MIDI messages to communicate its current setting.

A device receiving a Control Change message changes its operation to reflect the new control setting. A Control Change message conveys three different pieces of information: the number of the channel over which it's sent; a number from 0 to 121, called the *control value,* that identifies the control that's been moved or pushed; and a number from 0 to 127, called the *setting value,* that represents the new setting of the control or further definition of the control.

There are three kinds of controls that Control Change messages work for: *continuous controllers,* controllers that have a full range of settings; *switches,* controllers that are either on or off with no intermediate settings; and *data controllers,* controllers that can enter numerical data directly or by stepping through values at each push of a button.

The MIDI specifications assign a range of control numbers for each type of controller. Control numbers 0 to 63 are used for continuous controllers, control numbers 64 to 95 are used for switches (and can also be used for certain types of continuous controllers), and control numbers 96 to 101 are used for data controllers. Some control numbers are assigned to specific controllers. For example, control number 1 is the modulation control (a continous controller), and control number 64 is the sustain pedal (a switch). Many numbers have been left undefined, however, so that manufacturers can use them for miscellaneous controllers not defined in the MIDI specifications.

The setting value (0-127) conveys the new setting of a control that's been moved. For a continuous controller, the value can reflect 128 different settings, from 0 (turned or pushed all the way to the bottom of the controller's range) to 127 (turned or pushed all the way to the top of the range). If the continous controller needs more than 128 possible values to convey its setting precisely, then a MIDI device can send two linked Control Change messages. The setting value of the first message combines with the setting value of the second message to allow 16,384 different settings. The setting value for switches is simpler. Any value from 0 to 63 means the switch is turned off, and any value from 64 to 127 means the switch is turned on.

Conveying the new value for a data controller can take as many as three Control Change messages. The first two messages identify the attribute whose value is changing: The control values tell a receiving device that the messages are both data controller messages; the setting values indicate which of the synthesizer's operating attributes is affected. The receiving device combines the two setting values to come up with an attribute number in the range from 0 to 16,383. The third Control Change message defines the change in the setting: The control value tells the receiving device to move the setting up or down incrementally (by a set number of counts) or to move the setting to an entirely new value; the setting value tells the receiving device how far to increment or decrement the current value or what the entirely new value should be. If you want more details about sending data controller values using Control Change messages, see Appendix A.

Pitch Bend Change

The Pitch Bend Change message sends information about a new setting for a pitch bend controller. It is usually sent when you move the pitch bend controller on a synthesizer. A device receiving a Pitch Bend Change message changes the pitch of the notes it's playing by bending them up or down to the new setting. A Pitch Bend Change message conveys two different pieces of information: the channel number on which it's sent, and a number from 0 to 16,383 that gives the new setting of the pitch bend controller.

If the pitch bend controller is a pitch bend wheel, the setting value tells the location of the pitch bend wheel: 0 means the pitch bend wheel is turned all the way to the bottom of its range, so that the pitch bends down as far as it can go; 8192 means the wheel is set in the center, where it normally rests, producing no pitch bend; 16,383 means the wheel is turned all the way to the top of its range, so that the pitch bends as far up as it can go. Other numbers indicate various amounts of pitch bend between the maximum and minimum.

The amount of pitch bending that results from a Pitch Bend Change message varies from device to device and depends on the pitch bend range setting of each device. For example, one MIDI device might let you bend pitch up and down by three half-steps in each direction, while a second MIDI device lets you bend pitch up and down by an octave in each direction. If both devices receive the same Pitch Bend Change message telling them that the pitch bend setting is at 0 (all the way down), the results will be quite different. The first MIDI device will bend the pitch of all the notes it's playing down by three half-steps, while the second MIDI device will bend the pitch down by a whole octave. To be sure two devices bend pitch in unison, you need to set both to bend pitches over the same range.

Channel Mode Messages

Channel mode messages set the MIDI channel receiving modes for different MIDI devices, stop spurious notes from playing, and affect local control of a device. They're much simpler than the channel voice messages and don't carry so much data in each message.

Local Control

The Local Control message connects or disconnects the controls of a MIDI device from the device's own sound generators. It is usually sent by a sequencer or a computer controlling a synthesizer. This is a very handy message to send if you're using as a subordinate device a synthesizer with a keyboard, and you want it played only by incoming MIDI messages. By turning off the local control of the synthesizer, its keys won't make any sound, and its controls won't have any effect on the internal functions of the synthesizer.

It's also handy to turn off local control of a synthesizer if you want to use its keyboard and controls as a master keyboard. Any time you press keys or use controls, the results are sent only over MIDI cables to control other synthesizers and don't actually produce sounds with the synthesizer's own sound generators.

A Local Control message conveys two pieces of information: the channel on which it's sent and the status of local control, on or off.

All Notes Off   If a synthesizer has been sent Note On messages and is playing notes but
                         somehow doesn't receive all the Note Off messages it needs to turn off all
                         the notes, then some notes will play indefinitely. The All Notes Off mes-
                         sage is a convenient way to handle this situation. Rather than trying to find
                         the pitches of the notes still playing by sending Note Off messages for each
                         of the 128 possible pitches, a single All Notes Off message tells the receiv-
                         ing synthesizer to stop playing all notes.

                             An All Notes Off message conveys only the channel number that it's
                         being sent on. It doesn't need to specify anything further and so conveys no
                         additional data.

Omni Mode Off   When a MIDI device receives the Omni Mode Off message, it changes its
                         MIDI channel reception mode (described earlier in this chapter) so that the
                         device receives MIDI messages on discrete MIDI channels instead of re-
                         ceiving messages on all channels. If the device is already set to Omni Mode
                         Off, then this message has no effect.

                             The Omni Mode Off message is usually sent by a sequencer or a
                         computer controlling different MIDI devices. Because changing the chan-
                         nel reception mode of a device might leave it playing notes for which it can
                         no longer receive Note Off messages, a device receiving Omni Mode Off
                         automatically turns off all of its notes.

                             The Omni Mode Off message conveys only the channel number on
                         which the message is sent.

Omni Mode On   A MIDI device receiving the Omni Mode On message changes its MIDI
                         channel reception mode (if it's not already set to Omni Mode On) so that it
                         receives all MIDI channel messages regardless of the channel on which
                         they're sent. Like the Omni Mode Off message, Omni Mode On is usually
                         sent by a controlling sequencer or computer, and it automatically turns off
                         all notes being played by the receiving device. Omni Mode On conveys
                         only the channel number on which it's sent.

Mono Mode On   A MIDI device receiving the Mono Mode On message sets its MIDI chan-
                         nel reception mode so that it plays notes monophonically. This message is
                         usually sent by a sequencer or controlling computer. It automatically turns
                         off Poly Mode and stops all notes that the receiving device is playing.
                         Mono Mode On conveys only the channel number on which it's sent.

Poly Mode On   A MIDI device receiving the Poly Mode On message sets its MIDI channel
                         reception mode so that the device plays polyphonically. This message is

usually sent by a sequencer or controlling computer. It automatically turns off Mono Mode and stops all notes that the receiving device is playing. Poly Mode On conveys only the channel number on which it's sent.

Using these channel mode messages—Omni Mode Off, Omni Mode On, Mono Mode On, Poly Mode On—you can set any of the four possible MIDI channel reception modes for a device.

SYSTEM MESSAGES

MIDI devices send system messages without using channel numbers so that all the devices receiving the messages can act on them. There are three types of system messages: *system common messages, system real time messages,* and *system exclusive messages.* System common messages help coordinate song selection and tuning among MIDI devices, while system real time messages synchronize the timing among different sequencers during performance and recording. System exclusive messages send data between specific devices that can't be sent as any other kind of MIDI message.

To understand how the system messages that deal with sequencers work, it's important to understand what a *song* is in MIDI parlance. When a device with a sequencer (such as a drum machine, computer, or dedicated sequencer) records incoming messages, it records them in the order they're received and records the amount of time that elapses between the messages. This recording of messages is called a *sequence.* Most sequencers let you edit the messages in a sequence and link different sequences stored in memory. The finished sequence, ready for playback, is called a song.

Most sequencers store different songs in their memories, similar to the way a jukebox stores records. You can call up different songs by asking for them by title or number. Most drum machines, for example, have a set of buttons you can push to call up different songs. These buttons work something like patch buttons on a synthesizer: Each button you push brings up a different song. Once the song is ready to play, you play it as you do a song recorded on an audio cassette. One button starts the song playing; another button stops it.

You can usually start playing the song at any point, something like fast forwarding or rewinding a cassette in a cassette player to a section of a song you want to hear. A special feature of a sequencer lets you speed up or slow down the song as you play it back, usually by turning a knob or adjusting some other control.

System Real-Time Messages

System real-time messages are all very short and simple. They are only one byte long and carry no extra data with them, such as channel numbers, pitches, or velocity. Because these messages synchronize the timing of MIDI devices in performance, it's important that they be sent at precisely the time they are required. They must not be forced to wait for other long MIDI messages to be sent first. To avoid delays, system real-time messages are sent in the middle of other messages, if necessary. For example, a one-byte system real-time message can be inserted between the status byte and the first data byte of a channel message, as shown in Figure 5-8. When a receiving device receives a real-time message, it quickly acts on the message, and then returns to its previous activity.

Figure 5-8.
A real-time message can be inserted between the bytes of other messages.

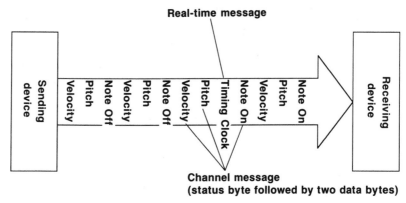

Timing Clock

The Timing Clock message (often called a *MIDI clock*) is the most important and frequently sent system real-time message; it helps keep separate sequencers in the same MIDI system playing at the same tempo. When a master sequencer plays a song, it sends out a stream of Timing Clock messages as it plays to convey the tempo to the other sequencers. The faster the Timing Clocks come in, the faster the receiving sequencer plays the song.

To keep a standard timing reference, the MIDI specifications state that 24 MIDI clocks equal one quarter note. This means, of course, that the other standard note lengths also have clock equivalents, as shown in the chart in Figure 5-9.

To see how Timing Clocks work, consider a sequencer that has a quarter note and two eighth notes to play. It receives a stream of Timing Clock messages from another sequencer that sets the performance tempo. The receiving sequencer starts playing its quarter note and then begins to count successive Timing Clocks as they come in. Once it has counted 24 clocks, it ends the quarter note and starts an eighth note. After counting 12

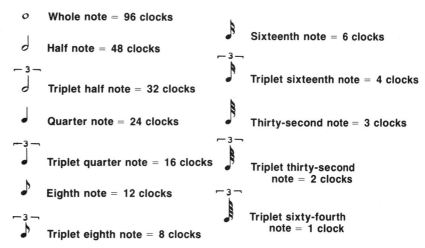

Figure 5-9.
MIDI reproduces traditional note lengths using MIDI clocks.

more clocks, it ends the eighth note and starts a second eighth note. After 12 more clocks, it ends the second eighth note. The rate of the incoming MIDI clocks sets the tempo of the notes the sequencer plays.

Start

The Start message is a simple message that tells the receiving sequencer to start playing at the beginning of whatever song it has ready to play.

Stop

The Stop message tells the receiving sequencer to stop playing its song.

Continue

The Continue message tells the receiving sequencer to start playing its song at whatever point it last stopped playing. This message differs from the Start message in that it doesn't ask the sequencer to start the song again at the beginning. The Continue message allows the sequencer to start at whatever point it received the last Stop message.

Active Sensing

In a perfect world, MIDI cables would never come unplugged when they weren't supposed to. In our imperfect world, cables do come unplugged, often with embarrassing consequences: You get no response as you pound on the master keyboard, and, even worse, notes playing on a disconnected subordinate device continue to play because the device is unable to receive Note Off or All Notes Off messages. Active Sensing messages can help you avoid this awkward situation.

When a device sends an Active Sensing message to another device, the receiving device detects that there is a good connection between the two devices. After the receiving device receives the first Active Sensing message, the device expects to receive Active Sensing messages regularly every 300 milliseconds (about 3 messages per second). If it doesn't receive regular Active Sensing messages, it assumes the connection has been broken and turns off all the notes it's playing. Active Sensing messages are used for connection testing because they come at regular intervals (even when the sending device isn't active in any other way), and because they don't create any reaction in the receiving device when they are received.

Few devices are equipped to send out or receive Active Sensing messages; however, this does not cause any compatibility problems. If a device equipped to receive Active Sensing messages doesn't receive one, then it doesn't expect them at regular intervals. And if a device unequipped to receive Active Sensing messages is in fact sent these mesages, it merely ignores them.

System Reset

The System Reset message asks the receiving device to reset itself to its *default* setting, the condition it's in when you first turn it on. The default setting usually means that the device is in MIDI channel reception Mode 1 (Omni On/Poly), that local control is on with all the voices turned off (no notes playing), that the song in a sequencer is set to play from the beginning, and that song playback is turned off. Because the default settings vary somewhat from device to device, the System Reset message can have different results on different devices.

System Common Messages

System common messages are commands that prepare sequencers and synthesizers to play a song. The various messages enable you to select a song, find a common starting place in the song, and tune all the synthesizers if they need tuning.

Song Select

The Song Select message asks a sequencer to load a specific song from its memory. Song Select identifies the song using a number from 0 to 127. The sequencer responds by finding and then loading the song stored under that particular number.

Song Position Pointer

The Song Position Pointer message sets a sequencer to begin playing a song at any point in the song. Song Position Pointer carries with it a value from 0 to 16,383 to set a new song position. This number tells the distance of the new song position in 6-clock increments from the beginning of the song. Because 6 MIDI clocks equal a sixteenth note, you can also think of the pointer value as the distance measured in sixteenth notes from the beginning of the song.

Song Position Pointer isn't meant to be used while the sequencer is already playing a song. If you use it while several sequencers are playing a song together, timing difficulties in sending and implementing the messages might throw the sequencers out of synchronization.

Tune Request

The Tune Request message asks all receiving MIDI devices to tune themselves. This message is rarely used, however. Digital synthesizers don't drift in and out of tune, and the analog synthesizers that do often lack the ability to tune themselves.

EOX: End of Exclusive

The EOX (End of Exclusive) message informs receiving MIDI devices that a system exclusive message has ended. The MIDI specifications classify EOX as a system common message, so it's mentioned in this section. Its function is explained in greater detail in the next section.

System Exclusive Messages

The format of a system exclusive message allows MIDI manufacturers to create customized MIDI messages to send between their MIDI devices. Each system exclusive message starts with a status byte that identifies it as a system exclusive message. The first data byte that follows is an identification number from 0 to 127, which identifies the manufacturer of the device sending the message. (For example, the number 67 means the manufacturer is Yamaha.)

When a device receives a system exclusive message, it reads the identification number to see if the message was sent by another device made by the same manufacturer. If so, the device tunes in to the rest of the message. But if the sending device was made by a different manufacturer, the receiving device ignores the rest of the message. Some devices, such as computers, can be programmed to receive and understand system exclusive messages sent by a device made by another manufacturer. Such devices can also send the system exclusive messages using identification numbers of different manufacturers.

A system exclusive message can have as many data bytes as the sending device wants to send. These data bytes (all numbers from 0 to 127) can represent anything the maker desires. Some manufacturers use system exclusive data bytes to send the information for patches back and forth between synthesizers, so that patches designed on one synthesizer can be loaded into a second similar synthesizer without your having to enter them on the control panel. Other manufacturers use system exclusive messages to send custom messages that use the special features of their equipment. For example, some Yamaha synthesizers use system exclusive messages to send special Note On and Note Off messages that can tune each note to be slightly sharp or flat.

When a device is finished sending a system exclusive message, it sends an EOX message to signal the end of the message. When the devices that are ignoring the system exclusive message receive the EOX message, they start paying attention to messages that arrive over the MIDI cable. Of course, some messages, such as Timing Clocks and other system real time messages, can be sent sandwiched between the data bytes of a system exclusive message. Because these messages comprise a single status byte (a number from 128 to 255), receiving devices that are ignoring the system exclusive data bytes (ranging from 0 to 127) can pick them out, act on them, and then go back to ignoring data bytes.

MIDI IN OPERATION

Now you've seen the kinds of messages that MIDI devices can send back and forth between themselves. When the devices actually use these messages, a few odds and ends have to be taken care of to ensure that the messages all work the way they should.

Transmitting Simultaneous Events

MIDI is a serial interface: It sends single messages through the cables one after the other. Musical events don't always happen one after the other. What happens, for example, if a player plays a chord by pressing three keys on a synthesizer at the same time? MIDI must somehow transmit those three simultaneous notes using successive messages.

MIDI gets around these problems by being faster than the human hand and ear. MIDI can send even the longest messages (with the exception of system exclusive messages) at the rate of at least 1040 messages per second. A MIDI device can read keypresses even faster than this. When a player plays a chord, what seem like simultaneous keypresses are usually separated by inaudible milliseconds. The keypresses are actually a series of notes played so close together that they sound simultaneous. The MIDI keyboard sends these chord notes one at a time at a rate so fast that you hear them as simultaneous notes.

Running Status

MIDI devices can use a technique called *running status* to make data transmission even faster. Running status allows a device to send a stream of messages of the same kind without repeating the status byte for each message. When the receiving device receives a status byte, it stays in that status mode until it receives a new status byte. It interprets any subsequent data bytes according to the established status mode.

For example, consider a series of Note On messages. Each Note On message usually has a status byte followed by two data bytes, one for pitch and one for velocity. To send a series of Note On messages using running status, a device sends a Note On status byte and then follows it with a pair of data bytes for each note. When the receiving device receives the first Note On message, it enters Note On mode. It interprets each pair of data bytes that follows as the pitch and velocity values for a new note. Because a note with a velocity of 0 has no volume, a pair of data bytes with 0 velocity can turn off a note without sending a Note Off message that would break up the stream of Note On data.

When the sending device wants to send another kind of message, it simply stops sending data and sends another message as it would normally. As soon as the receiving device receives a new status byte, it enters the appropriate status mode and interprets new data accordingly. By eliminating repeated status bytes, running status reduces the number of message bytes and speeds up note transmission.

Irrelevant Messages

MIDI messages convey information about a wide variety of MIDI device features. Unfortunately, not all MIDI devices have the full range of features, which means that a device occasionally receives a message that it can't possibly act on. For example, a synthesizer that can't bend the pitch of notes might receive a Pitch Bend Change message. Its response is simple: It ignores the message.

One important implication of irrelevant messages is this rule: The fact that you can send messages to a device doesn't mean the device has the features to respond. Connecting a velocity-sensing keyboard to a synthesizer, for example, doesn't mean the synthesizer will respond to the velocity information by playing notes louder and softer. The synthesizer needs the built-in features to respond to velocity. Because the MIDI specifications don't state how many features a MIDI device must have, a MIDI device need not be equipped to respond to all MIDI messages.

MIDI Messages on Parade

One of the best ways to see how MIDI messages work is to look at an example. The example that follows introduces a hypothetical MIDI system and then presents a simple stream of MIDI messages to show how the different types of messages can work together to make music.

A Hypothetical MIDI System

Figure 5-10 shows the MIDI system used in this example. The system has a sequencer, a drum machine with a built-in sequencer, and three synthesizers. The arrows in the figure show the direction of the message flow.

Figure 5-10.
A hypothetical MIDI system.

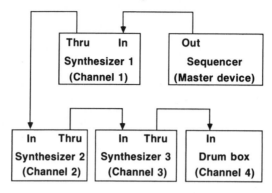

The sequencer is the master device; it sends messages to all the other devices in the system. The four other devices are set to receive messages in Mode 3 (Omni Off/Poly): Synthesizer 1 is set to receive MIDI channel 1, synthesizer 2 to receive channel 2, synthesizer 3 to receive channel 3, and the drum machine to receive channel 4.

Preparing to Play a Song

The first messages that the sequencer sends prepare the system to play. First, they transfer a patch stored in the sequencer's own memory to synthesizer 2. Next, they load a song in the drum machine and instruct the synthesizers to tune up. In the following table the messages sent by the sequencer are shown in the left column, with any data bytes indented below the status byte of the message. The results of the messages are listed in the right column.

Message	Result
System exclusive	All the devices wait to see if this affects them.
Manufacturer #61	Only synthesizer 2, made by manufacturer 61, tunes in.
A stream of data bytes	Synthesizer 2 gets a new patch.
EOX (End of Exclusive)	All devices tune in again.
Song Select	Devices that lack sequencers ignore this message.
Song #5	The drum machine loads song #5.
Tune Request	Synthesizer 3, an analog synthesizer, tunes up. The other devices ignore this message.

After the sequencer sets up the MIDI system to play, it starts to play the short piece of music shown in Figure 5-11. It sends the high notes to synthesizer 1, the middle notes to synthesizer 2, and the low notes to synthesizer 3. The drum machine starts playing its own song, a running pattern of sixteenth notes that mark time against the sequence of notes the synthesizers play.

Figure 5-11.
*The music the
sequencer plays.*

What follows are the messages that the sequencer sends. This list doesn't show the timing between messages, but there is a handy rule of thumb. Whenever you see Note On and Note Off messages in a cluster, the sequencer sent them out as close together as possible. Between Timing Clock messages, there is a regular time interval which keeps the drum machine playing at a tempo synchronized to the notes the sequencer plays.

Message	Result
Start	The drum machine plays a sixteenth note.

Note On, Channel 3
  Pitch 65
  Velocity 64
	Synthesizer 3 plays an F.

Note On, Channel 2
  Pitch 69
  Velocity 64
	Synthesizer 2 plays an A.

Note On, Channel 1
  Pitch 72
  Velocity 64
	Synthesizer 1 plays a C.

Timing Clock	
Timing Clock	
Timing Clock	
Timing Clock	
Timing Clock	
Timing Clock	After counting 6 clocks (the equivalent of a sixteenth note), the drum machine plays its next sixteenth note.
6 Timing Clocks	The drum machine plays another sixteenth note.
6 Timing Clocks	The drum machine plays another sixteenth note.
6 Timing Clocks	The drum machine plays another sixteenth note.

(continued)

Message	Result

Note Off, Channel 3
  Pitch 65
  Velocity 64
	Synthesizer 3 turns off its F.

Note Off, Channel 2
  Pitch 69
  Velocity 64
	Synthesizer 2 turns off its A.

Note Off, Channel 1
  Pitch 72
  Velocity 64
	Synthesizer 1 turns off its C.

Note On, Channel 3
  Pitch 65
  Velocity 64
	Synthesizer 3 plays an F.

Note On, Channel 2
  Pitch 70
  Velocity 64
	Synthesizer 2 plays a B♭.

Note On, Channel 1
  Pitch 74
  Velocity 64
	Synthesizer 1 plays a D.

6 Timing Clocks	The drum machine plays another sixteenth note.
6 Timing Clocks	The drum machine plays another sixteenth note.
6 Timing Clocks	The drum machine plays another sixteenth note.
6 Timing Clocks	The drum machine plays another sixteenth note.

Note Off, Channel 3
  Pitch 65
  Velocity 64
	Synthesizer 3 turns off its F.

Note Off, Channel 2
  Pitch 70
  Velocity 64
	Synthesizer 2 turns off its B♭.

Note Off, Channel 1
  Pitch 74
  Velocity 64
	Synthesizer 1 turns off its D.

Note On, Channel 3
  Pitch 65
  Velocity 64
	Synthesizer 3 plays an F.

Note On, Channel 2
  Pitch 69
  Velocity 64
	Synthesizer 2 plays an A.

Note On, Channel 1
  Pitch 72
  Velocity 64
	Synthesizer 1 plays a C.

6 Timing Clocks	The drum machine plays another sixteenth note.
6 Timing Clocks	The drum machine plays another sixteenth note.

(continued)

Message	Result
Note Off, Channel 3 Pitch 65 Velocity 64	Synthesizer 3 turns off its F.
Note Off, Channel 2 Pitch 69 Velocity 64	Synthesizer 2 turns off its A.
Note Off, Channel 1 Pitch 72 Velocity 64	Synthesizer 1 turns off its C.
Note On, Channel 3 Pitch 64 Velocity 64	Synthesizer 3 plays an E.
Note On, Channel 2 Pitch 67 Velocity 64	Synthesizer 2 plays a G.
Note On, Channel 1 Pitch 72 Velocity 64	Synthesizer 1 plays a C.
6 Timing Clocks	The drum machine plays another sixteenth note.
6 Timing Clocks	The drum machine plays another sixteenth note.
6 Timing Clocks	The drum machine plays another sixteenth note.
6 Timing Clocks	The drum machine plays another sixteenth note.
Note Off, Channel 3 Pitch 64 Velocity 64	Synthesizer 3 turns off its E.
Note Off, Channel 2 Pitch 67 Velocity 64	Synthesizer 2 turns off its G.
Note Off, Channel 1 Pitch 72 Velocity 64	Synthesizer 1 turns off its C.
Note On, Channel 3 Pitch 65 Velocity 64	Synthesizer 3 plays an F.
Note On, Channel 2 Pitch 69 Velocity 64	Synthesizer 2 plays an A.
Note On, Channel 1 Pitch 72 Velocity 64	Synthesizer 1 plays a C.
6 Timing Clocks	The drum machine plays another sixteenth note.
6 Timing Clocks	The drum machine plays another sixteenth note.

(continued)

Message	Result
6 Timing Clocks	The drum machine plays another sixteenth note.
6 Timing Clocks	The drum machine plays another sixteenth note.
Note Off, Channel 3 Pitch 65 Velocity 64	Synthesizer 3 turns off its F.
Note Off, Channel 2 Pitch 69 Velocity 64	Synthesizer 2 turns off its A.
Note Off, Channel 1 Pitch 72 Velocity 64	Synthesizer 1 turns off its C.
Stop	The drum machine stops playing its song.

All the data in the preceding table creates only a few seconds of music, the five chords and the percussion sounds indicated in Figure 5-11. The sequencer does not send Note On and Note Off messages for the percussion sounds because the drum machine sends those from its own sequencer.

In the last chapter, you learned about physical MIDI connections and, in this chapter, about the messages sent over the connections. With the information in both of these chapters, you have a good working knowledge of MIDI that will help you use MIDI systems confidently. If the material in these chapters has piqued your curiosity about the technical details of MIDI connections and MIDI messages, be sure to read Appendix A, "Getting Technical." It explains the fundamentals of serial data transmission and the specific, bit-by-bit format for each type of MIDI message.

Upcoming chapters show you how to use MIDI in practical applications and introduce you to actual MIDI systems and their users. The next chapter deals with one of the most exciting and versatile additions to any MIDI system: the computer.

6 | COMPUTERS AND MIDI

Computers excel at working with MIDI messages. After all, MIDI messages are nothing but numbers sent serially over a cable, and computers were originally designed to manipulate numbers. By adding a personal computer to your MIDI system, you can apply its computing power to notes, rests, patches, and other aspects of music communicated through MIDI messages. The computer can change its function depending on the software you use, effectively providing you with many different MIDI devices for the price of one.

In this chapter, you'll learn how a personal computer works in a MIDI system. If you've never used a personal computer before, read the first part of this chapter, a short introduction to computers that explains what they are, what parts they have, and what they do. The next part of the chapter tells you how a computer can be adapted to communicate by means of MIDI cables and MIDI messages. The last part of this chapter shows some of the many ways you can use a computer in a MIDI system.

A PERSONAL COMPUTER PRIMER

A computer is a device that has a *CPU* (central processing unit) that performs numerical calculations, *memory* to store numerical values, a set of controls that allow you to control the CPU, and an output of some sort that imparts the results of the computer's operations. Technically speaking, a digital synthesizer is a computer—it has a microprocessor that works as a CPU, memory to store patches and other synthesizer settings, keys and buttons to control the microprocessor, and a small display on which the microprocessor presents information. Other devices that are technically computers include household equipment such as programmable microwave ovens and compact disc players.

A personal computer is a general-purpose computer designed to be used by one person at a time. It differs from devices such as digital synthesizers and microwave ovens in that these other devices are *dedicated* computers, designed to perform a specific type of task. (They are "dedicated" to that task.) A personal computer has features that can be used for activities as diverse as cartoon animation and budget forecasting. These features are divided into two separate types: *hardware* and *software.* The physical components of the computer are the hardware. Software is invisible. It provides the computer a set of instructions, usually called a *program,* that occupies the computer's memory and guides its operation.

If you're not familiar with the concept of hardware and software, consider a familiar example: a cassette player. The player, its amplifier, batteries, speakers, and other physical components are the hardware. The cassettes you play are also hardware, but the music recorded on the cassettes, stored as magnetic impulses on tape, is software.

A Typical Personal Computer: Hardware

Most of today's personal computers are similar in overall design. Figure 6-1 shows a typical computer with its parts labeled. Refer to the figure as you read the following sections.

The System Unit

The system unit is the central part of a personal computer and houses the computer's internal circuitry, microchips, power supply, and other important components. Its internal parts control all other parts of the computer.

The microprocessor is the most important chip in the system unit. It is the computer's CPU—it performs calculations and follows the instructions you send it. The microprocessor also controls the other chips and components in the computer. It uses *memory chips* to store information. Most memory chips in the system unit are *RAM chips* (short for random access memory) that let you manipulate information very quickly. The microprocessor can write, erase, and transfer information from one section of RAM to another.

Figure 6-1.
*Front and back
views of a typical
personal computer.*

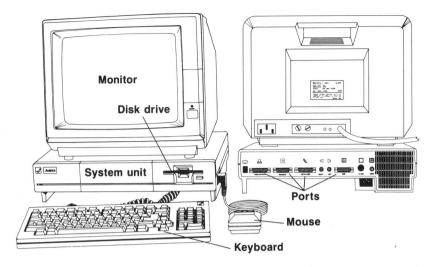

As a rule, RAM chips don't store information for long periods of time: They lose all their information when you turn off the electrical power, even if it's off for only a fraction of a second. A second type of memory chip, a *ROM chip* (short for read only memory), stores information permanently, even when the power is turned off. The information stored on a ROM chip is permanently engraved in the chip at the factory. The microprocessor can only read information from ROM; it can neither write over nor erase any information stored on a ROM chip.

Many computers have chips that can generate sound, usually referred to as *sound chips*. The microprocessor controls these chips to make music, so that the computer functions as a synthesizer. The quality of the sound produced by computer sound chips isn't usually very high, however. Expensive sound chips and the other electronic components required to create an excellent audio signal add a considerable amount to the cost of the computer, prompting most computer manufacturers to use less expensive audio chips and components to keep the final price down. Typical computer sound-generating capabilities support three or four voices with a very limited range of timbres. Some new computers do include high-quality sound chips, with results that are encouraging. These machines can use sampled sound and can have 8, 16, or even more voices.

The Keyboard

The keyboard is the primary means of controlling the computer. It enables you to type commands and enter data. Because its keys are usually arranged like a standard typewriter keyboard, it's often called a *QWERTY keyboard* (after the letters in the second row of the keyboard) to distinguish it from a music keyboard used with a synthesizer.

The Monitor

The computer uses the *monitor* to display information. On most computers, the monitor looks like a television set because it uses the same technology: a *CRT* (cathode ray tube) that displays the picture. Some small portable computers have flat displays that use *LCD* (liquid-crystal display) technology, the same technology that most digital watches use. The computer monitor can be separate from the system unit, connected by a cable, or built directly into it.

The Mouse

A *mouse* isn't standard equipment for all computers but is rapidly becoming a popular addition to the QWERTY keyboard for giving instructions to the computer. The mouse is connected to the system unit with a long cable. It has a small rolling ball on the bottom that the computer uses to sense motion as you slide the mouse across the desk.

When you move the mouse, you move a pointer displayed on the monitor to a different location on the screen. By clicking a button (or buttons) built into the mouse, you can give the computer instructions that pertain to the object or location you're pointing to on the screen. Using the mouse provides an alternative to memorizing a long list of computer commands and typing them on the keyboard.

Disk Drives

As a computer receives information—characters you type in or notes coming in over MIDI—it stores the information in RAM. This information is always at the mercy of the power supply, since the information will abruptly vanish the instant you turn off the computer. To provide safe, long-term storage, most computers use a *disk drive* to store information from one session to the next.

The most commonly used type of disk drive records information on a rotating *floppy disk*. A floppy disk (shown in Figure 6-2) is a thin, flexible disk made of the same material as audio recording tape and covered with a protective outer envelope.

Figure 6-2.
Two common types
of floppy disks:
5¹/₄-inch and
3¹/₂-inch.

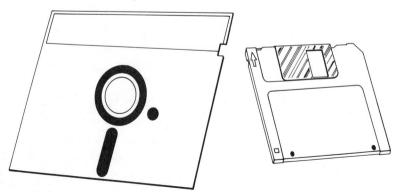

The disk drive uses a recording head much like a tape recorder head to record data magnetically on the floppy disk as it rotates in the drive. The disk drive can also read the information stored on the disk so that the computer can load whatever information it needs from the disk into RAM. Once the computer finishes sending and receiving data to and from a disk drive, the drive stops rotating, so you can remove the disk from the drive and put in another one.

A *hard disk drive* uses a rigid metal disk, instead of a floppy disk, to store information. Unlike floppy disks, the hard disk isn't removable, but it can store 40 or 50 (or more) times as much information as a floppy disk, so it's less important to be able to swap disks in the drive. A computer can also store and retrieve information much faster using a hard disk drive than it can using a floppy disk drive.

Disk drives are often built into the system unit, but they can also be external devices, connected to the console by a data-carrying cord. A computer is usually equipped to use more than one disk drive to increase its data storage capacity and to make copying information from one disk to another much easier.

Computer Ports

Most computers have a set of ports built into the system unit for connecting additional pieces of hardware (usually called *peripherals*). The two most common types of ports found on a computer are *serial ports* and *parallel ports*. As the names imply, a serial port sends data serially, as a MIDI port does, and a parallel port sends data in parallel, transmitting a number of bits simultaneously. The serial port is commonly used to connect a modem (a device that lets the computer send and receive data over the telephone lines), while the parallel port is commonly used to connect a printer.

Other computer ports connect the computer to external disk drives, monitors, keyboards, mice, and other peripherals. One of these additional ports, the audio port, is especially important to musicians. If the computer has sound chips, the audio signal they generate comes out through the audio port. By connecting the audio port to an amplifier and a speaker, you can hear the sound synthesized by the computer.

Printers

The printer, shown in Figure 6-3, is one of the most useful peripherals and is very commonly added to a computer system. It can print text on paper to create letters, reports, articles, and other documents. Most computer printers are *dot-matrix* printers. These printers create letters, numbers, and other characters by using small pins to hammer dots of ink on the page.

Figure 6-3.
*A typical dot-
matrix printer.*

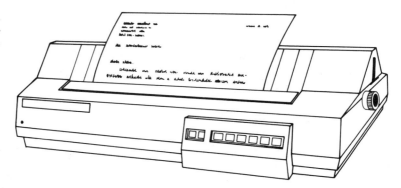

You can see an example of dot-matrix characters in Figure 6-4. Because the computer directly controls the pins in the printer head, it can use them to print any kind of image: pictures, mathematical symbols, and most important to musicians—music staves and notes.

Figure 6-4.
*This musical
notation was
printed on a
standard dot-
matrix printer.*

A Typical Personal Computer: Software

Software does not conform to a set of standards from computer to computer to the extent that hardware does; in fact, software for one kind of computer usually won't work on another kind of computer. But there are some basic categories of the software that personal computers use.

Operating System Software

The one type of software that all computers must have to be able to work is *operating system software.* The operating system is usually stored in part in ROM chips inside the computer so that the computer can run it immediately when you turn on the computer. Typically, the computer then loads additional operating system software from a disk. The operating system tells the computer how to perform fundamental tasks such as recognizing what you type on the keyboard and displaying text and pictures on the monitor. The operating system also tells the computer how to store information in different parts of its memory and on disks in attached disk drives. It's the operating system software that gives a computer much of its distinctive character.

Application Software

Once you turn a computer on so that it begins to run its operating system, the computer is like an idling car waiting to go somewhere. To use the computer for a particular task, you need *application software,* or simply, an *application.* An application is usually sold by a software publisher on a floppy disk. To run an application, you first load it from the disk drive into the computer's RAM.

Each application program makes the computer work in a different way. A word-processing program, for example, enables you to use the computer for entering and editing text. A graphics program has a different objective; it turns the computer into a drawing workstation. A music program turns the computer into a sequencer, a patch synthesizer, a patch librarian, or any of many different devices. Such applications are discussed later in this chapter.

MIDI INTERFACES

The right computer running the right software can become a valuable MIDI device to use in your MIDI system. There's only one problem: Because most personal computers don't come equipped to work in a MIDI system, you have to compensate for their lack of built-in MIDI ports. Fortunately, almost all computers do have a serial port, and it's a simple matter to turn the serial port into several MIDI ports by adding a *MIDI interface.*

A MIDI interface is usually a small piece of equipment that plugs directly into the serial port on the back of the computer, as shown in Figure 6-5 on the next page. In addition to the plug that goes into the serial port, the interface usually has at least one MIDI In port and one MIDI Out port. The electronic components inside the interface take signals coming from the computer through the serial port and convert them to the right voltage to send over a connected MIDI cable. They also convert incoming MIDI messages to the right voltage to send back into the computer through the serial port.

You can buy many different kinds of computer MIDI interfaces. Each is designed for a specific kind of computer and usually won't work with a different kind of computer. While some interfaces offer very few MIDI ports, others can have two MIDI In ports and as many as six or eight MIDI Out ports. Some interfaces also include a MIDI Thru port. When you buy a MIDI interface, it's important to get the appropriate one

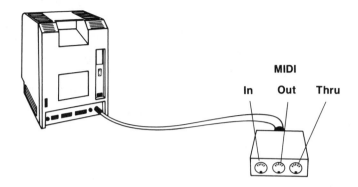

Figure 6-5.
*A MIDI interface
plugged into the
serial port of a
personal computer.*

for the computer you're using, with the right kind and number of MIDI ports for attaching the other devices in your MIDI system.

**Smart and Dumb
MIDI Interfaces**

If you disregard the various MIDI port configurations and the tailoring of interfaces for specific computers, there are two major types of MIDI interfaces: *smart* interfaces and *dumb* interfaces. A smart MIDI interface is a dedicated computer by itself. It has memory and its own software stored in ROM, and it runs on commands it receives through the serial port from the personal computer. When the smart interface acts on commands, it sends appropriate MIDI messages over its MIDI ports. The smart interface can also manipulate messages it receives through its MIDI ports and can send information about those messages back to the personal computer.

A dumb MIDI interface has no microprocessor; it doesn't send or receive MIDI messages on its own. A dumb interface simply ensures that the voltage of the signal coming from the computer's serial port is made compatible with MIDI, and it changes the voltage of incoming MIDI signals to voltages compatible with the computer's serial port. The personal computer, rather than the interface, carries out any processes that actually manipulate MIDI messages.

The main advantage of a smart MIDI interface is that it can perform tasks with very little supervision from the personal computer controlling it. For example, a smart interface can have as part of its built-in software a metronome that sends out regular MIDI clocks through the MIDI Out port to control the tempo of attached drum machines or sequencers. To run the metronome, the computer simply sends two messages to the interface: One sets the tempo, and the next tells the interface to start sending clocks. The interface does the rest of the work until it receives a message from the computer to stop. To create the same metronome using a dumb interface, the computer has to send its own MIDI clocks through the serial port to the interface, which then passes them on to attached MIDI devices. The computer must commit its own resources to calculating the interval between MIDI clocks to set the required tempo.

A smart interface has its disadvantages, as well. To begin with, it's much more expensive than a dumb interface because it requires its own expensive memory chips and a microprocessor. Also, the microprocessor and the program built into the smart interface are often redundant: A personal computer running the right software can be powerful enough by itself to send all its own MIDI messages without help. This is not always the case, though. The IBM PC, for instance, does need the help of a smart interface to send MIDI messages.

There can also be compatibility problems. Application software for the personal computer isn't always compatible with a smart interface. Because each different kind of smart interface has its own set of operating commands, your software might not know what commands to send to a particular interface to make it work. As a result, most applications aren't written to take advantage of a smart interface's own programming. These disadvantages have led most software publishers to sell applications written for dumb interfaces. And most musicians buy dumb interfaces to save expense and to avoid duplicating capabilities that the computer already has.

MIDI SOFTWARE

Once you have a computer connected to your MIDI system, you can run a variety of MIDI application programs. Although these programs have different features and aren't always easy to classify, they generally fall into four major categories:

♦ Music recording and performance applications

♦ Musical notation and printing applications

♦ Synthesizer patch editors and librarians

♦ Music education applications

Music recording and performance applications let you record MIDI messages as they enter the computer from other MIDI devices, and then they let you edit and play back the messages in performance. Musical notation and printing applications enable you to write music using traditional musical notation. You can then play the music using a performance program or print the music on paper for live performance or publication. Synthesizer patch editors and patch librarians are programs that store the information for different synthesizer patches in the computer's memory and disk drives and that allow you to edit the patches in the computer. Music education applications teach you different aspects of music using the computer monitor and the keyboards and other controllers of attached MIDI instruments.

MUSIC RECORDING AND PERFORMANCE

Software to record, edit, and play back MIDI messages is by far the most popular MIDI software for computers. Performers can use a computer running this software much as they'd use a multi-track tape deck in a music studio to record their performances for later playback: A single person can record a song one part at a time and then play back all the parts simultaneously to sound like a full band. Because the software functions like a recording studio, software publishers often call this kind of program a "MIDI recording studio," or more succinctly, a *MIDI recorder.*

Most MIDI recorders are modeled after a tape deck. Often, the screen displays controls that look like Play, Record, Fast Forward, Rewind, and Stop buttons and counters that keep track of MIDI clocks or quarter notes. (Figure 6-6 shows an example of this kind of MIDI recorder.) Unlike a tape deck, however, a MIDI recorder records only the MIDI messages you generate when you play, not the sound you create. In this way, it's more like the piano roll on an old-fashioned player piano; you create a recording of all the keys played and controls moved. When you play back that recording, it works as if you were using the same keys and controls again.

Figure 6-6.
The controls of a typical MIDI recorder resemble those of a standard tape deck (screen from Performer *by Mark of the Unicorn).*

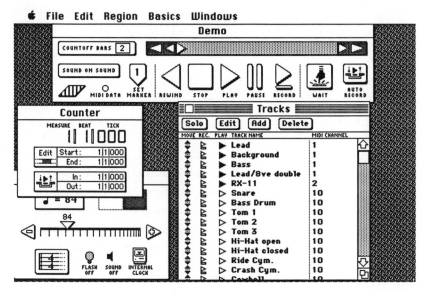

Recording MIDI Messages

Most MIDI recorders record music in *real time*—that is, the MIDI recorder stores MIDI messages in the computer's memory in the order the messages come through the MIDI In port, recording the exact time (usually counted in MIDI clocks or even smaller timing units) between messages. If you speed up or slow down as you play music, the MIDI recording will reflect that change when you play it back.

Step-Time Recording

Some MIDI recorders offer *step-time* recording. When the recorder receives MIDI messages in step time, it records them without noting the time between messages. You specify the time between messages as you record so that you can make the timing as precise as you want. For example, if you are recording a series of notes in step time, you play the first note and then enter the length of the note on the computer keyboard (perhaps 24 MIDI clocks—a quarter note). You then play a new note and enter its length (say, 12 MIDI clocks—an eighth note). By entering the notes a step at a time, specifying each note length exactly, you can create a perfect series of notes. The advantage of step-time recording is accuracy; its disadvantages are tedious note entry and the inability to capture spontaneous nuances of live performance.

Recorder Tracks

The tape recorder in a recording studio is usually a multi-track recorder, capable of recording many tracks at once on a single tape. Each track can store a different audio signal. By recording a different instrument on each track, a recording engineer can change the volume, tone, and other qualities of any individual instrument without affecting the sound of the instruments on other tracks. The use of separate tracks gives the engineer a chance to alter the sound of the playback without re-recording the entire performance.

MIDI recorders also offer separate tracks for recording. Each track records a stream of MIDI messages in a different section of the computer's memory. When the MIDI recorder plays the recording back, it starts all the tracks so that they play simultaneously. By setting each instrument in your MIDI system to send messages on a unique MIDI channel and then setting each track in the MIDI recorder to record one of those channels, you can record a separate instrument on each track.

If you want to record a composition using a single performer to play all the instruments, you can record the composition one part at a time, using a process called *overdubbing*. The first time through, you record one instrument playing on one track. You then stop the recorder and go to another instrument that is set to a second track. When you record this time, the first track plays back its recorded part so that the performer can listen to the first part and synchronize the playing. The next time through you can record a third instrument on a third track while the first two tracks play back their parts.

You can continue through as many tracks as you want (or as many as your recorder can handle) and then play back the entire song. All tracks will play back at once, sounding like many different players performing at the same time.

Punch In and Punch Out

Another handy MIDI recorder feature makes it easy to re-record a portion of a track. Once you've recorded a track full of MIDI messages, you can use *Punch In* to start recording over those messages at any point in the track and *Punch Out* to stop recording at any point.

This feature provides a useful way to correct mistakes in a real-time performance. For example, if you record the performance of a lifetime, perfect except for two botched notes toward the end of the track, you don't have to re-record the entire track. Instead, you play through the track and listen to the performance. When you reach the two botched notes, you punch in to start recording over those notes, and then you play them as they should be played. Immediately afterward, you punch out to stop recording so that you don't record over the notes at the end of the performance. Most MIDI recorders let you set the punch in and punch out points in the track before you play it back; the recorder automatically punches in and punches out at the correct times for you to correct your mistake.

Message Filters

Another useful MIDI recorder feature is a *message filter.* You can set a message filter on a track to ignore certain types of messages as you record. For example, if you don't want to record any Pitch Bend Change messages, set the message filter to filter out Pitch Bend Change messages. As you record, any Pitch Bend Change messages that come into the computer are ignored and not recorded. When you play back the recording, there will be no pitch bends in the music.

Message filters are useful in conserving memory as you record. Some types of messages, such as Pitch Bend Change and Channel Pressure messages, enter the computer in a steady stream as you use the pitch wheel and change the pressure on keyboard keys. These messages consume memory in a computer much faster than simple Note On and Note

Off messages. If you don't need to include some of the more profuse types of messages, you can conserve memory for the notes you play by setting the message filter to eliminate those types.

Editing MIDI Recordings

The biggest advantage of a MIDI recorder over a tape recorder is the ease with which you can make very precise editing changes to a recording. A recording engineer using a tape recorder can adjust the relative volume and tone of each track on a recording to change the overall sound of the recording. An engineer can also use a razor blade and splicing tape to cut out bad sections of the tape and splice together good performances. But it's next to impossible to change the quality of a single note on one instrument in a tape recording. This isn't so with a MIDI recorder. Because it records MIDI messages instead of the actual sounds of a performance, it's an easy job to change a single message in subtle ways to touch up the performance.

Changing Individual MIDI Messages

To make individual message editing easy, most MIDI recorders display all the messages recorded on a particular track. (See Figure 6-7 for an example.) You can choose any message and change the data it carries. A recorded Note On message, for example, has a pitch value and a velocity value. You can change either value to alter the pitch or the volume of the note. Also, a MIDI recorder usually shows the time (measured in MIDI clocks from the beginning of the recording) at which each message was recorded. You can change this time value to change the timing of the MIDI message when you replay the track.

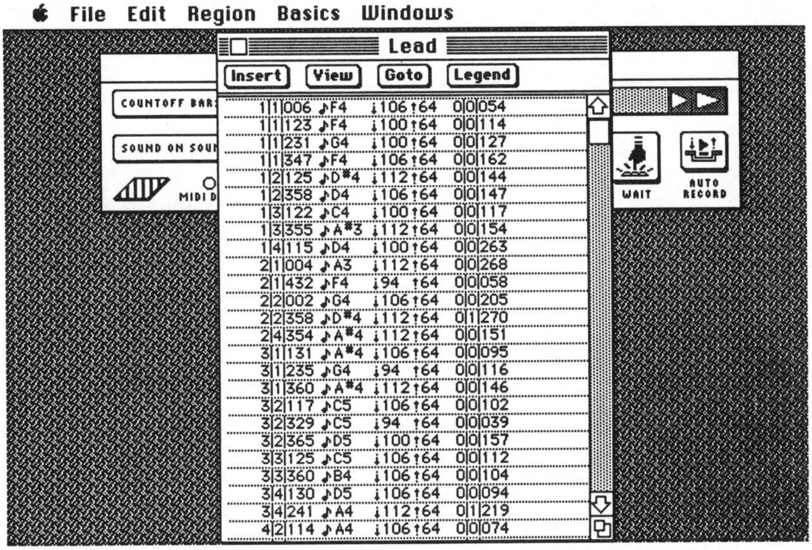

Figure 6-7.
These messages were recorded on a single track of a MIDI recorder (screen from Performer).

Inserting and Deleting MIDI Messages

A good MIDI recorder enables you not only to change messages, but also to add and subtract messages from a track. You can insert messages to add notes or effects where you need them. You can also delete messages for any notes that you mistakenly played while recording. In fact, you can insert and delete individual notes to create an entire song from scratch—without recording a single note. This process is both time consuming and tedious, but it does give you minute control over every facet of the song.

Quantization

Quantization is another editing feature of most MIDI recorders that helps you correct the timing of notes you record. Quantization lines up the notes in a track to fall on neatly spaced intervals of time. You can use this feature to clean up sloppy rhythms that were recorded in performance. For example, look at Figure 6-8. The left half of the figure shows a run of sixteenth notes that were played in uneven rhythm. The numbers in the left column represent the number of MIDI clocks that elapsed from the beginning of the recording to the beginning of the corresponding notes. These are sixteenth notes, each of which lasts 6 MIDI clocks, and they should be spaced at 6-clock intervals. Because they were played unevenly, they do not have a consistent interval of 6 clocks.

Figure 6-8. *Quantization cleans up the rhythm of the unevenly played sixteenth notes at left in this figure to produce the precise rhythm on the right side.*

Clocks	Note Played	Clocks	Note Played
0	Note A♮	0	Note A♮
7	Note B♭	6	Note B♭
13	Note C♯	12	Note C♯
17	Note D♮	18	Note D♮
24	Note E♮	24	Note E♮
32	Note F♯	30	Note F♯
37	Note G♯	36	Note G♯
40	Note A♮	42	Note A♮

If you choose to quantize the track, you first pick a quantization value of 6. The MIDI recorder then changes the timing value before each note to the nearest multiple of 6, as you can see in the right half of Figure 6-8. When you play back the track, you hear perfectly timed sixteenth notes.

Quantization is not a miracle cure for sloppy rhythm. When a MIDI recorder moves the beginnings of notes to the nearest multiple of the quantization value, it can move the note in the wrong direction if the rhythm is too sloppily played. Quantization also removes the rhythmic nuances created by deliberately playing notes slightly before or after the beat.

Cut and Paste   Not all editing features work on small details. Some features, such as *Cut* and *Paste,* let you work with large sections of a recording to change its overall structure. Cutting is a simple process: To cut a section of a track, you specify the MIDI message at the beginning and the MIDI message at the end of the segment you want to cut, and then you ask the MIDI recorder to cut that segment. The recorder cuts the segment from the track and joins the two remaining sections.

When the MIDI recorder cuts a segment of a track, it stores it in another area of the computer's memory called a *buffer* so that you can recall the segment later. The next time you cut a segment, the recorder puts the new segment in the buffer and erases the one that was there. The buffer contains only the last track segment you cut.

To paste a segment stored in the buffer, you select a point between two messages in a track and then ask the MIDI recorder to paste. The recorder makes a copy of the segment in the memory buffer and inserts the copy between the two messages in the track. The recorder spreads the track sections before and after the insertion point to make room for the new segment. (Some recorders paste the new segment over the messages on the existing track. Such programs typically provide an alternate feature, called *Insert,* that places the segment stored in the buffer between the sections of the existing track.)

Cutting by itself lets you get rid of whole blocks of music that you want to edit out of a track. Together, Cut and Paste let you cut a section of music in one location and move it to another location in the track. You can also use Cut and Paste to duplicate sections of music. For example, if you want to record a song that has four verses with a chorus between each one, you need only record the chorus once. Your recording can contain verse 1, verse 2, verse 3, verse 4, chorus. You can then cut the chorus to store it in the buffer and paste it into the track four times, once after each verse. Your final recording is verse 1, chorus, verse 2, chorus, verse 3, chorus, verse 4, chorus. Some MIDI recorders also let you cut and paste across several tracks at a time, which saves a lot of work if you're trying to rearrange sections of the whole recording.

Some MIDI recorders offer a feature called *Copy* that works much like Cut. It copies the segment you select to the buffer, but it doesn't actually cut the segment from the track. Then it's a simple matter to paste the segment elsewhere in the recording.

Sequences and Songs   Another editing technique for repeating segments of music is using *sequences* and *songs.* A sequence is a series of messages in a track. You can designate different segments of a track as different sequences, and in some recorders you can give names to the different sequences. A song is a list of directions that tells the recorder how to play the sequences—in what order to play them and what sequences to repeat. In the Cut and Paste process described earlier, you made a song with four verses and choruses by pasting the chorus four times. If the recorder you use allows you to build songs out of sequences, you could set up five sequences in the recorded track: the four verses and the chorus. You could then give the recorder directions to play the sequences in the order you want: verse 1, chorus, verse 2, chorus, verse 3, chorus, verse 4, chorus. You wouldn't actually have to copy the chorus four times.

Playing Back Recordings

Once you've recorded and edited a score on a MIDI recorder, you can change other sound qualities when you play it back. Most recorders offer you the same kind of playback controls you find on a standard tape deck: Play, which starts the recording playing; Fast Forward, which moves quickly forward to start playing at a spot further ahead in the score; Rewind, which moves quickly back to an earlier spot in the score; and Stop, which stops playback.

A standard MIDI recorder also has a counter that tells you how far you have progressed into the score, displaying either the number of MIDI clocks or the number of beats (usually set to equal quarter notes) since the beginning of the score. With some recorders, you can start the playback at any location in the score simply by specifying the counter setting for that location.

Individual Track Control

If you have music recorded on many different tracks, a MIDI recorder can play back all the tracks at once, or it can play back any single track or combination of tracks you choose. Individual track control lets you listen to any single part to simplify editing, or it lets you hear a few tracks at a time—to check synchronization between pairs or trios of tracks. If you want to record a new track to overdub a new instrument in a score, you can choose to play back other, previously recorded tracks as you record the new one.

Tempo Changes

When you play back a recording on a MIDI recorder, the recorder usually sends a stream of MIDI clocks along with the other messages it sends to attached MIDI devices. These MIDI clocks tell other MIDI devices with sequencers (such as drum machines) how fast the MIDI recorder is playing. If you change the tempo of a MIDI recording, any MIDI devices playing along with it change their tempos accordingly.

The ability to change the tempo of playback is very useful. Unlike a tape recorder, which raises and lowers the pitch of recorded music if you speed up or slow down the tempo, a MIDI recorder preserves the original pitch as you change the tempo. You can record a piece carefully at a slow tempo and then play the recording back at a brisk tempo. Tempo changes are also useful if you're recording music for the stage, in which case you might want to speed it up or slow it down to match a dance or other onstage action.

Transposition

Most MIDI recorders can also change the key of the recorded music when you play it back, a feature called *transposition*. For example, you can record a piece in the key of D and ask the recorder to play it back in the key of C. The recorder then plays back every note in the score two half-steps lower (the interval from D to C) than it was recorded. Transposition is useful for matching a recorded accompaniment to a singer. If the singer can't reach the high notes, you can transpose the music down until all the notes fall in the singer's range. If a singer wants to sing higher to sound more brilliant, you can transpose the playback up until it feels right.

MIDI
Accompaniment

It's easy to create a MIDI recording that you can play back as accompaniment to a live soloist, but it's hard to make the recorded accompaniment as responsive as a live accompanist. A human accompanist will listen to the soloist sing or play, and when the soloist speeds up or slows down for expressive purposes, the accompanist speeds up or slows down accordingly. A standard MIDI recorder keeps playing without regard for tempo variations by the soloist.

A few MIDI recorders and other special MIDI programs can "listen" to a live performer and change the playback tempo to accompany the performance. You first record all the accompaniment parts you need and record the solo part on a separate track from the accompaniment. You then feed MIDI messages from the soloist to the recorder. (If the soloist is a vocalist or plays an acoustic instrument, you can use a pitch tracker to convert the performance to MIDI messages.)

When you ask the MIDI program to accompany, it looks at the first note in the recorded solo track. As soon as it "hears" (receives a MIDI message for) that same note, it starts playing the accompaniment to go with it. As long as the notes coming in match the notes recorded in the solo track, the program keeps playing accompaniment. As the notes come in faster or slower, the program can speed up or slow down the accompaniment to match. If the soloist plays notes that aren't in the solo track, then the program stops playing and waits until it receives the right notes before it goes on with the accompaniment.

This accompaniment flexibility makes it easier to use a computer as a backup, but it still doesn't approach a human accompanist. It can't make allowances for mistakes and won't let the soloist deviate from the recorded solo line (not even for an inspired flight of improvisatory fancy).

Computer-Generated Music

There are programs that take MIDI music beyond playback feats of the recorder, programs that actually write the music themselves and then play it by sending the appropriate messages to your MIDI devices. Most of the programs depend on mathematical formulas to generate pitches, durations, amplitudes, and timbres. The music that results can range anywhere from tedious and boring to fascinating and mesmerizing.

At this writing, music-generating programs haven't been able to write very expressive music, but work with fractal mathematics (a branch of mathematics that can describe irregular natural shapes through equations) may produce music more acceptable to the general public. Although these programs seem to take the creativity out of composing music, they actually shift the creative focus from the composer to the software writer. More and more composers are finding that they can create the kind of music they're striving for by learning to program.

MUSICAL NOTATION AND PRINTING

Application programs designed to assist with musical notation and printing do their work in three areas:

◆ Translating musical notation into MIDI messages

◆ Translating sequences of messages in MIDI recordings into written music

◆ Printing music on a printer

Musical notation programs aren't as similar as MIDI recorder programs and so don't all have a standard set of features. Each has its own approach to musical notation and printing and its own methods of creating written music.

Entering Music

Most musical notation programs use the computer monitor to display the music you enter. The program draws a music staff on the screen, and you enter notes on the staff. (See Figure 6-9 for an example.) Computers with a

Figure 6-9.

*The screen of a
typical musical
notation program
(screen from
Deluxe Music
Construction Set).*

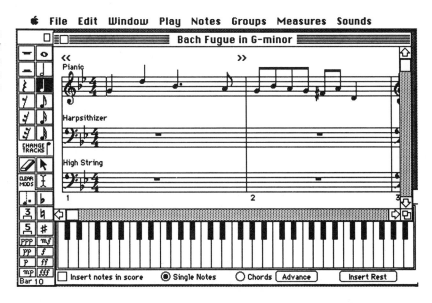

mouse let you point to notes, rests, and other musical symbols that you
want to use. You can then point to a location on the staff, and the computer
will draw the symbol there.

A comprehensive musical notation program provides a wide variety
of symbols for you to enter on the music staff. It offers note and rest lengths
ranging from a whole note down to a thirty-second note. It also offers triplets and, in some cases, even more esoteric note lengths such as quintuplets
and septuplets (notes that are played five or seven to the beat). A comprehensive program enables you to enter flats, sharps, and naturals as accidentals for any note on the staff. It also lets you enter dynamic markings,
such as *pp, mf,* and *ff,* as well as other important music symbols such as
ties, slurs, *crescendos,* and *diminuendos.* It's also important that you be
able to enter instrument (or patch) changes at any point in the score.

If you're entering music for later printing, you commonly need to add
text to your scores. You can use text to add lyrics to a song, to give tempo
markings, or to give instructions to the performer in the score. With suit-
able software, you can also enter special performance markings, such as
down-bows and up-bows (for string players) and guitar chord notation.

Some musical notation programs limit you to entering notes only on a
grand staff with its two components: an upper staff in treble clef and a
lower one in bass clef. This can work satisfactorily if you have no more
than two or three parts to enter but gets congested quickly as you enter
more parts. A good musical notation program gives you many staves

on which to enter parts. For example, if you want to enter a full orchestral score, you can easily use 20 or more staves. The program should enable you to choose the clef, key signature, and time signature for each staff.

Editing Features

Musical notation programs have editing features to help you correct and change the music on the screen. You can select a block of music on the screen and use Cut, Paste, and Copy the same way you can with a MIDI recorder to move or to repeat a segment of music. You can also delete individual notes and symbols from the score or insert symbols between those already in the score.

Most musical notation programs automatically space notes entered on a staff to place them in the correct rhythmic location relative to other notes. They also prevent you from entering too many notes in a measure. A comprehensive program gives you a number of options, as well, that help to reduce clutter and make notes more legible. You should, for example, have the option to space notes yourself, to determine the direction of note stems, and to beam eighth, sixteenth, and thirty-second notes together or to take the connecting beams away.

Alternative Musical Notation

If you know how to read and write traditional musical notation, then entering music on a staff is very natural. Otherwise, it can be torturous. Some musical notation programs offer alternative systems of notation. You can see an example of such a system in Figure 6-10. Most of these

Figure 6-10.
An example of alternative musical notation. Notice that the notes are graphed onto a grid (screen from Music Works).

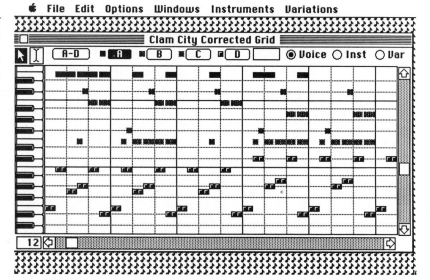

notation systems depict notes graphically. The higher the pitch of the note, the higher the note appears on the graph. The longer the note lasts, the longer it extends on the graph.

These alternative systems of notation make it possible to enter music (or at least noise) by drawing random shapes on the screen. Some notation systems have been well designed to give you a lot of control over the music you enter; others are designed poorly and give you little control of elements other than pitch and duration. Some programs have a feature that translates the music you enter in the alternative system into traditional musical notation on a staff with notes.

Translating Written Music into a Performance

Once you enter a score in a musical notation program, you can look forward to hearing it played on your MIDI system. This gives you an advantage over composers in the past who often waited years to hear their pieces played or never heard them at all. Some programs use the computer's own sound chips to play the music you entered. Others turn the music into MIDI messages and transmit them to external MIDI devices. Programs of either type are hybrid programs—part musical notation program, part music performance program. Like MIDI recorders, they can play back music (often with the ability to change tempo and to make transpositions); unlike a MIDI recorder, they don't record performances.

Some musical notation programs are unable to play back scores without assistance; they rely on a compatible MIDI recorder program to play back the music you enter. The notation program turns the music you enter into a sequence of MIDI messages that it stores on disk. Using your recorder program, you can then load the sequence from the disk and play the music on MIDI instruments.

Translating a Performance into Written Music

Musicians everywhere dream of an effortless means of turning a live performance into written music. As this shared dream is scripted, the artist performs the piece once, and then the computer turns it into sheet music, copyrights it automatically, and sends copies to be sold at music stores everywhere, all without the performer having to know one thing about traditional musical notation. Alas, it just isn't that simple.

Turning music into written notes is an interpretive art. When a musician hears a strain of music, there are usually many different ways to write it as music. The musician writing down the music can decide that a beat will be a quarter note, a half note, or any other note value, and then write the music a different way depending on the note value assigned to a beat. A series of short notes can be depicted as notes followed by rests or as staccato notes with no rests. The musician must use judgment to balance a variety of considerations, all in an effort to create the most legible and easily interpreted score.

Pity the poor computer then, powerfully short on intelligence and lacking a musical soul, to boot. What can it do to write down music? Actually, it can do quite a bit with the right software. Most computer owners use a MIDI recorder program to record a performance and store it on a disk. They then use a musical notation program to interpret the recorded MIDI messages as written music.

Interpreting MIDI Messages

The musical notation program can tell the pitch of the recorded MIDI notes by reading the pitch value of the Note On messages and can tell the duration of each note by reading the number of MIDI clocks that occur between Note On and Note Off. It can interpret the pitch value as a vertical position on the music staff and can turn the duration of the note into the correct note length value by using the clock-to-note equivalencies of the MIDI clock (shown in Figure 5-8 on page 85) or of a still more precise clock. Once the notes of a performance appear on the staff at the correct pitch and with the correct length, you can touch them up and make a few other decisions, such as key and time signature. The majority of the work is done by the computer.

Interpretation Problems

Still there are problems, particularly in the interpretation of note durations. When a musician (even a great one) plays notes in live performance, they aren't exactly sixteenth notes, eighth notes, quarter notes, and other standard note values. They're usually a little longer or shorter, sometimes as a result of expressive rhythm manipulation, sometimes as a result of uneven playing. The computer takes all these uneven lengths literally and turns them into very messy collections of thirty-second, sixty-fourth, and one-hundred-twenty-eighth notes tied together and appended with rests. Music translated in that fashion is almost impossible to read.

To solve the problem of unequal rhythms, you can always quantize the notes in a MIDI recording. This doesn't always work well, though. If you play a piece of music that has runs of thirty-second notes, then you can't quantize at a note length longer than a thirty-second note without turning all the thirty-second notes into sixteenth notes. And if you do quantize at thirty-seconds, then any quarter (or longer) notes you play that depart more than a thirty-second note from their prescribed lengths will show up wrong. The quantization won't correct them when it translates them to written music. Fortunately, you can go back to the written music and edit it to correct the notes. But you find yourself once again in a position where you need to know how to read music.

Printing Music

If your software enables you to print music (as well as enter and play it), you'll find that printing is usually an easy task. First, you'll probably have to break the music into pages on the screen and decide how wide to print each measure. With some software, you can add a title page and some text at the top and bottom of each music page (perhaps the title, the name of the composer, and a copyright notice). You might also be able to ask the computer to number the measures and add page numbers to each page. When you're ready to print, the program sends the music to an attached printer, which prints your "hard copy"—real ink on real paper that you can hold in your hands.

The quality of the music printout depends on the printer. Dot-matrix printers turn out legible, if not beautiful, copy. The attractiveness of the printed copy improves considerably as the density of the dots that produce the image increases. Perhaps the best results are produced on *laser printers,* which electromagnetically etch images on a steel drum with a laser. The steel drum picks up ink on its etching and bonds the ink to a sheet of paper. Laser-printed music can look as good as typeset music.

SYNTHESIZER PATCH EDITORS AND PATCH LIBRARIANS

Designing custom patches on a synthesizer is seldom enjoyable. Most synthesizers have very small displays that can't adequately show you what you're doing to a complicated patch. Also, synthesizers usually have limited memory for storing patches; you might run out of room after creating only 10 or 16 new patches. With patch-editor and patch-librarian software, however, you can design your patches on the much larger display area of the computer screen and store them in the abundant memory of the computer and its disk drives.

Patch Librarians

A patch librarian is the simplest patch program you can use on a computer. It receives patches from connected synthesizers in the form of system exclusive messages, stores them in memory and on disks, and allows you to recall them when you need them. Because each kind of synthesizer has its own method of creating and transmitting patches, you need to determine whether a given patch librarian works with the synthesizer you're using. If the two are incompatible, the program will be unable to receive patches from the synthesizer.

A patch librarian can receive patches individually or in *banks*. A bank of patches is a set of patches that corresponds to the complete set of patch buttons on a synthesizer. For example, a synthesizer with 16 patch buttons (one for each of 16 patches) stores 16 patches in each bank. You can rearrange and assign names to the patches in a bank, and you can store individual patches or entire banks on disk.

When you want to recall the patches you stored earlier, you can retrieve them from disk into the computer's memory. You can then send them, singly or as a complete bank, to the synthesizer. Because you can get access to a new set of stored patches simply by swapping disks or loading another file, your patch library is limited only by the number of disks you own.

If you're a performing artist, a patch librarian can make your life much easier. You can store sets of compatible patches as separate banks and load a bank into your synthesizer by pressing a few buttons. In a matter of seconds, you're ready to play, using the set of sounds you want. A patch librarian also makes it easy to swap patches with other synthesizer owners by trading disks full of patches.

Patch Editors

Patch librarians merely store and send patches they receive from the synthesizer without altering them. Patch editors actually let you change those patches when they're in the computer's memory. (See Figure 6-11 for an example.) Each synthesizer has its own method of synthesis and requires

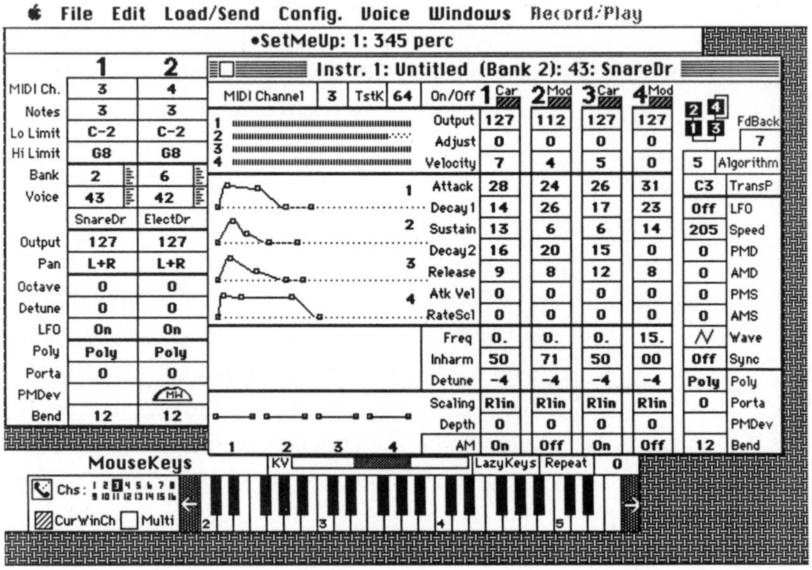

Figure 6-11.
The screen of a typical patch editor (screen from Opcode FB-01 Editor/Librarian).

its own kind of patch editing. Consequently, a patch editor, like a patch librarian, must be written to work with a certain type of synthesizer.

Despite major differences, most editors are alike in taking advantage of the full computer screen to show the current condition of the patch. The screen can show full patch envelopes and the settings of any oscillators or operators (a Yamaha term) that control the patch. You can alter any setting and see the results immediately. A good patch editor sends patch revisions directly to the synthesizer, providing you a chance to play a few notes to see how your revisions affect the patch. Almost all patch editor programs also include patch librarians. As you create and test a new set of patches, you can store them to disk in a bank and recall them later to send to your synthesizer.

MUSIC EDUCATION SOFTWARE

Music education software involving MIDI has been a neglected field when you compare the number of widely-distributed music education programs to the number of MIDI recorders, patch editors, and musical notation programs in circulation. You can expect to see more and more educational software as programmers and teachers realize the tremendous potential of programs that teach people the fundamentals of music at home and in the classroom.

Because the standards for music education software are still unsettled, the descriptions in this section dwell less on software specifics and more on current categories of educational programs and trends to anticipate in future programs. Some of these programs rely heavily on MIDI; others have little or no need for it. Certainly there are areas of music instruction, such as guitar and keyboard mechanics, that can clearly take advantage of MIDI and are due for further developments.

Piano Labs

One of the most natural settings for applying MIDI to music education is the piano laboratory. A piano lab is normally a classroom with 10 to 20 electric pianos. A student sits at each piano, and the teacher teaches from a master keyboard, playing examples and asking individual students to play different exercises. Because the pianos in a piano lab have headphones, students can practice different exercises at the same time without being lost in cacophony.

Using a MIDI system, a school can set up a piano lab with 16 synthesizers hooked to a computer and a master synthesizer. The students in the lab sit at the 16 synthesizers and listen to themselves play over head-phones. MIDI messages from each synthesizer in the lab enter the computer on a different MIDI channel. Meanwhile, the teacher can listen to any student or combination of students by choosing the MIDI channels that the computer will receive and play on the master synthesizer. If a student has something to demonstrate to the rest of the class, the teacher can send the messages from the student's keyboard through the master keyboard's amplified speaker system. A deluxe synthesizer lab can also include a musical notation program that can print out the music that a student plays.

Sight-Reading Training

Computers are also useful for teaching *sight reading,* the ability to play a piece from the sheet music without first practicing the piece. For example, a computer can flash a note on its screen for a mere fraction of a second. You attempt to play that note on a MIDI instrument, and the computer tells you if you played the right note. This exercise develops your ability to recognize pitch and note length quickly.

Computer programs can assist you in developing other sight-reading skills, as well. Some programs focus on your scanning technique. They display a piece of music on the screen and move a small box from note to note to teach you how best to scan.

Ear Training

Ear training is a field of music education that trains musicians to identify and to write down the pitch intervals and rhythms they hear in a piece of music. It also teaches them to sing without instrumental accompaniment lines of music written in traditional musical notation (sometimes distinguished from ear training as sight singing). Most of this work is done in a class where a teacher plays music and the students write it down, or where all the students sing music printed in books designed for ear training. It's very hard for the teacher to give each student individual training, and it's also hard for the student to practice outside of class without help.

An ear-training program can provide that help. It can play musical examples using the computer's own sound generating equipment or an attached synthesizer. The student then writes the music on the computer screen, where the computer can check the accuracy of the student's notation. An ear-training program can also display a piece of music on the monitor and ask the student to sing it. By incorporating a microphone and a pitch tracker into the setup, the student can learn from the program which notes were sung incorrectly and can even hear the correct melody or interval generated by the computer. This kind of programming gives ear-training students a chance to drill and develop their skills outside of class. It can also teach ear training to musicians who are unable to enroll in formal music classes.

Music Theory

There are many programs now on the market that teach music theory, an area of musical study that includes traditional musical notation, harmony, voice-leading, and other practical and sometimes esoteric facets of music. Some of these programs are little more than textbooks entered into the computer, programs that present textual information a screen at a time on the computer monitor and follow each section with a quiz to see what the student has learned.

Music theory is better taught with examples. Music theory programs that make use of an attached synthesizer to play examples and to ask the student to play examples are generally more effective than strictly textual and graphic programs. It's a simple matter to add MIDI control of a synthesizer to a music theory program, and so it is likely that more music theory programs will make use of MIDI.

In this chapter you've learned some fundamental facts about computers—what they are and how they're used in a MIDI system. You've seen how computers can be adapted to MIDI systems through a combination of hardware and software of various types. In the concluding section of this chapter, you've had a glimpse of the promise of the computer as a MIDI device—recording, playing, notating, storing, and teaching. So far, most of what you've learned has been theoretical. In the next chapter, you'll look at some real MIDI devices in real MIDI systems to see what's actually available today.

7 | REAL MIDI EQUIPMENT

Real MIDI systems aren't made up of typical synthesizers, typical drum machines, typical keyboards, and other typical devices any more than a real family has 2.4 children. A real MIDI system is composed of real equipment, each piece with its own unique features. To see how a MIDI system actually works, you need to go beyond an understanding of typical MIDI devices to learn the specifics of real MIDI devices.

This chapter introduces you to some of today's popular MIDI devices through a series of equipment profiles. The profiles present a variety of devices—several different kinds of synthesizers, a master keyboard, a drum machine, two different kinds of MIDI controllers, a MIDI Thru box—and describe their features and operation. The equipment profiled here doesn't represent the best or worst of the instruments on the market. Instead, each profile discusses an excellent example of a specific type of device, a device in common use today and likely to remain popular long after newer models replace it. Use the profiles in this chapter as yardsticks to help you evaluate equipment for your own MIDI system.

SYNTHESIZERS   Synthesizers can be categorized by their different methods of sound synthesis. You'll recall from Chapter 3 that most synthesizers today are digital
synthesizers that use digital oscillators to create sounds. Other digital synthesizers are sampling synthesizers that alter and play back sounds that
have been digitally pre-recorded. The four synthesizer profiles that follow
provide you with examples of both types of digital synthesis. The synthesizers, which vary greatly in price, are the Casio CZ-101, a simple, low-
price digital synthesizer; the Yamaha DX7, a more expensive, full-featured
digital synthesizer; the Yamaha FB-01, an inexpensive digital synthesizer
expander module; and the Ensoniq Mirage, a moderately-priced sampling
synthesizer.

A Profile of the   The Casio CZ-101 (shown in Figure 7-1) is an extremely popular syn
Casio CZ-101   thesizer, perhaps because it was one of the first synthesizers offered for
under $500 that delivers digital sound. Its small size makes it extremely
portable, and it can run on six D-cell batteries if AC power is unavailable.
Some enterprising street musicians even use the CZ-101 with a small, battery-powered, amplified speaker for street performances.

Figure 7-1.
The Casio CZ-101
synthesizer.

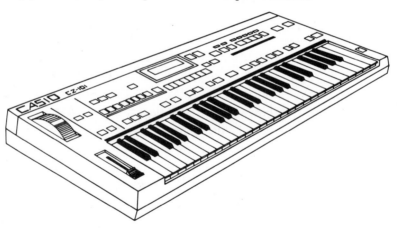

The CZ-101 keyboard spans four octaves and uses miniature keys, somewhat awkward to play if you're used to a full-size keyboard or if you have
large fingers. The keyboard is very simple—it sends Note On and Note
Off messages with no attack velocity, release velocity, or aftertouch. The
CZ-101 has a pitch bend wheel to the left of the keyboard.

There are eight sound generators inside the CZ-101, each capable of
producing waveforms that can be shaped by an amplitude envelope generator, a pitch envelope generator, a filter envelope generator, and an LFO
(for adding *vibrato*). The two envelope generators can create complex

envelopes; you can set as many as eight different levels with their attendant rates of change. Learning to use Casio's sound synthesis process, called *phase distortion synthesis* (PD synthesis, for short), is fairly easy.

The CZ-101 can play as many as eight notes at one time if all its sound generators are used separately, but the sound generators are usually paired in a patch to create chorusing effects (one voice slightly out of tune with another) and to make the sound richer. Pairing generators limits the CZ-101 to four simultaneous notes. It can, however, put these four available voices to good use: The CZ-101 is polytimbral. When controlled by another device, such as an external sequencer, through its MIDI In port, it can play four different patches simultaneously (each voice responding to messages coming in on a different MIDI channel).

The CZ-101 has 16 factory-programmed patches built into ROM and room in RAM for 16 additional patches that you program yourself. Plugging in an external RAM cartridge gives you room for 16 more programmable patches. The control panel provides a row of eight patch buttons, with four switching buttons, to let you select any patch, and it provides nearly 40 buttons to let you choose waveforms and set the LFO, envelopes, and other patch characteristics. A liquid-crystal display (LCD) with two rows of 16 characters identifies the patch you're currently using and shows the values you're setting as you work.

The CZ-101 has a MIDI In and a MIDI Out port but lacks a MIDI Thru port. It can receive MIDI messages on any single channel (Omni Off) or on all channels (Omni On) and can be set to Polyphonic or Monophonic mode. In Omni Off/Mono mode, you can use a different patch on each of the four channels (the polytimbral feature mentioned before). The CZ-101 responds to standard MIDI messages, excluding velocity or aftertouch information, and has a full set of system exclusive messages that allows it to swap patches over MIDI.

The CZ-101 and small synthesizers like it are not remarkably full-featured, but they're not meant to be. They offer high-quality sound, a keyboard for performance and note entry, and the means to create patches, all for a very low price. If you're on a small budget, they are an excellent way to start or add voices to a MIDI system.

A Profile of the Yamaha DX7

The Yamaha DX7 (shown in Figure 7-2 on the next page) is very popular with professional musicians because of the richness and variety of its sound. It was the first major synthesizer to use MIDI and was instrumental (if you'll excuse the expression) in firmly establishing MIDI as a standard with musicians and other synthesizer manufacturers.

Figure 7-2.
The Yamaha DX7
synthesizer.

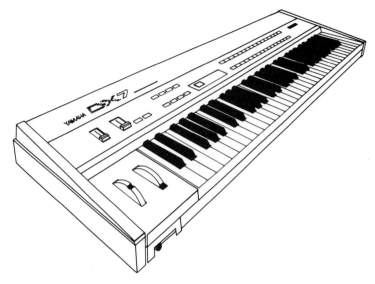

On the outside, the DX7 doesn't seem particularly imposing. It has a five-octave keyboard with full-size keys. The keyboard senses both attack velocity and aftertouch. To the left of the keyboard, the DX7 has a pitch bend wheel and a modulation wheel. It uses a display with two LED (light-emitting diode) characters and a 16-character LCD to show switch settings and patch selections. There are also two sliders in the control panel: a volume slider and a data entry slider that enables you to set values quickly as you program a patch.

The inside of the DX7 is more impressive and has changed in various ways as the machine and its MIDI capabilities have evolved. The DX7 has 16 sound generators that synthesize sound using a method called *FM synthesis* (short for frequency modulation), a patented Yamaha technique. FM synthesis works by combining the outputs of digital oscillators, called *operators* in FM synthesis parlance.

A DX7 patch uses six operators to create sound, each of which comprises a digital oscillator that generates a sine wave and an amplitude envelope generator that shapes the output of the oscillator. The envelope generator is a simple ADSR (attack, decay, sustain, and release) generator with four levels and rates that you can set. The sound produced by a single operator is bland, but when six of them work together, the sound is impressive.

To synthesize sounds, the DX7 combines the six operators using 32 different combinations, called *algorithms*. One algorithm simply mixes the output of all six operators together. Others use the output of one operator to modulate another operator to create complex harmonics in the output of the modulated operator. The principle is similar to that of FM radio, in that one signal, the *modulator,* is used to modify a second *carrier* signal.

To create a patch, you first select an algorithm and then set the frequencies, envelopes, and other operator parameters. This process sounds much simpler than it actually is. FM synthesis, though rich in possibilities, is not an intuitive process, and you'll find it very hard to learn if you're not willing to devote a lot of time and energy to understanding how it works.

Fortunately, there are some excellent patches already programmed into the DX7. It comes equipped with 32 pre-programmed patches in internal RAM. You can also buy ROM cartridges, each of which holds two banks of 32 patches. When you plug the cartridge into the DX7, you can use the patch select buttons on the control panel to select a patch in internal RAM or from the cartridge.

Once you are able to program your own patches, you can store them in internal RAM in place of the patches that are provided with the DX7, or you can store them on a RAM cartridge. The cartridge plugs into the DX7 in the same slot you use for a ROM cartridge. You can copy all 32 patches from the DX7's internal RAM into a RAM cartridge and remove the cartridge to store the patches outside the DX7. To recall the stored patches, simply plug in the RAM cartridge again: The DX7 can play patches directly from the RAM cartridge just as it can from a ROM cartridge. You can use RAM cartridges to build a library of patches and to trade patches with other musicians. Because the DX7 can swap patches over a MIDI cable by means of system exclusive messages, you can also use a computer to store and swap DX7 patches.

The DX7 is equipped with a MIDI In port, a MIDI Out port, and a MIDI Thru port to make it easy to connect to other MIDI devices. It responds to standard MIDI messages, including attack velocity and aftertouch information. It receives MIDI messages over all the MIDI channels (Omni On) or over any single channel (Omni Off), but because it is monotimbral, it can play only one patch at a time. The DX7 also has jacks for two foot pedals, two foot switches, and a breath controller.

The DX7 or some similar synthesizer in the $2,000 range is usually the heart of a MIDI system. The expense of such an instrument is justified by the quality of its sound and the versatility of its keyboard and controllers. Once you have the high-quality keyboard that comes with one of these synthesizers, you can expand your system with MIDI devices that lack built-in keyboards.

**A Profile of the
Yamaha FB-01**

The Yamaha FB-01 expansion unit (shown in Figure 7-3) is an inexpensive synthesizer (under $500) with no keyboard, pitch bend wheel, modulation wheel, or any other kind of controller. By itself, it does nothing; it must have an auxiliary controller such as a master keyboard or a sequencer to run it using MIDI messages.

Figure 7-3.
*The Yamaha FB-01
expansion unit.*

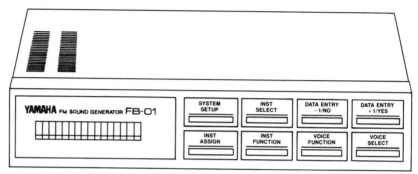

Because it has no keyboard, the FB-01 is a small and unobtrusive device, only slightly larger than this book. It has a front panel with a 16-character LED display that shows patches and other setting information. It also has a set of eight buttons that enable you to call up different patches, set MIDI modes and channels, control *glissando* and modulation, and set other operational variables. In the back of the FB-01 are three MIDI ports—In, Out, and Thru—and two audio ouputs, left and right. (The FB-01 produces stereo sound.)

Inside, the FB-01 has eight sound generators that create sound using FM synthesis. Unlike the DX7, which also uses FM synthesis, the FB-01 uses four, rather than six, operators per voice. With fewer operators, the FB-01 has fewer algorithms to work with, 8 instead of 32. While it isn't capable of producing sounds quite as complex as those of the DX7, it does synthesize some very rich sounds.

You can't create your own patches directly on the FB-01—it doesn't have the necessary controls—but if you have a computer with appropriate software connected to the FB-01, you can create your own patches on the computer and send them to the FB-01 using MIDI. The FB-01 has 96 patch locations in RAM (two banks of 48) to store the patches you create. If you don't want to use a computer for patch creation and storage, the FB-01 has 240 pre-programmed patches stored in five banks in ROM (48 patches in each bank). Altogether, you can have access to 336 patches.

The FB-01 also has memory to store 20 configurations. Each configuration sets the FB-01's MIDI mode and the MIDI receiving channels, calls up a bank of 48 patches for use, and defines a number of other settings, among them the pitch bend range and the amount of *portamento*. You can request a particular configuration by pressing a few buttons on the front panel.

The FB-01 works very well when connected to a master keyboard, such as the Yamaha KX-88 (described later in this chapter); another synthesizer with a responsive keyboard, such as the DX7; or an external sequencer. It can respond to all types of MIDI messages, including those that contain attack velocity, aftertouch, pitch bend, and program change information. By using a controlling keyboard, you can change patches using the keyboard's patch buttons and can play music with the keyboard and the pitch bend and modulation controllers.

The FB-01 can receive MIDI messages on all channels (Omni On) or on any single channel (Omni Off). It's polytimbral, so you can set it to Omni Off/Mono to play eight different patches simultaneously, each patch receiving messages on a different MIDI channel. The FB-01 also has a special Omni Off/Poly Mode so that you can set it up to receive notes on several discrete channels. Each channel can play polyphonically, provided that you assign it multiple voices.

The FB-01 performs other MIDI tricks, as well. In addition to the system exclusive messages it uses to swap patches, it also has a special set of system exclusive messages that offer special Note On and Note Off messages that let you tune each note in fractions of a half-step. You can program one FB-01 to play only odd pitch values and another to play only even values. Then, you can play them on the same MIDI channel to produce the effect of one large 16-voice FB-01 instead of two 8-voice synthesizers.

The FB-01 and similar expansion units are an excellent way to add high-quality voices to a MIDI system at a low cost because you don't pay for a keyboard or other built-in controllers included with a full-featured synthesizer. An expansion unit with polytimbral abilities also makes an excellent addition to a computer system. With a sequencing program, you can use the polytimbral patches as separate little synthesizers, all added for the cost of one expansion unit.

A Profile of the Ensoniq Mirage

Unlike the other synthesizers in this section, the Ensoniq Mirage (shown in Figure 7-4 on page 131) is a sampling synthesizer. The Mirage is a popular sampling synthesizer because it is one of the first decent-sounding samplers to be offered for well under $2,000.

PLAYING YOUR CARDS

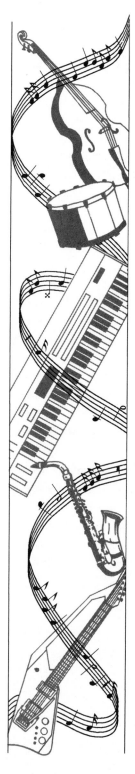

If you own an IBM personal computer, you have a unique option available to you if you want to add an expansion module to your computer. IBM now makes the IBM Music Feature, a synthesizer on a card that includes its own smart MIDI interface. This plug-in circuit board uses chips similar to those in the Yamaha FB-01, and it has all the same features—four-operator FM synthesis, eight voices, hundreds of built-in patches, special tuning by means of system exclusive messages—and other features that you read about in the FB-01 profile. To expand these capabilities further, you can interconnect a pair of Music Feature cards in your computer.

IBM personal computers are built to permit easy expansion. To add some extra hardware to the computer, you can buy expansion cards that contain the desired chips and circuitry. After removing the computer's cover (a simple task), you can plug a card into one of several expansion slots inside the computer so that the computer can run the extra hardware as an integral part of the machine. One type of plug-in card that is commonly used with MIDI is the smart MIDI interface (usually a Roland MPU-401 interface). This interface plugs into one of the slots and connects to an external box with three MIDI ports: In, Out, and Thru. This kind of card is essential if you want to use any external synthesizer or other MIDI device with an IBM personal computer.

Each Music Feature card combines a smart MIDI interface with a full synthesizer. The synthesizer is a single plug-in expansion card, and the MIDI interface is a small, separate box that connects to the back of the card. The interface has three MIDI ports—In, Out, and Thru—and the synthesizer card itself has stereo audio outputs and a stereo headphone jack for private listening. Once you plug the card into your computer, you can play the synthesizer directly from the IBM using sequencer software, or you can plug a MIDI keyboard into the MIDI interface and play the synthesizer from the keyboard without involving the computer's own microprocessor. You can use the Music Feature strictly as a MIDI interface to control an external MIDI system through the card's MIDI ports, or you can use external MIDI devices simultaneously with the Music Feature's own synthesizer.

IBM expects to sell the Music Feature to educational institutions and home users and has been working closely with software companies to create useful software for it.

Figure 7-4.
The Ensoniq
Mirage sampling
synthesizer.

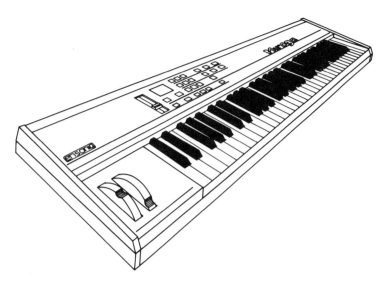

The keyboard of the Mirage is a standard synthesizer keyboard: five octaves of full-size keys with a pitch bend wheel and a modulation wheel.
The keyboard responds to attack velocity and aftertouch, and—a somewhat unusual feature—it also responds to release velocity. A jack in the
back of the Mirage lets you connect a foot switch or a foot pedal for playing
sustained notes. Above the keyboard is a two-digit LED display, a numeric
keypad similar to a calculator's, and a few extra buttons. These controls
together allow you to enter numeric values that control the Mirage's
patches and playback characteristics.

The Mirage has eight sound generators, each of which can play back
sampled sounds stored as waveform tables in the Mirage's internal RAM.
Each value in the waveform table is stored as an eight-bit value, which
means it can represent a number from 0 through 255. Other, more expensive sampling synthesizers use 12-bit or 16-bit samples, which increases
the dynamic range (the amplitude range) of the sample to produce samples
with higher fidelity.

The Mirage samples sounds at a rate of 30,000 samples per second,
fast enough to capture low- and mid-frequency sounds with fidelity, but a
little too slow to pick up very high-frequency sounds. (With additional
equipment, you can increase the sampling rate to 50,000 samples per second.) The rule of thumb is that a sampling rate must be at least double the
highest frequency you want to sample. Thus, you need at least 40,000
samples per second to sample a sound with a frequency of 20,000 cycles
per second. Higher sampling rates let you sample higher frequencies, and
they increase the *resolution* of the sound, making samples clearer and more

free of distortion. Unfortunately, faster sampling also uses up more RAM and drives up the cost of the sampler because you need more RAM chips.

The Mirage can play back sound samples at different pitches. It can also add an amplitude envelope and a filter envelope to the samples it plays back and can add *vibrato* with an LFO. For each envelope, you can set five separate levels and rates. A clever design feature allows you to create unique new sounds by mixing two separate sampled sounds as one patch. You can tie the blending feature to keyboard aftertouch or velocity so that the resulting sound will favor one or the other sound sample depending on how you press a key.

The Mirage doesn't have patches built into internal ROM. It stores them instead on $3\frac{1}{2}$-inch floppy disks, each of which can store as many as three patches. Recalling a patch is not instantaneous. Because of the amount of data it has to transfer, the Mirage requires a few seconds to load a patch from the disk into its own internal RAM. Each patch you load from disk is actually a dual patch; it has one sampled sound for the upper half of the keyboard and a second sampled sound for the lower half. By playing in different halves of the keyboard, you can play different sounds.

You can create your own patches by plugging a microphone or other audio source into the Mirage and recording short sound samples. You can then edit the sounds to loop the way you want them to, and you can set envelopes, LFO, and other characteristics using the numeric keypad and the two-digit LED display. It takes skill and perseverance on the Mirage or on any other sampling synthesizer to sample an acoustic sound and then touch it up so that it sounds natural.

The Mirage has a built-in sequencer with which you can record as many as 333 notes of performance on the keyboard and overdub on notes you've already recorded. You can store as many as eight of these sequences on a floppy disk along with your patches. If you want to expand the capacity of the sequencer, you can add a RAM cartridge to the Mirage which adds room for 1024 extra notes in the sequencer.

The Mirage is a full MIDI device, with both a MIDI In and a MIDI Out port. The MIDI Out port mixes the output of the Mirage with any MIDI messages coming into its MIDI In port so you can use the MIDI Out port in place of a MIDI Thru port if you want. The Mirage responds to all types of MIDI messages to play notes with attack and release velocity and aftertouch. You can also use MIDI to change patches on the Mirage by sending Program Change messages from an external MIDI device. In addition to the MIDI ports, the Mirage also has an external sync jack that lets you synchronize its sequencer playback with non-MIDI drum machines and sequencers.

Adding a Mirage or a similar sampling synthesizer to your MIDI system is an effective way to introduce an acoustic sound to an otherwise all-electronic system. It also enables you to play novelty sounds, including custom patches of your own voice, and allows you to create fat electronic-sounding patches by starting with an already rich acoustic sample.

MASTER KEYBOARDS

A master keyboard is the opposite of an expansion module: It has a music keyboard and a control panel but no internal sound generators. Because you can tailor its controls to send all types of MIDI messages, you can use a master keyboard to control synthesizers, drum machines, and sequencers that might be hard to control with a regular synthesizer keyboard.

A Profile of the Yamaha KX-88 Master Keyboard

The Yamaha KX-88 (shown in Figure 7-5) is a top-of-the-line master keyboard. It's not cheap, but its versatility and the feel of its keyboard make it popular with musicians.

Figure 7-5.
The Yamaha KX-88 master keyboard.

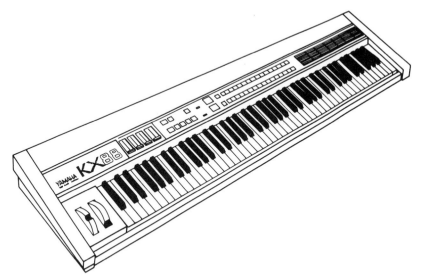

The KX-88 has 88 full-size weighted keys covering 7$\frac{1}{2}$ octaves, the same range as a standard piano keyboard. The keyboard senses attack velocity and aftertouch but doesn't sense release velocity. It has two wheels to the left of the keyboard that can be used for pitch bend and modulation. If you normally play a standard, light-touch synthesizer keyboard, you might need some time to adjust to the KX-88 keyboard. The keys have weight and resistance like piano keys. If you're accustomed to playing piano, then the KX-88 can help you achieve the same control of nuance you have on an acoustic piano.

The KX-88 has a full control panel. But because the KX-88 doesn't have its own sound generators, the controls have no rigidly defined functions: You can determine what variables they will control. There are two rows of 16 numbered buttons that are normally used to change patches on an auxiliary device. There are also four continuous sliders, two toggle switches (switches that alternate between two states each time you press them), and five momentary switches (switches that need only a single touch to select an action, something like a start switch). You can add extra controllers using jacks on the side of the keyboard: two foot-switch jacks, two foot-pedal jacks, and a breath-controller jack.

All the controls and auxilliary controllers on the KX-88 send out MIDI messages when you use them. You can determine the messages they send. For example, you can set one of the sliders to send Control Change messages that adjust the modulation so that you can use the slider instead of a modulation wheel to add modulation to notes. You can also set switches to send messages that operate switchable functions on a connected device.

When you first turn on the KX-88, it has a set of default MIDI messages that the controls will send. These default messages work with most MIDI devices. For example, the two rows of 16 buttons send out Program Change messages to call up new patches on an attached device. With these two rows of buttons, along with a bank-select button located next to them, you can select as many as 128 different patches.

You can affect the way the music keyboard sends channel voice messages. You can have it send messages over any single MIDI channel or over any two MIDI channels, a handy feature if you want to play two attached devices simultaneously. You can also split the KX-88 keyboard at any point you select, so that the lower half of the keyboard sends messages over one MIDI channel and the upper half of the keyboard sends messages over a second MIDI channel. You can program either half of the split keyboard (or the whole keyboard, for that matter) to transpose the notes you play up or down by as little as a half-step or as much as two octaves.

The KX-88 can save the characteristics of any keyboard setting you create: keyboard splits, transpositions, MIDI-message assignments for the controls, and so on. It has 16 memory slots for keyboard settings, and once you create and save a setting, you can recall it with a button push in much the same way that you recall a patch on a synthesizer.

The KX-88 is designed to control sequencers as well as synthesizers. It can send Song Select messages at the touch of a button and can also send a stream of MIDI clocks. You can set the rate of the clocks using one of the KX-88's sliders. You can also enter custom MIDI messages, such as system exclusive messages, by entering them byte by byte on the rows of patch keys. The KX-88 sends these messages in streams of 20 bytes.

There are two MIDI ports on the side of the KX-88: MIDI In and MIDI Out. Because the KX-88 is designed to control other devices, most of its activities involve sending rather than receiving MIDI messages. However, you can also send MIDI messages into its MIDI In port to set keyboard splits and transpositions, recall keyboard settings, and perform other controlling operations.

The KX-88 and other master keyboards are actually a cost-effective way to develop an extensive MIDI system. By spending money on a good master keyboard, you don't have to buy other synthesizers with keyboards. And many synthesizers, such as the Mirage and the DX7, come in *rackmount* versions that contain the sound generators of the regular synthesizer but lack the keyboard, the controllers, and most of the other buttons and switches. You can mount these synthesizer modules in a metal rack designed especially to hold such instruments. A master keyboard with a rack of add-on synthesizers is more convenient to transport than a system composed of full synthesizers and is usually less expensive in the long run.

DRUM MACHINES

A drum machine combines specialized sound generators designed to create percussion sounds with a built-in sequencer to provide steady backup rhythms for a performing group or to provide a rhythm track for a recording. Drum machines vary significantly in features and price. The profile that follows describes an inexpensive but versatile drum machine, the Roland TR-505.

A Profile of the Roland TR-505 Drum Machine

The Roland TR-505 drum machine (shown in Figure 7-6) is a small unit, measuring about 12 by 7 by 2 inches. It's easily portable and can run on six penlight batteries or on AC power. The controls on the front of the TR-505 are simple: There is a large liquid-crystal display in the upper left corner, volume and tempo knobs, and 16 rubber buttons, one for each sound the TR-505 plays. In addition, there are 15 buttons that control other characteristics of the TR-505.

Figure 7-6.
*The Roland TR-505
drum machine.*

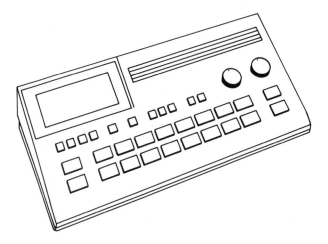

The sampled sounds available on the TR-505 have been pre-recorded by Roland and stored in internal ROM. They are all life-like percussion sounds, played on the TR-505's eight digital sound generators. The 16 available sounds are listed below:

Low and high congas	Snare drum
Low and high cowbells	Rimshot
Closed high-hat cymbal	Timbale
Open high-hat cymbal	Hand clap
Low, mid, and high tom drums	Crash cymbal
Bass drum	Ride cymbal

Each sound can be played at six different volume levels (communicated in MIDI as attack velocity) and can be accented for extra punch.

You can play the TR-505 in live performance by tapping out rhythms on the 16 percussion buttons—each time you press a button, the TR-505 plays the appropriate percussion sound. But the buttons are not designed for live use; they are small and hard to press with accuracy. The best way to use the TR-505's percussive offerings is to program rhythms in its built-in sequencer or in an external sequencer.

The internal sequencer stores 48 already-programmed "rhythm patterns," single-measure rhythmic figures (usually of three or four beats). It also has room for 48 more rhythm patterns that you can create by playing the percussion buttons in real time or by entering notes one at a time in step mode. After you record a rhythm pattern, you can edit it in various ways. You can copy rhythms you record to new rhythm patterns, or you can delete sections of rhythms. You can also insert new rhythms between notes of existing rhythms and can overdub rhythms you've already recorded, adding new notes to notes already in the sequencer's memory.

The TR-505 can repeat and combine the rhythm patterns in its memory to create a "rhythm track," which is a full rhythmic composition. You can play back a rhythm track in any tempo by using the tempo knob to set the playback speed. The TR-505 can store six different rhythm tracks that you can recall and play back at any time. If you want to store tracks outside the drum machine, you can attach a cassette recorder (or any other tape deck) to record the data signal for the track. Later, you can load the track into the sequencer's memory by playing the tape recording back into the drum machine.

The TR-505 has left and right audio ports to send stereo signals. The various percussion sounds have been imaged between channels so that the sounds seem to spread from left to right to create the illusion of a full percussion battery. There is also a headphone jack for listening in stereo without an amplifier, and there's a foot-switch jack that lets you start and stop the TR-505 with your foot.

The TR-505 has a MIDI In and a MIDI Out port. It can send Note On and Note Off messages for the percussion sounds it plays. Because the percussion sounds aren't pitched, the TR-505 matches each sound with a MIDI pitch value and sends that value whenever it plays the sound. When the TR-505 receives MIDI messages, the pitch values likewise determine which percussion sounds the device plays. You can set the sending and receiving pitch value for each of the sounds to be any convenient value. For example, you can set the bass drum to play on pitch value 36. When you play a C two octaves below middle C on an attached keyboard, the keyboard sends a Note On message with a pitch value of 36 and causes the bass drum to play.

Because the TR-505 also sends and receives MIDI clocks, you can synchronize it with other sequencers. It receives all the MIDI sequencer commands, such as Song Select, Song Position Pointer, and Continue, enabling you to control its operation from another source.

In place of a drummer, you can use a drum machine such as the TR-505 as a simple "rhythm box" in performance to grind out repetitive dance rhythms. In live performance, you can connect a drum machine to a drum pad controller, such as the one described later in this chapter. You can also use a drum machine creatively when you make recordings, or you can employ it as a very sophisticated metronome to produce complex rhythms and tempo changes.

AUXILIARY CONTROLLERS

Most MIDI performances are accomplished using a keyboard with pitch wheels, modulation wheels, and pedals. The current range of MIDI devices does, however, offer an alternative mode of performance for singers, guitar players, drummers, wind players, and other musicians who make music without using a keyboard. The two profiles that follow show you two types of auxiliary controllers: the IVL Pitchrider 4000 and the Roland PAD-8 Octapad.

A Profile of the IVL Pitchrider 4000

The IVL Pitchrider 4000 (shown in Figure 7-7) is a rack-mount unit—it's made with all its controls in a front panel so that it can be mounted in a rack with other equipment. Its controls are very simple: a two-digit LED display with a button on each side to increase or decrease the displayed value and a third button to change the operating mode of the Pitchrider. Lights on the front panel indicate the current mode.

Figure 7-7.
The IVL Pitchrider 4000.

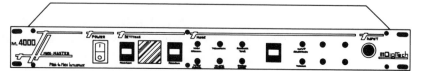

There are two jacks in the back of the Pitchrider: a Mic In jack and a Line In jack. Into the Mic In jack you can plug a cable carrying a low-level audio signal, such as the signal from a microphone. The Line In jack is intended for a stronger, line-level audio signal, such as that from a cassette deck or synthesizer. There is also a single MIDI Out port to send information from the Pitchrider to an auxiliary synthesizer, sequencer, or other MIDI device.

When you turn on the Pitchrider, it senses the incoming audio signal (through either the Mic In or Line In port) and quickly determines the pitch of the signal. The audio signal must be monophonic, such as a single singing voice or wind instrument. If you send a polyphonic audio signal such as a piano or guitar chord to the Pitchrider, the device will be unable to discern the different pitches in the chord.

The Pitchrider normally takes 10 milliseconds or slightly longer to determine the incoming pitch before it sends a Note On message to an auxiliary instrument. The Note On message conveys the pitch value and attack velocity (the volume) of the note. As soon as the sound dies away or moves to a new pitch, the Pitchrider sends a Note Off message and a new Note On message if there is a new pitch.

The Pitchrider is highly sensitive to changes in pitch. As it senses an incoming pitch, it indicates on its LED display whether the pitch is flat or sharp, using different segments of the display to show if the pitch is slightly out of tune or significantly out of tune. The Pitchrider can also transmit Pitch Bend Change messages as the incoming pitch moves up and down, enabling an attached synthesizer to bend the pitch up and down with the audio source. If the sound gets louder or softer, the Pitchrider can send Aftertouch messages to change the volume of the note generated on the attached synthesizer.

You can adjust the Pitchrider's response to incoming audio signals. For example, the Pitchrider is programmed to respond to standard tuning centered around an A♮ at 440 cycles per second. You can tune it up to an A460 or down to an A390 to make it work correctly with an out-of-tune instrument. You can also change the time the Pitchrider takes to determine a pitch, slowing it from its 10 millisecond optimum recognition time. This makes the Pitchrider less sensitive to sudden changes in pitch. Other useful adjustments allow you to transpose outgoing notes by one to twelve half-steps up or down or to change the pitch bend range of outgoing messages over a range of one half-step to a full octave. You can also set the sensitivity of the Pitchrider to the incoming audio signal so that it responds to the softest signals or so that it ignores all but the loudest signals.

The Pitchrider is a convenient way to play a single melodic line on a synthesizer by singing or playing a wind instrument into a microphone. In a similar way, you can use it to record a melody into a MIDI sequencer. The Pitchrider isn't infallible, however. Feedback from the speaker to the microphone can produce random notes, or a slow response time from the Pitchrider can cause problems. You can improve the device's response by using a contact microphone; it rests directly on an instrument and picks up vibrations without picking up speaker feedback traveling through the air. And a little practice will help you learn the Pitchrider's limitations and get the best possible results from it.

A Profile of the Roland PAD-8 Octapad

The Roland PAD-8 Octapad (shown in Figure 7-8) is a controller for drummers. It has eight touch-sensitive, flexible plastic pads that feel like drum heads. Each pad sends Note On and Note Off messages as it's struck. You can set each pad to send messages over a different MIDI channel, and you can also set each pad to send a different Note On pitch value. By adjusting the touch sensitivity of a pad, you can set it to respond in different ways to soft and hard strikes. You can also set the gate time of each pad to control the interval between a Note On message and the subsequent Note Off message. The gate time corresponds to the length of the note that the pad plays.

Figure 7-8.
The Roland PAD-8 Octapad.

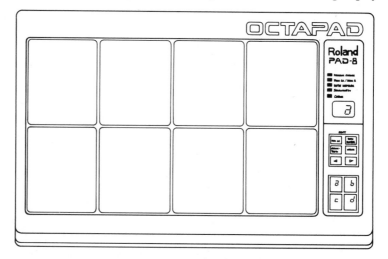

The Octapad has a simple set of ten control buttons you use to set all the pad characteristics. A two-digit LED display shows you the different values as you set them. Once you set all the pads, you can save the entire arrangement as a "patch preset" and store as many as four patch presets in the Octapad's memory. You can change the patch preset by pressing a single button or by using an external foot switch plugged into the Octapad. You can also use the Octapad to send a Program Change message to an attached synthesizer to change a patch as you play.

The Octapad has six jacks for plugging in extra pads—individual, touch-sensitive pads like those on the Octapad. There are also two footswitch jacks. The Octapad has two MIDI ports: MIDI In and MIDI Out. It uses the MIDI Out port to send its controlling MIDI messages to attached MIDI devices. The Octopad itself does not respond to incoming MIDI messages. You can use the MIDI In port to connect a second Octapad. The incoming messages from the second Octapad are mixed with the first Octapad's own messages, and both sets of messages are sent to the attached synthesizer or drum machine. Using the MIDI In port in this way lets you expand from 8 pads to 16 pads.

The Octapad works best with drum machines. In fact, Roland designed it with a special patch preset to work with the Roland TR-707 drum machine or another similar drum machine. Considering the amount of equipment the average drummer has to haul back and forth between gigs, the low weight and small size of an Octapad and a good drum machine or two offer some clear advantages.

MIDI THRU BOXES

MIDI Thru boxes are simple devices that become increasingly important as your MIDI system grows and requires more complex MIDI connections. The next profile describes a typical Thru box, the Casio TB-1.

A Profile of the Casio TB-1 MIDI Thru Box

The Casio TB-1 MIDI Thru box (shown in Figure 7-9) has two MIDI In ports, labeled A and B, and eight MIDI Thru ports. Each Thru port has a switch that connects it to either MIDI In port A or MIDI In port B. This arrangement effectively gives you two Thru boxes; you can connect a different MIDI source to each MIDI In port and then connect as many MIDI Thru ports as you need for each MIDI source (limited to eight, of course) by setting the appropriate switches.

Figure 7-9.
The Casio TB-1 MIDI Thru box.

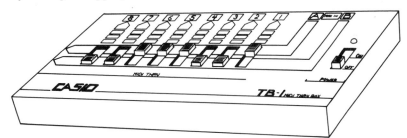

The TB-1 requires its own power source to keep the MIDI signals clean and powerful as they pass from the MIDI In ports to the MIDI Thru ports. You can power the TB-1 with six penlight batteries or with an AC-to-DC converter.

MIDI Thru boxes are necessary any time you set up a large MIDI system—at times, to make up for the fact that some of the MIDI devices don't have their own MIDI Thru ports, but also to simplify MIDI connections and to keep the MIDI messages from being garbled by slow Thru ports in long daisy-chain connections.

In this chapter you've seen some of the different kinds of MIDI equipment used today in MIDI systems, and you've become familiar with their features, operation, and uses. Some of these devices will doubtless be replaced over time by more powerful or less expensive pieces of equipment—manufacturers never stop improving products in their search for new customers—but the features you read about in these profiles will continue to be common features in new products. The next chapter combines some of the products profiled in this chapter into an actual MIDI system controlled by a computer.

8 | COMPUTERIZED MIDI SYSTEMS

A computer can be one of the most significant and useful additions you can make to your MIDI system. It can also be one of the most complicated. This chapter gives you an opportunity to look closely at some real computers and the software they run.

The first part of the chapter introduces you to two different computers. You can see what kind of equipment each includes and how it runs. The next section describes some of the software you can run on these computers: sequencers, patch editors, and musical notation editors. You'll get a rundown on the features that make these programs useful to you. The last section spotlights a complete MIDI system with a computer, a synthesizer, a drum machine, and an expansion module—devices introduced in this and the previous chapter—and shows you how to make MIDI connections to run different software on the computer.

The profiles in this chapter, like those in the last chapter, are not in-depth reviews of equipment and software. They concentrate instead on describing popular products that typify a certain category of hardware or software. In most cases, you'll find two profiles in each category. The first profile introduces a low-cost product; the second describes a product that costs considerably more. By reading both profiles, you can decide whether you can get what you want from the less expensive product, or whether it's worth shelling out some extra cash to get additional features.

PERSONAL COMPUTERS

In this section, you'll find profiles of two popular MIDI computers: the low-priced Atari 520ST computer and the higher-priced Macintosh Plus computer. Of course, there are numerous other personal computers that can run MIDI software, among them the popular Apple II, the very inexpensive Commodore 64 and Atari 800 computers, the versatile Amiga computer, and the all-pervasive IBM Personal Computer. All of these computers have their devotees and their own impressive MIDI software, but it's impossible to describe them all in the space of this chapter. The two profiles that follow will give you a concrete idea of what a personal computer can contribute to your MIDI system.

A Profile of the Atari 520ST Computer

The Atari 520ST personal computer (shown in Figure 8-1) combines powerful features with a low price. It's the lower-priced half of the Atari ST line of computers, which also includes the higher-priced (and higher-powered) Atari 1040ST computer.

Figure 8-1.
*The Atari 520ST
personal computer.*

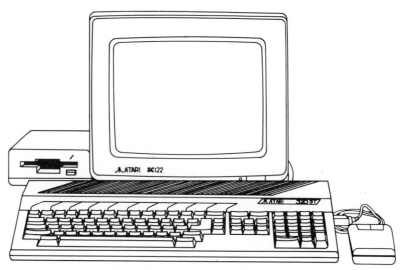

The Atari 520ST has some good, inexpensive MIDI software written for it, and it has a special bonus for MIDI users: built-in MIDI ports. The 520ST doesn't require a MIDI adaptor to work in a MIDI system.

*Parts of the Atari
520ST*

The heart of the 520ST is housed in a system unit that includes a built-in keyboard. The keyboard has all the standard keys you find on a typewriter, as well as a numeric keypad, ten function keys (whose purpose varies depending on the software you run), and a set of cursor control keys for moving a *cursor* on the monitor screen. (The cursor is a flashing symbol that moves throughout text on a screen to show you where you're typing.)

The 520ST also has a two-button mouse that you can use to move a pointer displayed on the screen.

Inside the system unit is a Motorola 68000 microprocessor, a powerful chip that handles 32 bits of data at a time. (Compare that to the microprocessors in most synthesizers that typically handle 4 or 8 bits of data at a time.) The 520ST has 512 kilobytes of RAM to store data and 16 kilobytes of ROM to store operating system software. The 520ST also has a sound chip that produces three voices. The sound chip can produce frequencies from 30 Hz to 125,000 Hz (far above the range of human hearing), but the sound quality is too low to use in a MIDI system.

The system unit is only one part of the 520ST computer setup. You also need a monitor to display information and a disk drive to store data. For your monitor, you have a number of options. You can use a standard television set, an Atari SC1224 color monitor, or an Atari SM124 black-and-white monitor. The 520ST can produce color graphics with as many as 16 colors on the color monitor.

You also have a choice of floppy disk drives for the 520ST. You can buy a single-sided disk drive that stores 360 kilobytes of data on each disk, or a (more expensive) double-sided disk drive that stores 720 kilobytes on each disk. Both drives use $3^1/_2$-inch floppy disks. You can attach as many as two disk drives to the 520ST. You can also add a hard disk drive if you need the data storage capacity more than the respectable sum a hard disk will cost you.

Operating System Software

The operating system for the 520ST is *icon-based*. It shows programs and data files on the monitor as small pictures (icons). You can use the programs and files by pointing at corresponding icons with the mouse pointer and clicking a mouse button. You can also choose commands from *pull-down menus,* lists of commands that appear when you move the mouse pointer to the top of the screen. An icon-based operating system contrasts with a *command-line operating system,* one that prints the names of your programs and files on the screen. To use the programs and files, you type your commands on the keyboard. In general, icon-based operating systems are easier to learn than command-line operating systems.

Ports

The 520ST has many different ports across the back of the system unit that you can use to add peripheral equipment. It has a monitor port for connecting an Atari monitor, a parallel port for connecting a printer, a serial port for a modem (or other serial device), ports for a floppy disk drive and a hard disk drive, and two controller ports for a mouse or other controller (such as a joystick). Most important to MIDI users are two MIDI ports: MIDI In and MIDI Out.

The MIDI Out port has an interesting feature. You'll recall from Chapter 4 that the MIDI 5-pin plug uses only three of its pins, two for the signal and one for the ground. The 520ST uses the two normally unused pins in the MIDI Out port to send a MIDI Thru signal. If you plug a special adaptor into the MIDI Out port, you can have both a MIDI Out and a MIDI Thru port.

The Atari 520ST is well suited as a computer for a home MIDI studio; it's inexpensive and has a good variety of MIDI software available for it. It's not a good computer to use in live performance though: Both the system unit and the external drive need a bulky external AC power supply, giving you a total of at least five pieces of equipment to carry with you—the system unit, the monitor, a disk drive, and two power supplies. And when you set it all up, you'll need a relatively large, flat area and a tangle of cables to connect all the components. Still, considering the 520ST's impressively low cost, you might be willing to tolerate a few more cables and cords in a MIDI system already filled with them.

A Profile of the Apple Macintosh Plus Computer

The Apple Macintosh computer has been around for several years in several different versions. It started out as the plain, old Macintosh with 128 kilobytes of RAM, was upgraded with 512 kilobytes of RAM as the "Fat Mac," and was then thoroughly revamped with a new operating system and other features as the Macintosh Plus (shown in Figure 8-2).

The different Macintoshes are *upwardly compatible,* which means that programs written for an earlier version of the Mac run on later versions but that programs written for later versions don't necessarily run on earlier versions (although most do).

Parts of the Macintosh Plus

The Macintosh Plus looks much like its predecessors: a central unit that contains a 9-inch black-and-white monitor, a $3^1/_2$-inch floppy disk drive, and all the internal circuitry, including the microprocessor and memory. It has a detachable keyboard that connects to the central unit with a coiled cable; you can put the keyboard on your lap, on the table top, or anyplace you find it convenient to type. There is also a one-button mouse that plugs into the back of the central unit.

Figure 8-2.
*The Apple
Macintosh Plus
computer.*

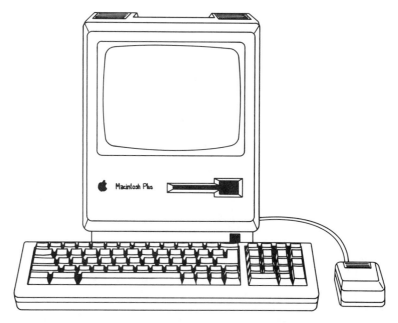

Like the Atari 520ST, the Macintosh Plus uses a Motorola 68000 microprocessor, but it has 1024 kilobytes of RAM, twice as much as the 520ST, and 128 kilobytes of ROM, compared to 16 kilobytes in the 520ST. With the sound chips on the Macintosh Plus, you can synthesize four voices of music at a time and play back sampled-sound waveform tables from the Mac's memory. These sound chips aren't sufficiently sophisticated, however, to give the Mac a sound comparable to that of a regular synthesizer.

The Mac keyboard has a full set of standard typewriter keys, a numeric keypad, and cursor control keys. Its internal disk drive is a double-sided 3½-inch drive that stores 800 kilobytes of data per disk. You can add an external double-sided 3½-inch drive, and for extremely large data storage capacity, you can add a hard disk drive.

Ports

The ports in the back of the Mac's central unit accommodate a range of peripheral equipment. There is one serial port for attaching a printer, a second serial port for attaching a modem, a floppy disk port for attaching an external disk drive, a mouse port to plug in the Mac's mouse, a SCSI port (an acronym for Small Computer Serial Interface, pronounced "scuzzy") that you can use to connect a hard disk drive (among other things), and an audio port that you can connect to an amplifier and speaker to play the Mac's audio signal over a high-quality sound system. (The Mac does have a built-in speaker, but it's small and sounds no better than the speaker on a small television set.)

The Mac does not have any MIDI ports, but you can plug a MIDI interface into either serial port. Because this serial port doesn't supply power to the interface, any interface you plug in here must have its own power supply. Some types of MIDI interfaces plug into both serial ports, giving you the advantage of two interfaces in one.

Software

The operating system software for the Macintosh Plus is one of its strongest features. Apple was the first personal computer company to come out with an icon-based operating system in a home computer, and their experience is certainly evident. The monitor shows a crisp black-and-white picture with icons and pull-down menus that you can manipulate with the mouse pointer. Almost all Mac programs use the same *user interface* (the method the program uses to communicate with you), and this consistency makes it easier to learn new programs.

Because the Macintosh Plus is a very popular computer among musicians, software developers have written quite a number of professional-quality MIDI programs for the Mac. One distinct advantage of the Mac is that its system software and its monitor display are designed to make it very easy to print whatever you see on the screen on an attached printer. Musical notation programs work especially well on the Mac, because you can see exactly where you are placing notes and musical markings on the screen before you print the score.

Portability

The Macintosh Plus is very compact, easy to set up, and easy to pack up and carry around. A minimum system has only two main parts: the central unit and the keyboard. If you've added an external floppy disk drive, you don't need an additional power supply; it runs on power provided by the central unit. Apple and other manufacturers make inexpensive, padded nylon carrying cases that carry all the separate components, including an extra disk drive. Packed into such a case, the computer is small enough to carry under the seat of an airplane.

Setting up the Mac is relatively simple. Place the central unit on a small flat area and plug it into an AC socket. Then plug the mouse in the back and the keyboard in the front, and you're ready to turn it on.

MIDI INTERFACES

All computers today (with the exception of the Atari ST) need to have MIDI interfaces before you can plug them into your MIDI system. Dumb interfaces are far more common than smart ones because of their simplicity, compatibility with the software, and lower cost. The following profile describes a typical MIDI interface for the Macintosh Plus computer.

A Profile of the Austin MIDIface MIDI Interface

The Austin MIDIface MIDI adaptor (shown in Figure 8-3) is a very simple MIDI interface that comes in two versions, one for the Macintosh Plus and a second version for the two older Macintosh models. (The first Macs and the Fat Macs have a different kind of RS-422 serial port than the Mac Plus has.) The MIDIface consists of a box with one MIDI In port and two MIDI Out ports. Leading away from the box are a cord that you plug into the Mac's RS-422 serial interface and an AC power cord to plug into a power outlet. After you make these two connections, you can use the MIDI Out and MIDI In ports to connect the Mac to your MIDI system.

Figure 8-3.
The Austin MIDIface MIDI interface.

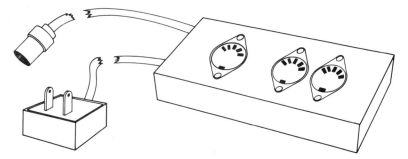

Most dumb MIDI interfaces for personal computers are similar to the MIDIface. Some can function without their own power supply, because some computers provide a power source through the serial port. Other MIDI interfaces include a Thru port so that you can pass MIDI messages through the interface without running MIDI software on the computer. In all cases, the really important feature is that you can get MIDI messages into and out of the computer.

SEQUENCER SOFTWARE

Most people who add a computer to their MIDI system use it to run sequencer software. The sequencer programs available today run the gamut from limited and simple programs to those that are full-featured and complicated. The two profiles that follow introduce you to two of these programs: *Midisoft Studio,* created and marketed by Midisoft Corporation; and *Performer,* created and marketed by Mark of the Unicorn. *Midisoft*

Studio is a simple sequencer, deliberately designed with limited features to keep it easy to use. *Performer,* which costs about three times as much as *Midisoft Studio,* is one of the most powerful sequencers currently available and has a very full range of features.

A Profile of
Midisoft Studio

Midisoft Studio (shown in Figure 8-4) is a sequencer program for the Atari 520ST or 1040ST computer. To use the program, you need an Atari computer system with a monitor and a floppy disk drive, a synthesizer (or several synthesizers), and at least two MIDI cables to connect the synthesizer to the Atari.

Figure 8-4.
A screen from
Midisoft Studio, *a*
sequencer program
for the Atari ST
computer.

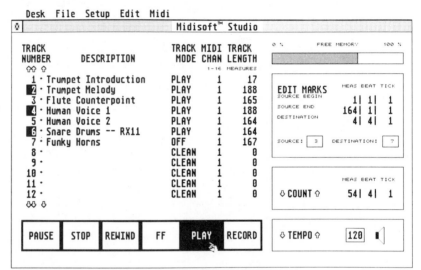

Tracks

Midisoft Studio offers 32 different tracks that you can use for recording or playback. Each track can be set to one of five modes: Clean—an empty track; Record—a track set to record MIDI messages; Play—an already-recorded track set to play back its contents; Off—a recorded track that won't record or play back; and Solo—a recorded track set to play by itself. You can set the mode of each track individually. This makes it possible to record on one track while other tracks are simultaneously playing back and still others are inactive. Once you've recorded on a track, you can protect it from accidental erasure by turning on its Protect feature.

Studio displays the status of its 32 tracks in a window on the program's main screen. Each line in the track window describes a single track with a track number, a symbol that shows whether or not the track is protected, a 24-character label for the track, the current mode of the track, the

MIDI channel number over which the track plays, and the length (in measures) of the recorded music in the track. The combined capacity of all these tracks is approximately 38,000 notes in the Atari 520ST.

Controls

Once you've set the modes of the tracks, you can use a set of controls on the program's main screen to record and play back tracks. These controls resemble tape recorder controls. A Play button initiates playback on all tracks set to Play mode (while tracks set to Record do nothing). A Record button records on the track set to Record mode and simultaneously plays all tracks set to Play mode. To move to a new spot in a recorded score, you can use Fast Forward or Rewind. The Fast Forward button plays back your recorded score at double speed; the Rewind button moves the counter toward the beginning of the track. The Stop button stops recording and playback, and (if you so stipulate) it automatically sets the score back to the beginning. The Pause button pauses playback or recording; you can resume playback at the same point in the score at which you interrupted it by using the Pause button a second time.

The Counter

To indicate your location in a score, *Studio* provides an on-screen counter that works much like a tape recorder counter. As you play or record, it counts music in measures, beats, and ticks. You can set the number of beats per measure, as you would in writing a time signature. To record a waltz, for example, you'd set three beats per measure. Each beat is a quarter note and is divided into 240 ticks, providing an internal tick rate that is 10 times faster than the standard MIDI clock rate (24 clocks per quarter note). This fast rate lets *Studio* record your rhythms with more accuracy than it could using the MIDI clock rate.

The Metronome

Midisoft Studio has a built-in metronome that uses the Atari's own speaker to click on each beat as you play or record. It makes a loud click on the downbeat of each measure, followed by softer clicks for each of the other beats in the measure. You can set the tempo of the metronome anywhere from 30 beats per minute to 480 beats per minute. The tempo you set affects the playback: Changing the metronome tempo speeds up and slows down playback of the score. If you want to establish a tempo before you begin recording a score, you can set the metronome to play a few lead-in measures before *Studio* starts playing or recording. You can also turn off the metronome at any time to silence the clicks.

Recording

Recording in real time is simple. You first set the metronome to play a few lead-in bars and set the metronome tempo to your performance tempo. You can then set a track to Record mode and use the Record button to start recording. The metronome plays a set number of lead-in bars, and then *Studio* starts recording. Each recording track records messages that arrive on any MIDI channel (an Omni On state for each track). When you finish recording, press the Stop button.

You can also record music in step time. First, pick a standard note length, such as a quarter note or a dotted eighth note (or any length defined by ticks and beats), for the interval between note beginnings (the step time). Then press the Record button. *Studio* waits for you to play music on a keyboard. When you press a key, the program records a note of the corresponding pitch. When you press a second key, *Studio* enters the second note, separating it from the first note by the step time you set. If you press more than one key at a time, *Studio* enters a chord at the step. Special buttons are provided to enter rests or to retract a mistake.

You can change step time on the *Studio* screen at anytime. As you use step time, you can change the spacing of notes by reserving a percentage of each note's length as silent space between notes. When you finish recording, use the Exit button to stop step-time recording.

Editing

Studio has editing features that help you edit individual tracks or segments of a track. (*Studio* doesn't let you edit individual MIDI messages.) You can erase the contents of any single track or transfer the entire contents of one track to another. You can also copy the contents of one track into any number of other tracks, and you can combine the contents of two tracks into a single track. If your recordings aren't rhythmically precise, you can quantize the contents of a track.

To make changes within a track, you first define the segment you want to edit. While playing back the score, you click the mouse button once when you hear the beginning of the segment you want to edit, and a second time when you hear the end of the segment. You can also establish the beginning and ending points by entering each location using measures, beats, and ticks. A third way is to Step Play the track, note by note, and click the mouse button to define the boundaries of the segment exactly.

After you define a segment, you can copy it into a buffer and insert it in another location in the same track or in another track. (Set the insertion point the same way you set the beginning or ending point of the track segment.) When you insert a segment, all notes following the insertion point shift back to make room for the inserted segment. You can also overlay a segment at an insertion point, in which case the music under the newly overlaid segment is erased.

There are two ways to eliminate the segment that you've defined. You can delete the segment, in which case the music following the segment moves up to fill in the deleted section. Or you can erase the segment, an operation that replaces the notes in the segment with rests.

Working with
External Devices

Midisoft Studio can record a full set of MIDI messages (except system exclusive messages). It can also respond to external MIDI clocks, and to Start, Stop, Continue, and Song Position Pointer messages so that you can synchronize playback with an external drum machine or other sequencer. You can ask *Studio* to send a System Reset, Tune Request, Song Select, or All Notes Off message at any time to help control your attached MIDI devices. If you want to control an attached sequencer with *Studio,* the program sends MIDI clocks as you play a score (one clock for every 10 of its internal ticks) and sends Start, Stop, and Continue commands when you use the Playback and Record controls. If you use Fast Forward or Rewind, *Studio* sends out a Song Position Pointer message to tell an attached sequencer where in the score you stopped.

Disk Storage

Midisoft Studio works with the Atari disk drive to store any of your recorded scores on floppy disk. You can build your own score library on disks and use them to exchange sequences with other musicians running *Studio* on an Atari ST computer.

A Profile of
Performer

Performer (shown in Figure 8-5 on the next page) works in many ways like *Midisoft Studio,* but it has many more features than *Studio.* To use *Performer,* you need a Macintosh computer with at least 512 kilobytes of RAM, a MIDI interface, a synthesizer (or synthesizers), and at least two MIDI cables to make connections.

Tracks

Unlike *Midisoft Studio, Performer* doesn't offer a fixed number of tracks to use. You can create tracks as you need them and can create more than 200 tracks in all. You can set each track so that it will play, record, do neither, or do both at the same time. You can also choose any MIDI channel (or multiple MIDI channels) for the track to record from or for subsequent playback of the recorded track.

Performer identifies each track as a line in a track window. You can scroll through the track list in the window to see each track. Each track line

Figure 8-5.
A screen from
Performer, *a*
sequencer program
for the Macintosh.

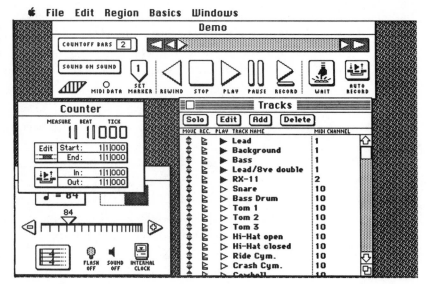

shows whether the track is set to record or play, displays the name that you entered for that track, and shows the MIDI channels for which the track is set. Controls at the top of the track list let you create and delete tracks. By using the mouse pointer, you can move any track to a new location in the list.

Controls

Like *Studio, Performer* uses standard tape recorder controls to play and record the score. Displayed above the controls is a slider that you can use to set the playback location anywhere in the length of the score. You adjust the position of the slider with the mouse pointer. A counter in the display shows your current location in the score using measures, beats, and ticks. You can set the number of beats per measure and the note value that is equivalent to a beat. *Performer* uses 480 ticks per quarter note, an internal clocking resolution 20 times as fine as MIDI's 24 clocks per quarter note.

The Metronome

Performer has a metronome that uses the Macintosh's speaker to sound a click on each beat, accenting the downbeat of each measure. You can set the metronome rate from 20 to 400 beats per minute. That rate, in turn, controls the playback and recording tempo of the sequencer. You can also set the metronome to play a few lead-in bars before you play back or record a score to help you establish a tempo. To make the metronome's beats visible, you can turn on a light that flashes on the Macintosh screen with each beat. You can turn off both the flashing light and the audible metronome click at any time.

Recording

Recording works much the same way that it does with *Studio,* but *Performer* provides some extra recording features. With either program, you can instruct the sequencer to start recording only when it receives a MIDI message from an external device. In this way, you can start a recording simply by playing the first note of your performance. *Performer* also lets you add notes to what is already recorded on a track. Of course, you can also record in the usual way, replacing the previous contents of the track. If you want to record over a single segment of a score without touching recorded music before and after the section, you can use Punch In and Punch Out to automatically start and stop the recording mode at the appropriate spots. You can set the punch-in and punch-out locations in a special display that identifies both locations in measures, beats, and ticks.

You can record in step time using any note value from a breve (double the length of a whole note) to a one-hundred-twenty-eighth note, any type of -tuplet note (quintuplet sixteenths, septuplet quarters, or whatever your imagination can invent), or any number of ticks. A special step-time display shows where you are in the measure as you record and lets you enter rests, notes, and chords with equal ease using an external keyboard and a mouse to specify note lengths.

If you want to filter incoming MIDI messages as you record, a filter display lets you specify the types of MIDI messages you wish to exclude. *Performer* will filter out almost any kind of MIDI messages and data, from Aftertouch to Pitch Bend Change messages. This helps you conserve memory as you record a performance.

Editing

Performer's real strength is its editing features. You can add and delete tracks, move and rename them, and reassign their MIDI channels. You can work on several tracks at one time if you want and can also define regions within tracks in much the same way you do in *Studio.* Once you define a region, you can cut, copy, paste (insert), erase, and merge the contents of the region. You can also undo any editing command you may have carried out by mistake. As you perform these operations, you can set a filtering feature so the editing commands work only on the types of MIDI messages you specify. For example, if you set the filter to work only on Program Change messages, you can use the Cut command to remove all the Program Change messages from a region.

In addition to the standard Cut and Paste commands, *Performer* offers a set of exotic, yet very useful, editing commands to fine tune your recorded scores. You can transpose all pitches within a region up or down by any number of half-steps. You can quantize all notes in a region to clean up rhythms, and you can *de-flam* a region, a process that lines up all the notes in chords so that their attacks are simultaneous. If you want to turn melodies upside down, you can ask *Performer* to invert all the pitches in a region. (It inverts them around any pitch you set.) You can also ask it to reverse the note order of any region so that the recorded notes play backward.

To change the duration of all the notes in a region, you can instruct *Performer* to make all notes equal in duration or to lengthen or shorten all durations by a percentage you set. If you want to affect the velocity of notes in a region, *Performer* can set all velocities to the same value, or it can increase or decrease all velocities by the same amount. It can also set a smooth *crescendo* or *diminuendo* within a region by setting the velocities to increase or decrease over the length of the region. *Performer* can control pitch bend data, modulation data, or other controller setting information in the same way that it controls velocity data. *Performer* has still other esoteric editing features, among them commands that let you change controller messages in a region from one controller to another.

If these editing features don't enable you to get the editing results you want, *Performer* can display the full contents of any individual track as a complete list of the MIDI messages in the order they were recorded. Each message is shown with the time it occurred (measured in measures, beats, and ticks), the type of musical event it is, its accompanying data, and the length of the event. For example, notes are shown with pitch, attack velocity, and release velocity data. You can choose any message and change its type, its accompanying data, its location in the track, or its duration. You can also delete any message or group of messages and add new ones at whatever point you want them. If you really want to create a score from scratch, you can create a series of messages in a track without recording them and then set them to be the notes, pitch bend values, program changes, and other messages that you want for playback.

Performer offers many other minor features that make editing, recording, and playback easy and flexible. It has full disk-storage abilities, so that you can build score libraries on disk. It also saves scores in a form that another Mark of the Unicorn product, *Professional Composer,* can read and convert to printed music. You'll find more about this feature in the *Professional Composer* profile later in this chapter.

**MUSICAL
NOTATION
SOFTWARE**

Musical notation software is useful for composers and arrangers who want to avoid the time-consuming task of copying their quickly penciled scores in ink and then recopying individual parts for musicians to play. Musical notation software combined with a sequencer is also useful for musicians who don't want to record live performances, preferring to play back music directly from their written scores.

The profiles in this section show you two musical notation programs. The first program, *Deluxe Music Construction Set* (sold by Electronic Arts), combines a musical notation program with music playback software. *Deluxe Music* plays back any entered scores on attached MIDI instruments without requiring additional software. The second program, *Professional Composer* (sold by Mark of the Unicorn), takes a different approach. *Composer* concentrates on offering a very complete set of musical notation program capabilities. Without the use of additional software, however, it offers very limited playback opportunities (although you can play back scores well if you use *Performer*). There is also a price difference: *Professional Composer* costs about five times as much as *Deluxe Music Construction Set*.

**A Profile of
*Deluxe Music
Construction Set***

Deluxe Music Construction Set (shown in Figure 8-6) runs on any Macintosh computer, from the 128-kilobyte Mac to the Macintosh Plus with its megabyte of memory. There is also a slightly different version for the Amiga computer.

Figure 8-6.
A screen from
Deluxe Music
Construction Set, *a
musical notation
program for the
Macintosh Plus,
showing three of its
windows.*

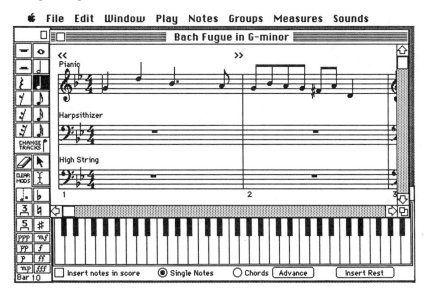

To print the scores you create, you need a printer, of course; *Deluxe Music* works with either a dot-matrix printer or a laser printer. If you want to play back the scores you create, you'll also need a MIDI adaptor, at least one synthesizer, and at least two MIDI cables to connect the synthesizer.

The Display

When you run *Deluxe Music* on the Macintosh, the program displays five windows on the monitor: the Score window, the Keyboard window, the Score Setup window, the Note Palette window, and the Memory window. Each window is a bordered section of the monitor screen with its own icons and activities.

The Score window is the region in which you actually create your score. It can contain as many as eight staves. You won't be able to see all eight at once, but you can scroll the contents of the window up and down to see all the staves. The staves can each be unbroken, extending continuously from left to right without page breaks, or they can be broken into pages. When they're unbroken, you can scroll the window from left to right to see the contents of a complete staff. When they're broken into pages, you can scroll up and down to see the contents of any page.

The Score Setup window lets you set the number of staves in a score and assign a clef (from a choice of four different clefs) for each staff. You can determine the number of measures to run across the width of a page, and you can also set the spacing of the page when it's printed. The Score Setup window also includes controls that set the volume and tempo of a score when you play it back and other controls for determining the appearance of staves on the page and selecting playback options.

The Note Palette window illustrates the different notes, rests, dynamic markings, accidental signs, and editing pointers you can use in creating your scores. There is a range of notes and rests from whole notes and rests to thirty-second notes and rests. You can dot any of these notes or turn them into triplets or quintuplets. There are also eight dynamic markings you can use that range from *ppp* to *fff* and three accidentals—flat, sharp, and natural.

The Keyboard window displays a music keyboard on the monitor screen. You can point to the keys with the mouse pointer to play the notes or to enter them on the staves in the score. The Memory window simply shows how much memory you've used and how much remains.

Entering Music

Entering notes, rests, and other symbols in a score is an easy task with *Deluxe Music*. You first set the meter, the time signature, and clefs for the different staves in the score. You then use the mouse pointer to select a symbol from the Note Palette, move to the staff you want, and click on the position at which you want to enter the symbol. *Deluxe Music* plays the pitches of notes as you enter them so that you can hear what you're entering. As you continue to enter symbols, *Deluxe Music* automatically draws bar lines at the appropriate intervals and spaces notes and rests so that they line up correctly on the beats. If you don't like the way the symbols are spaced, you can move them anywhere you want with the mouse pointer.

If you want to enter notes by playing on a music keyboard, you can use a step mode that works much like the step mode on a sequencer program. You select a note value on the Note Palette and then play a key (or keys) on an attached MIDI keyboard or on the keyboard in the Keyboard window (using the mouse pointer). *Deluxe Music* enters a note (or chord) of the selected length at the pitch you played. If you hold down the key for a long period of time, the value of the note you are entering will start to lengthen. For example, if you've chosen an eighth note from the Note Palette, and you hold a key for a brief period, you enter an eighth note on the staff. If you press the key for a longer time, the note begins to grow in increments of an eighth note, going from an eighth to a quarter to a dotted quarter to a half note, and so on until you release the key.

You normally enter one voice per staff, each voice playing a melody of single notes or chords. You can also set individual staves to carry two voices: One voice is written with note stems pointing up, the second with note stems pointing down. If you set all eight staves to carry two voices, you can enter a total of 16 voices using *Deluxe Music*.

Editing

Once you've entered music on the score's staves, you can edit it for better appearance and to achieve different playback effects. You can tie, slur, and beam notes together (connect their flags as horizontal bars). You can also set *crescendos, diminuendos,* and octave transpositions for different segments of music in a staff. At the beginning of any measure you can change the meter or the clef of the staff. You can also insert repeats with first and second endings.

If you're writing choral music, or if you want to add written directions to performers, you can add text at any location in the score by pointing with the mouse pointer to that location and then typing the text. You

3

160

MUSIC THROUGH MIDI

can choose from a variety of text fonts and styles, including one font that has standard musical symbols such as guitar-chording symbols, *fermatas,* trills, turns, and others. Once you've entered a block of text, you can move it elsewhere in the score.

Deluxe Music also offers standard editing functions. You can cut, copy, paste, and clear segments of the score and transpose any segment up or down by any number of half-steps. You can also halve or double the length of all notes and rests within a segment. If you have chords on a staff, you can invert a chord up or down to achieve a different sound with the same pitches. Other functions affect individual measures. You can split a measure in two, combine two measures into one, insert a new measure into the score, or delete a measure from the score. If you use a command and dislike the result, you can easily undo the effects of the command.

Score Playback

You can play back any score you enter using the four voices that the Macintosh generates, or you can play it back using attached MIDI instruments. As you enter the score, you can define an instrument to play each staff. That instrument can be one of the internal patches provided for the Macintosh voices, or it can be an external patch consisting of a single MIDI channel with an external patch number.

When you play back the score, *Deluxe Music* uses the instruments you assigned to play the music in the staves. It plays Mac patches using the Mac's own voices. To play an external instrument, *Deluxe Music* first sends a Program Change message with the patch number you specify over the MIDI channel you set for the instrument. The software then sends the contents of the staff over the same MIDI channel. *Deluxe Music* can change instruments in the playback wherever you assign a different instrument in the score.

When you play back a score, you can set the tempo anywhere from 1 to 240 beats per minute. You can also enter tempo changes at any point in a score, changes that modify the overall tempo during playback. If you want to control the overall volume level (relative volumes being controlled by dynamic markings within the score), you can set the volume level for playback to one of eight different settings. The controls in the Score Setup window enable you to transpose the playback of any individual staff up or down by an octave or to turn off any staff completely during playback.

During playback, *Deluxe Music* responds to all the dynamic markings, clef changes, meter changes, and other score entries you made by sending the appropriate series of MIDI messages or instructions for the Macintosh voices. *Deluxe Music* plays any repeats you entered, complete with first and second endings. *Deluxe Music* also flashes notes on the screen as they play and flashes the keys in the Keyboard window to show you the pitches being played. If you find the visual displays distracting, you can turn them off.

Printing Scores

To produce printed copies of the scores you enter, ask *Deluxe Music* to print, and it will reproduce the score exactly as you see it in the Score window. If you don't like the way it looks on paper, you can adjust the number of bars across the width of the page. You can also adjust the width of the score on the page to alter the spacing between notes and rests. If you want to print different parts from the score, you can specify the staves that you want to exclude. By excluding all the staves except the part you want to print, you can employ *Deluxe Music* to print that part separately.

Deluxe Music prints respectable-looking scores using a dot-matrix printer, but for cleaner, sharper results, use a laser printer. *Deluxe Music* uses a language called Adobe POSTSCRIPT to send musical symbols to the laser printer in a font called Sonata. It is not essential that the laser printer use the Sonata font, but the results achieved with Sonata are fast and attractive and approach the quality of typeset copy.

Deluxe Music has one more very useful feature. It works with another piece of Macintosh software, a sequencer called *Sequencer 2.5* (sold by Opcode Systems). You can save a set of sequences you record on *Sequencer 2.5* as a *Deluxe Music* score. When you run *Deluxe Music*, you can load that score, and *Deluxe Music* will convert it into notes, rests, and other symbols on the staves, so that each sequencer track becomes a separate staff.

A Profile of
Professional
Composer

Professional Composer (shown in Figure 8-7 on the next page) runs on a Macintosh with a minimum of 512 kilobytes of RAM. Because *Professional Composer* doesn't play back scores on external devices or allow note entry from an external keyboard, you don't need a MIDI interface or external MIDI devices to run the program. You do need a printer, however. *Professional Composer* works with either a dot-matrix printer or a laser printer.

Figure 8-7.
A screen from
Professional
Composer, *a*
musical notation
program for the
Macintosh.

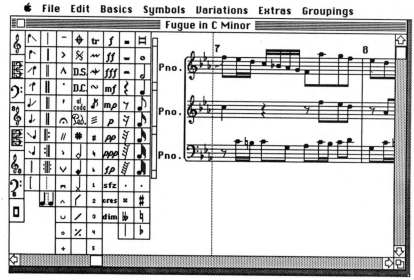

The Display

Professional Composer has a simple screen display. One window shows the staves of the score and can optionally display the complete assortment of notes, rests, and other symbols you can put in the score. You can work on as many as 40 staves at once and can scroll up and down to display any particular staff. The symbols available to you are notes ranging from a breve to a one-hundred-twenty-eighth note, rests ranging from a whole rest to a one-hundred-twenty-eighth rest, five different kinds of accidentals (including double sharps and double flats), dots for any of the notes, and repeat signs. There are also seven kinds of clefs, eight different dynamic markings, accent marks, percussion note heads, and a set of ornaments that includes trills, turns, and mordents. The program provides a set of bar lines that includes double bars and repeats with first, second, and third endings and a special set of markings that includes glisses and other commonly used jazz markings.

Entering Music

To enter music, you first set the number of staves you want in your score. If you like, you can tie them together along their left ends using braces and brackets. Then, choose a clef for each staff and a time signature for the score. *Professional Composer* lets you select an instrument for each staff; it shows you a menu with a list of acoustic and electronic instruments. Each instrument in the menu includes the actual pitch range (upper and lower pitch limits) of that instrument, as well as the transposition of the instrument if it transposes. (For example, a French horn usually transposes everything it plays down by seven half-steps.) When you choose an instrument for a staff, *Professional Composer* automatically imposes the upper and lower pitch limits on notes entered in that staff and sets the staff to transpose properly when you play back the score.

To enter symbols on the staff, you first point with the mouse pointer to the type of symbol you want and then point to the spot in the score where you want to enter it. Because notes and rests are the most frequently entered symbols, *Composer* offers two time-saving methods for entering them. The first alternative method is to choose the type of note or rest you want using the Macintosh's keyboard—different keys on the keyboard choose different notes and rests. You then move the mouse pointer to the location where you want to enter the note or rest and click the mouse to enter it. This method lets you use one hand on the mouse and the other hand on the keyboard to enter notes and rests with minimal mouse movement. If you want to avoid the mouse altogether, the second alternative method lets you use the keyboard to choose not only the notes and rests, but also their location in the score. If you are a touch typist, you'll find this to be a very quick method once you've memorized the keys for the various symbols and pointer movements.

As you enter notes and rests, *Composer* automatically lines them up to fall on the correct beats within each measure. If you want to space them differently, you can enter a space instead of a symbol to shift the locations of subsequent symbols.

Modifying Notes and Adding Lyrics

Once you have notes and rests entered, you can modify them. You can change any group of notes to any type of -tuplet notes—quintuplets, septuplets, nontuplets, and others—that you desire. You can also tie, slur, and beam groups of notes. Using other available symbols, you can add dynamic markings, *crescendos,* and *decrescendos* to the score and change meters and clefs at any point in the score. The program also enables you to add repeat signs, including first, second, and third endings for the repeats.

If you're entering vocal music, you can add lyrics beneath a staff. *Professional Composer* lines up each syllable to fall directly beneath a note if you ask it to. If your lyric has more than one verse, you can add multiple lines of text beneath a staff. The program supplies a variety of text fonts and styles, including a font that is designed to print chordal notation for jazz musicians.

Editing

Once you've entered a score, you can use editing features in *Composer*. You can cut, copy, and paste sections of a score and can also halve, double, or otherwise stretch and shrink note and rest values within a section. If you want to transpose a section, you can move it to a new key or transpose it up or down by any number of half-steps. At any time, you can have *Composer* check the score for excess notes in a bar and rebar the entire score to put the correct number of beats in each measure. If you find you're running out of staves to use, you can merge the contents of any two staves into one and can control the process so that one voice appears with note stems pointing up and the other appears with note stems turned down.

Playing Back Scores

Professional Composer can play back your scores, but only in a restricted manner. It is limited to the Macintosh's four voices and can employ only a small set of patches for those voices. The program is also limited to three tempos—fast, medium, and slow. When you play back a score, *Composer* plays the notes, rests, and dynamics but ignores other markings such as ornaments and repeats. To play back a score using MIDI instruments, you do have the option of saving it to disk and then loading it using *Performer* (described earlier in this chapter). *Performer* turns the notes and rests into MIDI messages and plays back the score using the pitches, durations, and dynamics laid down in the score. It also plays the notes using the articulation marks you set, so that *staccato* notes are short and *legato* notes long. *Performer* doesn't play any of the repeats, however, and can't change tempos in the middle of the score.

As mentioned in the *Performer* profile, you can load *Performer* scores into *Professional Composer*. *Professional Composer* turns a *Performer* score into printed music, converting each track to a separate staff and using the key signature and tempo settings from *Performer* to set the keys and tempo markings in the printed score. You must be sure to quantize and de-flam your *Performer* scores before you transfer them to *Composer,* however, or you'll see thickets of one-hundred-twenty-eighth notes in the printed score where you never intended them.

Printing Scores

When you ask *Professional Composer* to print, it prints the score almost exactly as you see it on the screen, breaking the long staves into pages. Before you print each page, you can preview it in a condensed form on the Macintosh's monitor. If you are satisfied with what you see, you can print that page; otherwise, you can stop printing and alter the score until you are content with it. If no amount of alteration satisfies you, you can save the page to disk as a graphics file. By loading the file into *MacPaint,* a standard

Macintosh graphics program, you can draw whatever features you want and then print the page.

If you want to print an individual part from the score, you can ask *Composer* to print only that part, and it will page the printed copy exactly as it does a full score. To make your scores look professional, you can also use *Composer* to create a title page for the score or part. For still greater refinement, you can create headers and footers, lines of text that appear at the top and the bottom of each page. *Composer* also automatically numbers each page in any part or score it prints.

PATCH EDITORS

A good patch editor is an important piece of software if you want to design your own synthesizer patches or collect patches from other sources. Unfortunately, there isn't a patch editor program that works for all synthesizers. Each patch editor is written to work on a specific computer and is designed to create patches for only one type of synthesizer. If you have several different kinds of synthesizers, you need several different patch editing programs, one for each synthesizer.

The profiles in this section show you two distinctly different types of patch editors. The first, *CZ Patch* (created and sold by Dr. T's Music Software), is an inexpensive patch editor for the Casio CZ-101 synthesizer. Because creating a patch for the CZ-101 is relatively straightforward, *CZ Patch* is a simple program. The second patch editor, *Sound Lab* (created by Blank Software and sold by Ensoniq), is written for the Ensoniq Mirage, a sampling synthesizer. Because it works with sampled-sound patches, it is necessarily more complex, with tools for altering the waveform tables used in the patches.

A Profile of *CZ Patch*

CZ Patch (shown in Figure 8-8 on the next page) can run on either the Atari 520ST or the 1040ST computer and works with the Casio CZ-101 synthesizer. It also works with Casio CZ-1000, CZ-3000, and CZ-5000 synthesizers, which use the same type of sound synthesis and the same sort of patches as the CZ-101. To run the program, you need a disk drive and monitor for the Atari and two MIDI cables to connect the computer and the synthesizer.

CZ Patch performs two functions. As a patch editor, it lets you design your own CZ-101 patches; as a patch librarian, it helps you sort and store those patches. To keep the two functions distinct, *CZ Patch* offers two different screens—the Librarian screen and the Edit screen—and lets you choose the screen you need.

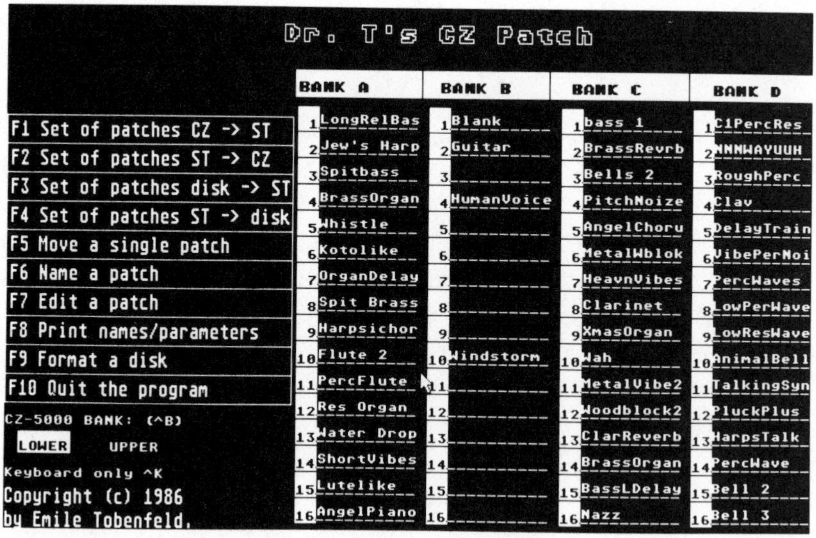

Figure 8-8.
The Edit screen from CZ Patch, *a patch editor for the Atari ST computers and the Casio CZ-101 synthesizer.*

Dr. T's CZ Patch

	BANK A	BANK B	BANK C	BANK D
F1 Set of patches CZ -> ST	1 LongRelBas	1 Blank	1 bass 1	1 C1PercRes
F2 Set of patches ST -> CZ	2 Jew's Harp	2 Guitar	2 BrassReverb	2 MMMWAYUUH
F3 Set of patches disk -> ST	3 Spitbass	3	3 Bells 2	3 RoughPerc
F4 Set of patches ST -> disk	4 BrassOrgan	4 HumanVoice	4 PitchNoize	4 Clav
F5 Move a single patch	5 Whistle	5	5 AngelChoru	5 DelayTrain
F6 Name a patch	6 Kotolike	6	6 MetalWblok	6 VibePerMoi
F7 Edit a patch	7 OrganDelay	7	7 HeavnVibes	7 PercWaves
F8 Print names/parameters	8 Spit Brass	8	8 Clarinet	8 LowPerWave
F9 Format a disk	9 Harpsichor	9	9 XmasOrgan	9 LowResWave
F10 Quit the program	10 Flute 2	10 Windstorm	10 Wah	10 AnimalBell
	11 PercFlute	11	11 MetalVibe2	11 TalkingSyn
CZ-5000 BANK: (^B)	12 Res Organ	12	12 Woodblock2	12 PluckPlus
LOWER UPPER	13 Water Drop	13	13 ClarReverb	13 HarpsTalk
Keyboard only ^K	14 ShortVibes	14	14 BrassOrgan	14 PercWave
Copyright (c) 1986	15 Lutelike	15	15 BassLDelay	15 Bell 2
by Emile Tobenfeld.	16 AngelPiano	16	16 Nazz	16 Bell 3

The Librarian Screen

The Librarian screen is the simpler screen. It displays four banks of 16 patches. Each bank is a column of patches, showing the name and number of each patch. For convenience, these banks of patches contain the same number of patches as the CZ-101's own banks.

To the left of the banks of patches are ten commands for manipulating the stored patches. The first command loads a bank of patches from the CZ-101 into one of the banks on the screen (and into the Atari's RAM), and the second does the reverse, loading a bank of patches on the screen into the CZ-101. In a similar way, the third and fourth commands transfer a bank of patches between the disk drive and the computer. The fifth command lets you move any single patch shown on the Librarian screen to any other location on the screen or in the CZ-101's memory, and the sixth command lets you assign a name for any patch on the screen. (These names are used only in the Atari and aren't stored in the CZ-101.)

You can use the seventh command to choose a patch for editing and to call up the Edit screen. If you have a printer connected to the Atari, you can use the eighth command to print a list of the patch names in a bank or all the settings of any patch, a useful reference sheet to keep with your synthesizer. The ninth command formats a blank disk (a necessary process to prepare a floppy disk for storing patches), and the last command quits the program.

The Edit Screen   If you choose to edit a patch, the Librarian screen disappears and the Edit screen appears. The Edit screen shows the control settings for the patch you chose. These settings show the rates and levels for the three different CZ-101 envelopes: the amplitude envelope, the filter envelope, and the pitch envelope. They identify the waveform you selected for the sound generator and the setting for the LFO. The Edit screen also tells you whether two sound generators are ganged together. If so, it tells you whether they're detuned and by how much. In short, the Edit screen displays all the characteristics that you can set in a CZ-101 patch.

You can change any patch setting by first selecting the setting you want and then using the mouse pointer to move a slider on the screen. As you move the slider, the screen displays new values for the setting. If you prefer, you can use two cursor keys on the Atari's keyboard to move the values up and down, or you can type the new value directly using the Atari keyboard.

Because setting the patch envelopes is the most complicated part of creating a patch, *CZ Patch* displays the shapes of all three envelopes at the bottom of the screen, each one displayed in a different color. As you make changes, the shapes of the envelopes change to reflect the new settings. At any time, you can hear what the patch change sounds like by pressing a mouse button. The CZ-101 then plays a note using your altered patch.

To make using envelopes even easier, *CZ Patch* lets you stretch or shrink all the rates or levels for an envelope. This operation is much easier than entering an entire set of new rate or level settings. Once you design (or locate in another patch) an envelope you like, you can copy it from one patch to another or you can save the envelope to disk for later recall. When you finish editing, you can return to the Librarian screen to put your patch in a bank and then save the bank to disk.

CZ Patch provides a much easier way to create patches for the CZ-101 than using the synthesizer's own controls and tiny display. In addition, it expands the storage capacity of the CZ-101. In live performance, using *CZ Patch* gives you quick access to a far more extensive selection of patches than the synthesizer alone can offer. And you get a bonus with *CZ Patch*: 14 banks of patches that come with the program.

A Profile of   *Sound Lab* (shown in Figure 8-9 on the next page) edits patches for the
Sound Lab   Ensoniq Mirage synthesizer. To run the program, you need a Macintosh computer with a minimum of 512 kilobytes of RAM, a MIDI interface for the Macintosh, and two MIDI cables to connect the Mirage to the Macintosh.

168

MUSIC THROUGH MIDI

Figure 8-9.
A screen from
Sound Lab, *a*
patch editor for the
Macintosh
computer and the
Ensoniq Mirage
synthesizer.

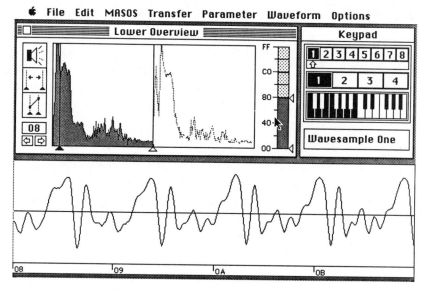

The Display

Sound Lab works with sampled sounds, so its windows are primarily devoted to showing waveforms of sampled sounds. One window gives an overview of the entire waveform table used in a patch. Another provides a closeup of a single section of the waveform table. A third, smaller window contains controls you can use to select one of two waveform tables and specify the sections of the table you want to work with. (Remember from the Mirage profile in the last chapter that each Mirage patch has two separate waveforms, one for the upper keyboard, the second for the lower keyboard.) As you work on a waveform table, the control windows give you various means of directly and indirectly modifying the sound that the waveform produces.

Editing a Waveform Table

Sound Lab has some powerful tools to edit a waveform table directly. You can look at any section of the waveform and actually redraw that section to change the shape of the waveform. You can also define a section of the waveform and use Cut, Copy, Paste, and Clear functions (much as you would with notes and MIDI messages in a sequencer program) to move, remove, and insert sections anywhere in the waveform table. Another editing function—Add—lets you combine two waveforms to create an entirely new waveform. You can also set looping points for a waveform.

    Sound Lab incorporates the full set of waveform manipulation functions included in MASOS, a special operating system that the Mirage uses for shaping sampled sounds. These functions—Fade, Scale, Reverse, Invert, Rotate, Replicate, Compress, Interpolate, and Filter Zeroes—let you change the shapes of waveform sections in useful ways without requiring you to draw exactly what you want.

Setting Envelopes and Other Characteristics

Sound Lab has other controls that let you indirectly modify the sound of a waveform. The program makes it easy to set envelopes for a patch; the screen displays the shapes of both the amplitude and the filter envelopes in an envelope window. You can alter the shape of either envelope using the mouse pointer. You can also change the way waveforms are mixed together and adjust the filtering process, the LFO rate, and other characteristics by using simple graphic controls in *Sound Lab* windows. A separate window displays a keyboard and provides a simple control for changing the split point on the keyboard.

Sampling Sounds

To make your own sampled sound patches, you can use *Sound Lab* to control the Mirage to let you set the sampling rate, the sampling threshold, the filter roll-off frequency, and other important factors that allow you to record the best possible sound in the Mirage's memory. Of course, once you sample a sound, you can edit it to refine its waveform table in the same way that you edit any other Mirage patch.

As you work with a patch, you can listen to it on the Macintosh's speaker, or you can play it back over the Mirage itself. Once you've created a patch you like, you can save it on a disk, or you can transfer it to the Mirage to store on the Mirage's own floppy disks. *Sound Lab* can act as a librarian for the Mirage, storing patches on Macintosh's disks to transfer later to the Mirage, but this method is impractical for live performance due to MIDI's data transmission rate. You can load a patch directly from a Mirage disk much faster than you can recall one from the computer's disk and then transmit it to the Mirage using MIDI.

A program such as *Sound Lab* is a necessity for anyone serious about editing sampled sound patches. The keypad and two-character display of the Mirage make it almost impossible to visualize what you're working with as you edit patches. *Sound Lab* shows you all the information you need in an easily alterable form.

A SIMPLE MIDI SYSTEM

The profiles in this and the last chapter describe single MIDI devices. Connecting two of these devices by means of MIDI and using them together is an easy task. When you begin to add more devices to the system, including a computer running different MIDI programs, things begin to get a little more complicated, as you'll see in the examples that follow.

The Components

To create a simple MIDI system, start with the basics: a synthesizer to let you play keyboard music, a drum machine to add a rhythm section to your performance, an expansion module to add more voices and patch variety to your synthesizer's sounds, and a computer to record sequences and edit patches. In this example, you use some familiar equipment: a Yamaha DX7 as the synthesizer, a Roland TR-505 as the drum machine, a Yamaha FB-01 as the expansion module, and a Macintosh Plus as the computer.

To use the Macintosh effectively in this system, you need a sequencer program such as *Professional Composer,* a patch editor for the DX7, and another patch editor for the FB-01. (You also need an amplifier, speakers, and a small mixing panel to play audio signals from the synthesizer, expansion module, and drum box. But these are common, non-MIDI pieces of equipment, and we won't need to discuss them.)

Connections

You need to do some thinking before you connect the four MIDI devices. In fact, setting up a MIDI system, even a simple one like this, is a problem that resembles one of those brain teasers in the back pages of a science magazine. The problem is this: If you want to run the sequencer program, the Macintosh has to receive MIDI messages from the DX7 keyboard so that it can record your performances. The Mac must also be able to send MIDI messages to the other three MIDI devices if you expect it to play back the scores you create. To use the DX7 patch editor, the Mac must send and receive messages from the DX7. And to use the FB-01 patch editor, it must send and receive messages from the FB-01. To play the FB-01 and the TR-505 from the keyboard, the DX7 must be able to send messages to both these devices. You have an unlimited number of MIDI cables but only a limited number of MIDI In, MIDI Out, and MIDI Thru ports, as shown in Figure 8-10. How do you connect the devices?

Alas, there isn't a perfect answer. The configuration shown in Figure 8-10 fulfills most of the MIDI message communication needs, but not all of them. It is essentially a daisy chain, passing messages from the Macintosh computer to the other three devices. A connection from the DX7 to the Macintosh sends messages from the DX7 keyboard and control panel to the Macintosh.

This configuration works best for running the sequencer on the Macintosh. The sequencer can play the three other devices, controlling each one on a separate MIDI channel (channel 1 for the DX7, channel 2 for the FB-01, and channel 3 for the TR-505). It can also record performances

Figure 8-10.
*Connecting a
simple MIDI
system so that you
can use the
computer for
running a
sequencer.*

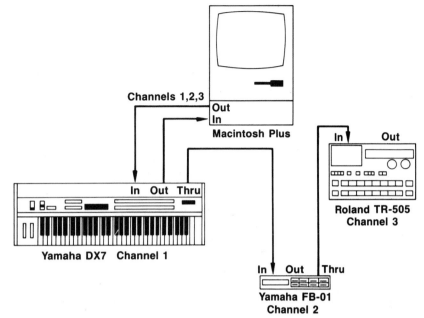

from the DX7 keyboard. You can play any other device from the keyboard because the sequencer can pass incoming messages to the Mac's MIDI Out port over any number of MIDI channels.

This configuration also lets you run the DX7 patch editor because the Macintosh can both send and receive messages from the DX7, but it doesn't let you run an FB-01 patch editor because the Mac can send but can't receive messages from the FB-01. Anytime you want to run your FB-01 patch editor, you can make one simple cable change: Disconnect the cable that plugs into the DX7 MIDI Out port, and plug it into the FB-01 MIDI Out port, as shown in Figure 8-11 on the next page. This configuration enables you to edit FB-01 patches, but it doesn't permit the computer to receive any keyboard messages or patches from the DX7. When you finish working with FB-01 patches, you can reconnect the cable to the DX7 MIDI Out port.

If you have a sequencer program that doesn't pass incoming messages through the Macintosh's MIDI Out port (unfortunately a common feature), then you have to change connections entirely to control the other devices with the DX7 keyboard. Figure 8-12 on the next page shows you this new configuration, essentially a daisy chain that passes messages from the DX7 to the other three devices, with an additional cable that sends messages from the Macintosh to the DX7. Unfortunately, you can't use this

Figure 8-11.
*This configuration
lets you use a
Yamaha FB-01
patch editor.*

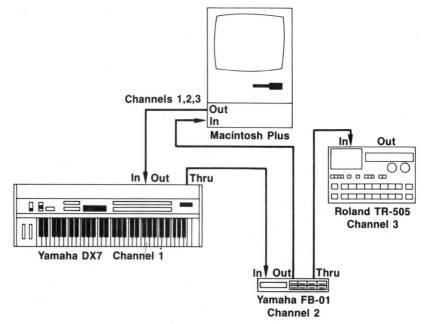

Figure 8-12.
*This configuration
lets you control
some of the other
MIDI devices from
the Yamaha DX7
keyboard.*

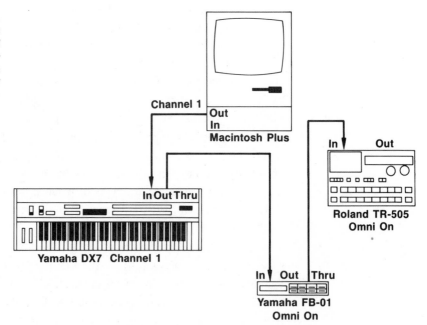

configuration to record your performances on the Macintosh because the DX7 uses its MIDI Out port to send messages to the FB-01, and the TR-505 at the end of the chain has no MIDI Thru port to pass messages back to the Macintosh.

To simplify matters, you can add a MIDI Thru box such as the Casio TB-1 to a system running a sequencer that doesn't pass through MIDI messages. Connect the MIDI In port of each MIDI device to a Thru port on the TB-1. You can then set up the Macintosh and the DX7 as master controllers by connecting their MIDI Out ports to the MIDI In ports, A and B, on the TB-1. A switch on the MIDI Thru box enables you to determine which set of incoming messages, those from A or from B, are passed to the MIDI Thru ports. This switching feature enables you to control the system from either the Mac or the DX7. You can see this configuration below in Figure 8-13.

Figure 8-13.
Using a MIDI Thru box to simplify connections.

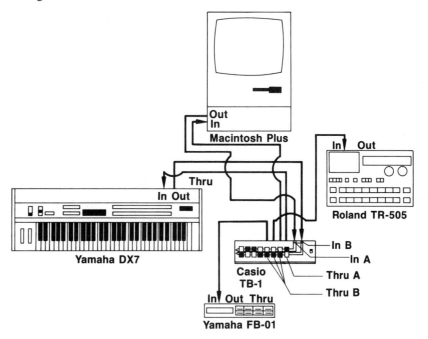

Using a MIDI Thru box as illustrated above saves you some cable switching, but it doesn't solve all your problems. For example, you still can't use the FB-01 patch editor without moving some cables because the only devices that can send messages on the system are the Macintosh and the DX7. The solution to this problem is to use a more extensive Thru box with more than two MIDI In ports, or to gang several TB-1s. These are, at best, expensive options. Another solution is simply to become proficient at switching cables. In any case, it's a good idea to label all your cables so that you know which one leads where.

A computer with the right software can, as you've seen, greatly expand the capabilities of a MIDI system. You've taken a close look at actual products—computers and software—and you've seen the necessity of thinking through MIDI connections when you use a computer in your system. In the next chapter, you'll see how keyboard player Tim Gorman uses his MIDI system in live performance.

9 | MIDI IN LIVE PERFORMANCE

With the many complex MIDI systems available today, it's easy to lose sight of the fact that MIDI was originally designed simply to tie synthesizers together in live performance. But it's still this straightforward use of MIDI that is most popular today; synthesizer players around the world use MIDI to set up master keyboards that control other synthesizers. Even though the MIDI connections are simple in most live performance situations of this kind, it takes time and consideration to set up a system that satisfies your needs as a musician.

In this chapter, you can read about Tim Gorman and his synthesizer system. Currently the keyboard player for the KBC Band and formerly with The Who, Gorman has years of experience playing synthesizers all over the world, and he knows how to set up a system that does the best job for him. You can take a close look at that system to see how he does it. You'll also find inserts in the chapter that explain some of the equipment used in a typical synthesizer system and show how to read MIDI specification sheets—all material that can help you set up your own MIDI system for live performance.

Tim Gorman

**TIM GORMAN,
KEYBOARD
ARTIST**

Tim Gorman rehearses regularly with the KBC Band in a church located in the small Marin County town of San Anselmo, just north of San Francisco. This church, a small and weathered old building, is The Church. Converted to a rehearsal space for rock musicians, it's filled with synthesizers, percussion equipment, mixing panels, amplifiers, speakers, and other rock band paraphernalia. The walls and ceilings are covered with spray-on insulation to allow maximum volume inside with minimum disturbance outside.

The KBC Band is a relatively new band made up of old hands. Its leader, Paul Kantner, was the leader of Jefferson Airplane and later The Starship. He plays rhythm guitar along with Marty Balin, who does lead vocals. Jack Casady plays bass; Tim Gorman, keyboards; Slick Aguilar, lead guitar; Darrell Verdusco, drums; and Keith Crossan, tenor sax. Over the last two years, they've rehearsed intensively, played concerts around the Bay Area, and put out their first album, *KBC Band*. At this writing, they've signed with Arista Records to record six more albums and are about to go on their first national tour, where they'll be taped for MTV. They play classic rock, a clean and powerful sound with a beat that brings audiences to their feet.

As the keyboardist for the group, Tim Gorman plays a variety of synthesizers, something he's had a lot of experience doing. He started playing music as a child in Oakland, and by 1962 he'd put together his own band. "By the time I was 10," he says, "I had a little group together. It was non-electric. I managed to get hold of some Beach Boys records and found out that they used these things called electric guitars and electric organs."

It didn't take him long to acquire electric instruments himself. "I got a little Farfisa organ and through the years modified it heavily. It was my first electronic keyboard. From that, I graduated to electric pianos, using the organ with them, and then eventually to the synthesizer." His first synthesizer was a Mini-Moog, an instrument he played along with electric piano in bands to make extra money through high school and college. He recalls, "It was one of the first ones that Bob Moog ever made, and it was actually hand-wired. There are no printed circuit cards in it—just 75,000 wires. I made the mistake once of taking the back plate off to see what made it tick, and it took me a day just to get all the wires back in there."

When Gorman went to college at the University of Portland in Oregon, he studied composition, music theory, music education, and piano performance. While developing his keyboard skills, he also worked on building an electronic music lab for the school, started a small recording studio, and briefly taught electronic music while a senior. After graduating, he started studio session work at a small studio in Portland. From there, he moved to Seattle to become a staff session player at a prominent studio, where he continued to build his experience with synthesizers. "I often was hired to work on other people's records," he says. "I was using ARP string ensembles and the Mini-Moogs at that time. Everything was still very much analog in those days. There was no digital to speak of."

At the invitation of producer Glenn Johns, Gorman moved to England to join a studio band. Gorman was the keyboard player called in to work with the artists on the records that Johns produced. At that time, he began to work closely with the Moog company, endorsing their synthesizers and getting bigger and better synthesizers from them to play. As his reputation spread, he was invited to join The Who as a keyboardist.

Before taking on Gorman, The Who had changed keyboard players often. "They went through keyboard players like underwear," he laughs. They must have liked Gorman, however. He played with them for four years, until the band retired and the members went their separate ways.

On his first tour with the band, Gorman took along nine synthesizers and an electric organ to give him the range of sounds he needed. These were pre-MIDI days; he would set up all the keyboards on stage and reach from keyboard to keyboard to play the instrument he wanted. "It was seagull stuff," he says, stretching his arms out. As the tour progressed, he worked to make it simpler. "Towards the third week of the first leg of the tour in America, I managed to figure out how I could use fewer keyboards, and I got the total down to five for the majority of the tour."

The System

After the breakup of The Who, Gorman returned to his home stomping grounds in the San Francisco area, where he was soon invited to join the KBC Band. The synthesizer system he now uses with the band reflects the simplicity he worked to achieve while on tour with The Who. He has three synthesizers with built-in keyboards, two rack-mount synthesizers, a master controller keyboard, a portable keyboard for mobile performance, and rack-mount audio equipment.

Equipment

Gorman's synthesizers are carefully chosen to give him the variety of sounds he likes to use in performance. His oldest synthesizer is a Memory Moog Plus, an analog synthesizer (built before the advent of MIDI) that was modified to include MIDI ports. He's had the Memory Moog for a long time and likes its sound. "It's actually serial number one," he says. "Believe it or not, it does sound different from other Memory Moogs—maybe because it's a prototype." Gorman also uses the Emulator II, a sampling synthesizer that lacks MIDI capability, to add sampled sounds to his system, and a digital synthesizer, a Roland JX-8P, to add digital sound.

Gorman's two rack-mount synthesizers are a Roland MKS-80 Super Jupiter analog synthesizer and a Roland MKS-20 digital piano module. The Super Jupiter is an eight-voice analog synthesizer that provides digital controls to set its patches. The MKS-20 digital piano is a 16-voice synthesizer whose sole purpose is to emulate realistically the sound of an acoustic piano, with options available to alter that basic sound.

Gorman uses a Roland MKB-1000 controller to play the MKS-20 via a MIDI connection. The MKB-1000 is a master keyboard with a full set of 88 weighted keys and no synthesizer voices of its own. Gorman likes the MKB-1000 because its feel and action are similar to those of the acoustic pianos on which he was trained. He also uses a Roland Axis MIDI keyboard, a hand-held MIDI keyboard controller that resembles a guitar, to play his Super Jupiter synthesizer by means of MIDI. The Axis has a keyboard with a three-and-a-half-octave range that he can play with his right hand; meanwhile, with his left hand, he works the controls—bending pitch, adjusting modulation and volume, and setting patches, key transposition, and other qualities. The Axis is fun for Gorman; it makes it possible for him to get out from behind his regular keyboards and to perform in front with the rest of the band.

Mounted in Gorman's equipment rack below the Super Jupiter analog synthesizer and the digital piano is a Roland MPG-80 Super Jupiter programmer, a Yamaha digital reverb unit, an Ibanez analog reverb unit, a Studiomaster mixing console, and a JBL amplifier which drives his two monitor speakers. (See the special section on the next page for a side glance at effects units. Figure 9-1 depicts some common rack-mount effects—not Gorman's, but typical of the equipment that is available.) The MPG-80 provides an alternate set of patch controls for the Super Jupiter module. The Super Jupiter's own controls are buttons with a small liquid-crystal display, but Gorman prefers the MPG-80's controls. Its dials and sliders work much more like traditional analog synthesizer controls. The MPG-80 is connected by means of MIDI to the Super Jupiter so that any of its controls automatically change the Super Jupiter's current patch. "Some people are just more comfortable with a dial than a button," he says.

Gorman uses the two reverb units in the rack to add effects and warmth to the sounds coming from his synthesizers. Because one is digital and the other is analog, they add two different qualities of reverb, a fact that Gorman exploits to advantage. "The reason I use them," he explains, "is that a good friend of mine—Tom Coster, who plays keyboards for Santana—taught me that if you overdrive an analog delay, you get a great warmth to it, almost guitarlike. You can make the delays fold into each other when you bend a note; it's a very smooth bend, a warmer sound. Then, to get it brighter, I run it through the Yamaha for the digital reverb sound, and that cleans it up at the same time. You get the dirt and you get the clean sound."

To mix the audio signals coming from all his equipment, Gorman has a Studiomaster 6-2-1 mixing console, a piece of equipment that accepts six

Figure 9-1.
A series of rack-
mounted effects
commonly used
in performance.

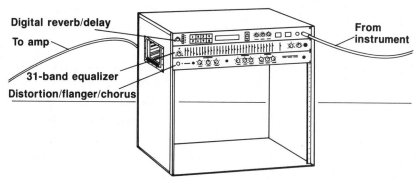

Digital reverb/delay

To amp

From instrument

31-band equalizer
Distortion/flanger/chorus

incoming signals. Its controls let Gorman adjust the relative volume of each signal. The mixer combines the six incoming signals into two outgoing signals that feed directly to the JBL power amplifier in the rack, which amplifies the signal and feeds it to two PAS monitor speakers.

Gorman mounts his synthesizers and other rack-mount equipment in a portable rack, a very sturdy metal shipping case with a removable front cover. The rack stands upright with the equipment bolted in, facing forward. Wheels on the bottom of the rack make it easy to move around onstage, and when a performance is over, the front cover of the rack can be latched closed, and the entire rack can be easily hauled to the next concert.

Connections

The connections between the devices in Gorman's system are simple. The diagram that follows in Figure 9-2 shows how the equipment (in the following list) is connected.

Components of Tim Gorman's Synthesizer System

Synthesizers
  A Memory Moog Plus analog synthesizer (MIDI)
  An Emulator II sampling synthesizer (no MIDI)
  A Roland JX-8P digital synthesizer (MIDI)
  A Roland MKS-20 digital piano (rack-mount with MIDI)
  A Roland MKS-80 Super Jupiter analog synthesizer (rack-mount with MIDI)

Controllers
  A Roland MKB-1000 controller (full keyboard with MIDI)
  A Roland Axis MIDI keyboard (hand-held keyboard with MIDI)
  A Roland MPG-80 Super Jupiter programmer (rack-mount with MIDI)

Effects
  A Yamaha SPX90 digital reverb unit (rack-mount with MIDI)
  An Ibanez AD-230 analog reverb unit (rack-mount, no MIDI)

Audio equipment
  A Studiomaster 6-2-1 mixing console
  A JBL 6230 power amplifier
  Two PAS (Professional Audio Systems) monitor speakers

SIGNAL PROCESSORS

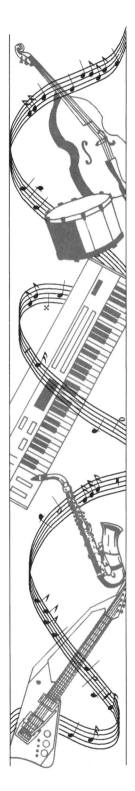

Signal processors, more popularly known as *effects,* are an important part of any electronic music system. They take the audio signal coming from an instrument such as a synthesizer or an electric guitar, modify the signal to give it a characteristic sound, and then pass it on to a mixer or an amplifier. Common types of effects are *distortion* and *overdrive,* which add a heavy-metal sound to an instrument; *chorusing,* which makes one instrument sound like several; and *flanging,* which imparts a sharp, metallic flavor to the sound.

Delay is one of electronic music's most popular and versatile effects. It adds a slightly delayed version (or versions) of the incoming audio signal to the original signal to create a synthetic echo or reverberation. When a signal is played through loudspeakers, this effect changes the apparent acoustic feel of the room the player and listeners are in. A good delay unit can make a synthesizer playing in a tiny, soundproof room sound like it's in the middle of a large cathedral, at the front of a large concert hall, or even inside a tin can (if the musician wants it to sound that way).

Delays vary greatly in price and features. Some allow a wide range of settings that let you create the acoustic feel of any size room; others have only a few settings. Some are analog and work by directly altering the incoming audio signal. But most sophisticated delay units are digital—the incoming signal is turned into a series of numbers, and the microprocessor inside the delay manipulates those numbers easily and precisely to give you the effect you specify. Once the effects have been introduced mathematically, the digital delay turns the digital sound back into an analog signal that goes to a mixer or a loudspeaker.

A delay commonly has a built-in microprocessor that offers additional control features. It can, for example, let you save your delay settings as a patch, to be recalled at a push of a single button. Some effects units are even MIDI compatible, enabling you to set individual delay controls by sending Control Change messages or to choose between different delay patches by sending Program Change messages. Figure 9-1 gives you a look at some typical rack-mounted signal processors.

Figure 9-2.
A diagram of
Tim Gorman's
synthesizer system.
Connections
appear
as follows:
MIDI
_____

Audio
- - - - - - -

Stereo audio
= = = = = =

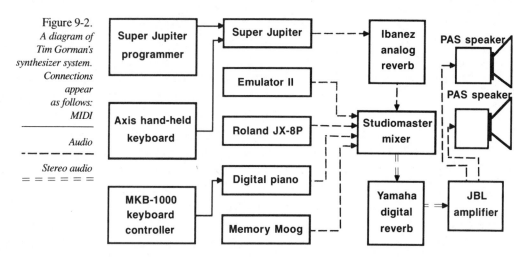

To make his equipment easy to play and control in rehearsal, Gorman arranges it so that everything is close at hand, arrayed as in Figure 9-3 around a central stool where he sits. Although the equipment rack is next to him in rehearsals, it's often backstage in performance, controlled entirely through MIDI and by the band's technical crew.

Figure 9-3.
Tim Gorman's
rehearsal
equipment
arrangement.

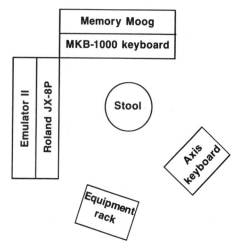

Design Philosophy

Gorman works at keeping his synthesizer setup simple. "I think simpler is better," he says, "especially in a live performance situation, because you never know what's going to go wrong. Somebody running backstage or crossing behind the main line of amps or speaker cabinets can trip over something—something can get pulled over, pulled out, knocked down, believe me, anything can happen." To keep the system simple, he limits the number of synthesizers, choosing them carefully to get the widest range of sounds possible.

"I've heard a lot of keyboard players remark that you've got to have them all," says Gorman. "Certain circuitry designs that are inherent to the way a company makes an instrument give it a certain sound—a certain warmth or a certain brittleness. To me, no other synthesizer sounds like a Yamaha DX7. And no other synthesizer has the warmth of a Memory Moog or a Super Jupiter for analog stuff. I know that there is a difference between analog and digital, and sure, you can say digital is always going to be more brittle, but I've heard really good digital synthesizers that were really warm."

The effort to keep a performance setup simple can get complicated. As Gorman observes, "It really depends on the songs you're playing and what the writer wants or what the performers that you're working with want in terms of the sound. You've got to ask yourself, 'How can I get by with the least actual tonnage of gear without sacrificing the sound?'"

To keep his system working, Gorman relies on the technical crew that supports the KBC band, a group of four people who work full time with the band, on tour and off. "We have a great crew," Gorman says. "When anything breaks down at rehearsal, they're there to fix it. They're also in charge of making sure all the MIDI cords and the audio phone plug cords are in perfect working order. No buzzes, no clicks, pops, any of that." The crew also sets up and tears down the equipment before and after concerts. "Your performance would suffer," says Gorman, "if you had to set up the gear *and* travel."

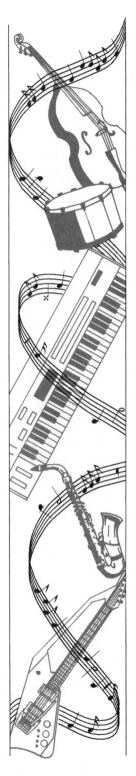

READING A MIDI IMPLEMENTATION CHART

It's important to be sure that the MIDI devices you buy can work well with each other. Although communicating simple MIDI events such as Note On and Note Off is usually no problem, you might have less success communicating other MIDI events. The problem might be that the receiving device simply lacks the features you require. For example, if you connect a synthesizer with a pitch bend wheel to an expansion module that doesn't recognize Pitch Bend messages, no amount of pitch wheel twiddling on your part will make the expansion module bend its pitches, even though your synthesizer is sending it Pitch Bend messages. The module merely ignores them.

There is a convenient way to find out what kinds of messages two MIDI devices can communicate: You can read their MIDI implementation charts. A MIDI implementation chart, such as the one shown in Figure 9-4, lists basic MIDI features and identifies those features that a device can use. Because the MIDI Manufacturers Association asks all its members to include a MIDI implementation chart with each MIDI product, you should be able to find one for any synthesizer you're thinking about buying.

The MMA specifies that MIDI implementation charts be printed the same size, using the same four-column format. The first column lists the features, or functions; the second shows whether the features are transmitted by the device; the next column shows whether the features are recognized (received) by the device; and the last gives the manufacturer's comments about the features. An ○ indicates that a feature is transmitted or received, and an × indicates that a feature is not transmitted or not received. For some features, the chart indicates a range rather than a simple × or ○ to indicate the limits within which a feature has been implemented.

To check feature compatibility between two MIDI devices, fold their MIDI implementation sheets vertically along the line between the Transmitted and Recognized columns. Put the Transmitted column of the device you'll use to send MIDI messages next to the Recognized column of the receiving device. Then, compare the sending and receiving

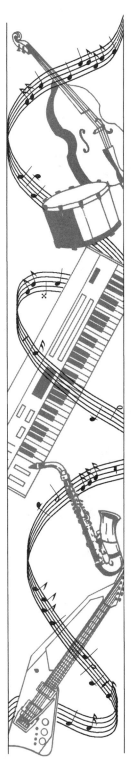

features to see what features are compatible between devices. If a feature is followed by matching ○s, then the devices can use that feature together by means of MIDI. If either feature is marked with an ×, then the two devices can't use that feature together. Features that show ranges of numbers can be used together only in the values that overlap within the two ranges.

MIDI Implementation Chart

Function		Transmitted	Recognized	Remarks
Basic Channel	Default	1-16	1-16	Can be stored in memory
	Changed	1-16	1-16	
Mode	Default	Mode 3	Mode 3/Mode 4	MONO M = 1 only
	Messages	×	POLY, MONO	
	Altered	****************	×	
Note		36-96	0-127	0-7 = 24-31 8-19 = 20-31
Number:	True voice	****************	20-108	109-120 = 97-108
				121-127 = 97-103
Velocity	Note ON	○ 9n v = 1-127	○ 9n v = 1-127	× × = not related
	Note OFF	○ 9n = 0	○ 9n v = 0, 8n v = × ×	
After-	Key's	×	×	
touch	Ch's	○	○	
Pitch Bender		○	○	Number of effective bits: 8 0-12 half tones
Control	1	○	○	MODULATION WHEEL
Change	5	×	○	PORTAMENTO TIME
	7	×	○	MAIN VOLUME
	64	○	○	SUSTAIN PEDAL
	65	○	○	PORTAMENTO ON/OFF
Prog		○ 0-63	○ 0-63	Tone/operation memory
Change:	True #	****************		
System Exclusive		○	○	Tone data, operation Memory data, other
System	: Song Pos	×	×	
	: Song Sel	×	×	
Common	: Tune	×	×	
System	: Clock	×	×	
Real Time:	Commands	×	×	
Aux	: Local ON/OFF	×	○	
	: All notes OFF	×	×	
Mes-	: Active Sense	×	×	
sages	: Reset	×	×	
Notes				

Figure 9-4. *A typical MIDI implementation chart.*

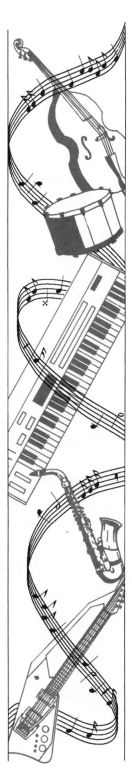

The MIDI implementation chart isn't self-explanatory. Even if you know MIDI messages, you might appreciate a little explanation. Refer to Figure 9-4 as you read the descriptions that follow.

◆ Basic Channel: Shows the MIDI channels that the device uses to send and receive messages. **Default** is the channel (or channels) in use when you first turn on the device; **Changed** is the channel (or channels) over which you can set the device to send and receive after it's turned on.

◆ Mode: Indicates the MIDI channel modes the device can use. **Default** is the channel mode the device is in when you first turn it on; **Messages** are the mode messages the device can send or receive (such as Poly On and Omni Off); **Altered** refers to the mode messages the device can't implement (because it can't enter that mode), followed by the mode the device enters when it receives a request for an unavailable mode.

◆ Note Number: Lists the pitch range of the device, expressed in terms of the pitch values used by Note On and Note Off messages. **Note Number** specifies the range of MIDI messages the device sends and receives; **True Voice** lists the range of notes that the device's voices can actually play. (Many synthesizers can send or receive higher and lower Note On messages than they can play. They transpose those out-of-range notes one or several octaves higher or lower so that they fall within the range of the synthesizer's voices.)

◆ Velocity: Shows whether the device can send and receive attack and release velocities. **Note ON** refers to attack velocity, and **Note OFF** refers to release velocity.

◆ Aftertouch: Shows whether the device can transmit and receive aftertouch information. **Key's** refers to polyphonic aftertouch; **Ch's** refers to channel aftertouch.

◆ Pitch Bender: Indicates whether the device can send and receive pitch bend information.

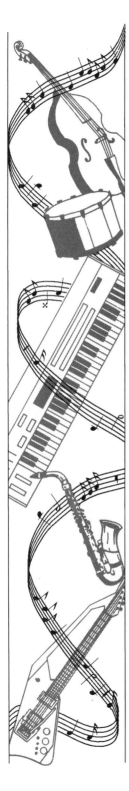

♦ Control Change: Indicates whether the device can transmit and receive control change information. The manufacturer should list the controls that send and receive this information, along with the control number used in the MIDI messages for each control.

♦ Program Change: Indicates whether the device can send and receive program change information (× or ○). **True #** lists the range of numbers that work with the device's program change buttons.

♦ System Exclusive: Tells you whether the device can send and receive system exclusive messages.

♦ System Common: Shows whether the device can send and receive different system common messages. **Song Pos** indicates the ability to send and receive Song Position messages. Likewise, **Song Sel** refers to Song Select messages, and **Tune** refers to Tune messages.

♦ System Real Time: Indicates whether the device can send and receive system real-time messages. **Clock** refers to the ability to send and receive Clock messages; **Commands** refers to the ability to send and receive Start, Stop, and Continue messages.

♦ Aux Messages: Shows whether the device can send and receive other types of messages. **Local ON/OFF** refers to Local Control On and Local Control Off messages; **All Notes OFF**, All Notes Off messages; **Active Sense,** Active Sensing messages; **Reset**, System Reset messages.

♦ Notes: Explains any permutations of MIDI features that the manufacturer can't describe under a particular function.

When you compare two charts by folding them vertically, as described earlier, remember that you're checking compatibility for MIDI messages sent in one direction only. To check compatibility for the MIDI messges sent in the other direction, switch the charts so that the original receiving device shows the Transmitted column and the original sending device shows the Recognized column. If the charts don't show you what you need to know, be sure your dealer can provide the information.

Although the tech crew usually takes care of cables, Gorman doesn't lack experience with MIDI cables breaking. "MIDI cords seem to wear out quicker than any other kind of cords," he says. "I don't know why. Maybe it's because they get patched so much—pulled in and out. You're trying different things. In the studio, I'm all over the place with them. I'm through here, in, out—whatever it takes to get the sound. Usually for a live setup, once you're set, you're set. It doesn't change until you move on to the next tour or the next record. They're counting on the show coming off exactly the same way every single night." Crew member Joe Healey, who works closely with Gorman, buys MIDI cables for the band. He tries to get sturdy, heavy-gauge cables, the shorter, the better.

Even with the best equipment and cables available, things can and will break down, often in concert. This is when it's important for a musician to know the system well and to have a responsive crew. "A minor bug like a MIDI cord going out," says Gorman, "must be traced quickly. For a live system, which is what this is, you've just got to be able to get to it quickly, that's all. If you've gone over it with your tech guy and you know where all the Ins and Outs are, you can just point to it. That's one reason why simple systems work pretty well."

The crew does more than take care of equipment glitches and manage the equipment on tours. They also help the band members keep up to date on new equipment. "The crew members do a lot of research independently at music stores," says Gorman. "They have a relationship with two or three music stores that they like to use. They might go in and have a piece of gear demonstrated to them or call in to ask if there is anything new that we should know about. In turn, the store sometimes calls us and says, 'You've got to come in and check out this instrument.' Then if the instrument seems pretty amazing, sometimes the store gives us a loaner and we try stuff out."

Replacing equipment in his system is very important to Gorman. "We're constantly updating the gear," he says. "That seems to be a religion now to me. I think it's just part of the business. Because the technology moves so quickly, you've got to be able to move with it. It's not like being a guitar player and hanging on to that '52 Les Paul for your whole life." To date, Gorman hasn't used computers with his MIDI system, but he's very interested in them. First, he has to find the time to learn about them. "As musicians," he says, "we spend so much of our time playing that redirecting our thinking is hard sometimes."

Gorman is also interested in some of the advanced synthesizers available now for prohibitively high prices. In a recent conversation, another keyboardist told Gorman that he was having great luck with a Fairlight 3, a top-of-the-line sampling synthesizer. "I asked him if it had a pool and an upstairs," Gorman says. "That's a lot of money to spend. It costs as much as a house. My dream is to see quality instruments like that come down in price so that more musicians at other levels of the business can afford them and use them—which I think would only increase the popularity of the instrument."

Gorman likes the flexibility that MIDI gives him in adding new equipment. It frees him from keeping everything on stage with him. "MIDI's been a big breakthough," he says. "It's allowed people to clean up the stage so it doesn't look like there's a music store up there, so the musician can interact with the audience a little better. The equipment can be rack-mounted off stage. It doesn't have to be seen. You could have no gear on stage nowadays—just the drums, the mikes, and hand-held instruments"—and musicians such as Tim Gorman, playing their music to appreciative audiences.

10 | MIDI IN THE RECORDING STUDIO

The recording studio has changed the music of this century more than any other musical tool. Musicians in a recording studio can create music impossible to play in a live performance. They can weed out performance mistakes, make a few musicians sound like a multitude, balance instruments of unequal loudness, and work on a piece of music the way a sculptor works with clay—molding sound at their leisure to create a finely crafted piece of music. The finished product is a recording on tape that can be played back at the push of a button to audiences worldwide. A composer in a recording studio has much more control over the final musical outcome than has ever before been possible.

Until recently, the most important implements in a recording studio were the mixing panel and the multi-track tape deck. Although musicians can accomplish an extraordinary amount with these devices, the amount of work involved can also become extraordinary. For example, replacing a single bad note in taped performance is very difficult and requires a new recording or extensive tape editing. Enter MIDI. With synthesizers under the control of computers, musicians can record performances without tape and alter them in ways not possible with tape recorders and mixers. MIDI allows musicians to make subtle changes to tempo, volume, timbre, and pitch not possible with tape decks and mixers alone.

Tom Scott

In this chapter, you'll enter a recording studio to meet Tom Scott, an active television and film composer in Los Angeles. Scott has his own studio, an electronic sound laboratory in which he uses MIDI, synthesizers, and computers along with the traditional tools of a recording studio to create television and film scores. You'll see how he uses his equipment to time his music to match activities in the films and videos he scores, to synchronize all the instruments playing a score, and to record the end result onto a tape he can deliver to the film studio. Separate sections within the chapter explain SMPTE, a timing standard used in the world of film and video, and MIDI sync, a method of synchronizing MIDI devices by means of MIDI clocks recorded on tape.

TOM SCOTT, FILM COMPOSER

Tom Scott is a composer with a wide audience that, for the most part, doesn't know who he is. His scores, like the music of many of his fellow film and television composers, play a supportive role in the shows they accompany and often escape conscious notice by audiences. Don't underestimate the importance of his music, though. It tells the hidden story behind what you see on the screen—the tension slowly building beneath an ordinary-sounding conversation, the solemnity of a sermon, the passion of a love scene. It's a demanding art to communicate all this emotional content while introducing the music as an integral part of the film, and Tom Scott is very good at it.

Scott is no stranger to the music business. His father, also a composer, worked as Bing Crosby's radio musical director and went on to score television shows such as *Wagon Train, Twilight Zone, Lassie,* and other popular series. Scott grew up in his father's world of music and developed his own musical talents. At the age of eight he started to play clarinet, and in junior high school he began to play the saxophone, as well. At the same time, he began to compose small pieces and songs, and in high school he wrote his first film score. "I wrote the score for a movie for the California school system when I was about sixteen. Automated egg processing," he laughs. "It was called 'Eggs to Market.'"

Scott's first successes came as a saxophonist. Beginning at age thirteen he played at weddings, for bar mitzvahs, and in small bands at country clubs. He also taught other players. By the time he was seventeen, he had about 20 saxophone and clarinet students. Record producer Bob Field heard him and asked him to record an album. Scott says, "It was one of those stories, you know: 'Kid. Hey, kid. You play good. You wanna do an album for me?'" That first album led to several more.

Scott also formed a jazz quartet, the Tom Scott Quartet, that played at the Baked Potato, a local L.A. jazz club. The group drew big crowds. "Suddenly people started jamming into this night club every Tuesday," he says. "It became an event here in town. We were looking at ourselves and saying, 'Gee, I guess we have a band here. We better give this thing a name.' So that became L.A. Express." L.A. Express went on to record with Joni Mitchell on an album and toured with her for a year.

When Scott returned to Los Angeles, he became active in recording studios as both a player and composer. His first break in score writing came in television. "Everybody remembers the first time they wrote for television," he says. "I wrote for an episode of Dan August, which was the Burt Reynolds TV show. I was in seventh heaven. It was one of the most exciting moments—the thrill of my life to have all these heavy studio guys that I knew playing my music." His first scores were entirely acoustic, with live performers playing winds, strings, and percussion. He had to write out parts by hand, paying close attention to parts for transposing instruments. "Nowadays, of course," he says, "things are different. We have computers to do some of this stuff."

Scott has kept both his composition and performance careers working simultaneously. In the past, he would record an album a year, which took from one-and-a-half to three months, and spend the rest of the year working on scores. He avoided going on tours so that he could keep composing. "I always enjoyed doing the writing," he says, "and wanted to stay in L.A. most of the time to be available for that kind of stuff when it came along." He found time to score films such as *The Sure Thing, Stir Crazy,* and *Uptown Saturday Night* as well as many television shows. Today he's cut back on his performance career to make more time for scoring, although he still likes to play, performing with jazz artists such as Dave Grusin and Lee Ritenour.

The Studio

Scott stays close to home when he works; he has his own recording studio on the first floor of his house in the Hollywood hills. He has managed to pack a surprising amount of equipment into a room only a little larger than an average bedroom and is able to score a film entirely by himself, with only the equipment in the studio. Even so, he often uses outside musicians and sometimes takes his work into a larger, commercial studio.

Equipment

Scott uses a variety of synthesizers to get the sounds he wants. He has a Yamaha DX7 for FM digital sounds, a Yamaha TX7 FM expansion module for additional FM voices, a Roland Planet S synthesizer which gives him a cut-down version of Super Jupiter synthesized sounds, a Moog Model 12 synthesizer and an Oberheim Expander synthesizer for analog sounds, a MIDI = Bass synthesizer (made by 360 Systems) for sampled-sound bass notes, a Roland digital piano for piano sounds, and a Linn Drum with a built-in sequencer for sampled percussion sounds. For the most part, he controls these synthesizers with a Yamaha KX76 master keyboard. He also has a Macintosh computer system that he uses for MIDI recording and playback, and a Lyricon, which is a controller device that looks like a metal clarinet, fingers like a saxophone, and sends out notes via MIDI.

The studio's computer system is a Macintosh Plus computer with an external floppy disk drive, a DataFrame XP Twenty 20-megabyte hard disk drive, and an Opcode Studio Plus MIDI Interface. The Opcode interface has two different sets of MIDI ports; one set plugs into the Mac's printer port, while the other plugs into the Mac's modem port. Each set of ports has its own MIDI In port and three MIDI Out ports. With the right software, the Macintosh Plus can receive, mix, and send MIDI messages on both sets of ports simultaneously. Scott uses the Opcode *DX/TX Editor/ Librarian* on the Mac to create and store patches for his two Yamaha synthesizers; he has *Performer* for recording performances and *Professional Composer* for musical notation.

Scott has a sophisticated recording system that both records and plays the audio signal from his synthesizer system. His main tape recorder is a Fostex B16D half-inch tape deck that has 16 independent channels for recording with a fast tape speed of 30 inches per second and Dolby C noise reduction for very clean sound. He has a Fostex Model E2 quarter-inch tape deck and a Technics 2 Track 1500 quarter-inch tape deck, both with two channels, that he uses to record mixed-down recordings from the 16-track tape deck. He also has a simple Technics M07 cassette deck for making cassette recordings of his work.

Tying all the synthesizers to the tape decks is a large RAMSA audio mixer with 16 inputs, four monitor channels, and two output channels. Scott can feed any audio inputs to the mixer, set their relative volume levels, and record them directly to the 16-track tape deck. He can also mix incoming signals down to two tracks for recording on the two-track decks. The mixer sends audio signals after they're mixed to a large amplifier that drives stereo speakers.

To sweeten and otherwise alter the sounds coming from his synthesizers, Scott's studio has a full set of effects through which he can run any audio signal. These include a Rockman Sustainer that Scott calls "heavy metal in a box," a Kepex II sound enhancer that imposes new envelopes on any incoming audio signal, a Lexicon Model 200 digital reverberator that Scott is very fond of, and a Fostex Compressor/Limiter Model 3070 that compresses signals, flattening out the sound to Scott's liking. He uses it mostly for recorded bass players and vocalists.

Of course, all this is strictly for the sound of the scores. Scott also needs video equipment to display the moving images he's working with as he scores. This part of the studio is simple in contrast to the rest of his

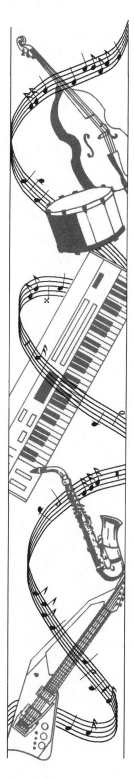

SMPTE

Anyone working extensively with film or video will sooner or later encounter the term SMPTE. Technically, SMPTE (pronounced simp´ty) is the acronym for the Society of Motion Picture and Television Engineers, but over the past few years, it's also become the name for a timing standard for film, video, and audio devices, a standard that the Society has set and promoted for use by film and video engineers.

The SMPTE timing standard was originally developed by NASA as a way to mark incoming data from different tracking stations so that receiving computers could tell exactly what time each piece of data was created. In the film and video version promoted by the Society, SMPTE acts as a very precise clock that stamps its time readings on each frame and fraction of a frame, counting from the beginning of the film or video. To make these time readings precise, SMPTE breaks time into hours, minutes, seconds, frames, and bits.

SMPTE uses a 24-hour clock, counting from 0 to 23 before it recycles to 0 again. It counts 60 minutes per hour and 60 seconds per minute, as with standard clocks. The number of frames in a second differs depending on the type of visual medium. In television, there are 30 frames per second; in film, there are usually 24 frames per second, occasionally 25. SMPTE counts frames differently depending on the type of visual medium used. To divide time even more precisely, SMPTE breaks each frame into 80 bits (not to be confused with the binary digit bits you read about in earlier chapters). When SMPTE is counting bits in a frame, it's dividing time into segments as small as one twenty-five-hundredth of a second.

To use SMPTE with a film or with a piece of video or audio tape, a SMPTE generator sends a stream of SMPTE signals that are recorded on the film or tape, usually on an audio track, starting at the beginning of the film or tape and continuing to the end. Each SMPTE signal contains the complete time reading at the exact moment it was generated, so that reading any one signal gives you its exact time location from the beginning of the film or tape. SMPTE-equipped video equipment can usually read and display the timing as a movie or video plays, showing time in the format hours:minutes:seconds:frames:bits. For example, if you stopped the video on a single frame, the SMPTE counter might display 01:25:52:06:73, which means that that frame is 1 hour, 25 minutes, 52 seconds, 6 frames, and 73 bits from the beginning of the video.

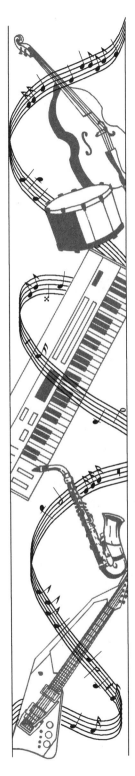

Many video devices don't keep track of bits, so it's likely that the device won't show you a bit value.

SMPTE is very useful for tying separate tape decks together. To do so, a SMPTE generator transmits a series of SMPTE signals that are recorded on one track of a tape on each tape deck that must be synchronized. After the SMPTE signals are laid down on tape, the tape decks can be set to record or play at the same time. As all the tapes on separate machines start to roll, each machine plays back its stream of SMPTE signals to a device called a *SMPTE synchronizer* that compares them and ensures all the SMPTE times match. If one machine is faster or slower than it should be, the synchronizer asks it to alter speed slightly to coordinate its timing with the other machines.

You can also use a SMPTE device called an *autolocator* to ask the synchronized machines to move to any point in a recording or film. By punching in the hour, minute, second, frame, and sometimes even the bit value, you can have the autolocator set each synchronized machine to that timing location in its recording. The autolocator then fast forwards or rewinds the machines it controls to the location you specified and remains there, ready to start recording or playback.

For the most part, SMPTE is used to make different tape decks and film machines work together. You can use SMPTE to tie two 16-track audio recorders together to act as a 30-track machine. (One channel on each recorder records the SMPTE signals.) You can also tie an audio and a video recorder together to integrate the video recording with a sound track on the audio recorder.

Because many film composers now record their music on a MIDI recorder, it's desirable to synchronize the MIDI recorder with video equipment. A SMPTE synchronizer should be able to give a time location to the MIDI recorder so it will move to that location in the MIDI score to start playback or recording. Unfortunately, MIDI recorders can't use incoming SMPTE signals to control their recording and playback. They expect to receive MIDI clocks instead.

There is a solution to this problem in the form of special equipment, a *MIDI/SMPTE synchronizer* such as the Roland SBX-80 or the Fostex 4050 (shown in Figure 10-1) that converts SMPTE to MIDI and vice versa. Because SMPTE signals come at very regular intervals—they are, after all, nothing more than highly refined clock ticks—converting these signals directly to MIDI clocks won't work. The rate of MIDI clocks varies with the tempo of the music, while the "tempo"

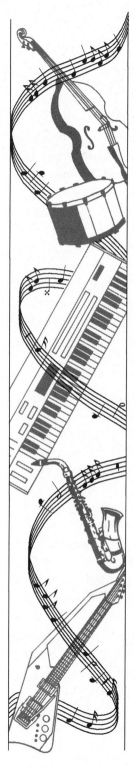

of SMPTE ticks is preset and unchanging. What the MIDI/SMPTE synchronizer does is to let you specify the tempos you want and the exact points in SMPTE timing at which you want each tempo to start, change, and stop.

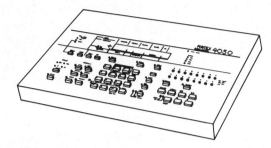

Figure 10-1. *The Fostex 4050 MIDI/SMPTE synchronizer/autolocator.*

The synchronizer keeps these tempos and timing points in memory. As a SMPTE video deck plays and sends a stream of SMPTE times to the synchronizer, the synchronizer checks the incoming time and sends out MIDI clocks at the tempo it's supposed to use at that time. If you fast forward or rewind the video tape to a new location, the MIDI/SMPTE synchronizer converts the new SMPTE time location into the number of MIDI clocks that have elapsed since the beginning of the MIDI score. It then sends a Song Position Pointer message to the MIDI recorder to tell it to start playback or recording at the new location. When the video deck begins to play again, the synchronizer sends MIDI clocks at the right tempo to start the MIDI recorder playing or recording again. The net result is that the MIDI recorder is synchronized to the SMPTE equipment in the same way that it would be synchronized if it were a regular SMPTE tape deck.

equipment. He uses a JVC BR8600U VHS video cassette recorder. This is a special VCR that records SMPTE signals on its audio track so that any location in a tape can be identified in hours, minutes, seconds, and frames on the screen. (For more information on SMPTE, read the SMPTE section in this chapter.) The VCR can also send SMPTE signals to other equipment to synchronize it with locations in the video tape. The video signal the JVC transmits is played on a 13-inch Sony monitor.

Connections and Synchronization

Connecting Scott's equipment so that it works well together isn't a trivial task. It requires many cables, a few helping devices, and a lot of thought to make the setup as versatile and controllable as possible. Scott uses various types of connections to make it all work: MIDI ties synthesizers, sequencers, and computers together; audio cables tie synthesizers, drum boxes, mixers, and tape decks together; SMPTE ties the VCR with the audio tape decks and the MIDI system; and an older, pre-MIDI drum machine is tied to a controller with a non-MIDI clock system. To see how all these connections are made, take a close look at Figure 10-3 later in this chapter.

To help make MIDI connections, Scott uses a simple Casio TB-1 MIDI Thru box. Because he has two main controllers—the KX76 controller keyboard and the Macintosh Plus computer—he uses the two MIDI In ports on the TB-1 to switch back and forth between the controllers as he needs them. The TB-1's eight MIDI Thru ports send outgoing MIDI messages to all the synthesizers and also feed MIDI messages back to the Mac so that it can record notes from the KX76.

Scott's Lyricon, used exclusively with the Moog Model 12 synthesizer, does have MIDI capabilities, but it's tied to the Moog with an older, non-MIDI control voltage arrangement. Because neither device is connected by means of MIDI to any other device, both are outside Scott's regular MIDI system.

Scott uses some special equipment to incorporate his Linn Drum percussion device into his MIDI system. Because the Linn Drum uses a non-MIDI timing clock system, he uses a Garfield Electronics Doctor Click, a timing device that sends and receives non-MIDI clocks to and from the Linn Drum and controls the tempo of its sequencer. To permit the Linn Drum to send its sequencer timing into the MIDI system, the non-MIDI clocks from the Linn Drum go to the Doctor Click, which sends them on to a J.L. Cooper MIDI Sync box, a specialized device that turns

MIDI Sync

SMPTE equipment is specialized and expensive; most MIDI users can't afford SMPTE tape decks, synchronizers, autolocators, and the other equipment necessary to make a MIDI system work with SMPTE. Fortunately, there is another, less expensive option available if you want to record synchronized MIDI scores on tape: *MIDI sync*.

MIDI sync is a method of recording MIDI clocks directly on tape and then playing them back to control a MIDI recorder externally. To use MIDI sync, you need a MIDI sync converter box, such as the Yamaha YMC10 (shown in Figure 10-2), because MIDI clocks arriving over a MIDI cable are in a digital form that won't record on a standard audio tape deck. The MIDI sync converter changes each digital MIDI clock message to a separate, audible tone and sends the tones to a single track of a tape deck to be recorded. When you play back the tape with the recorded clock track, the sync converter changes the tones back into digital MIDI clock messages and sends them through a MIDI Out port.

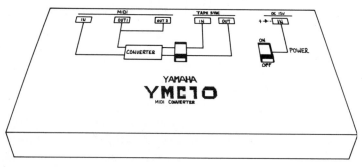

Figure 10-2. *The Yamaha YMC10 MIDI sync converter.*

MIDI sync is a very useful synchronization tool if you have only a few synthesizers and want to overdub on a multi-track tape recorder to make them sound like many synthesizers. To use MIDI sync in this way, you first record a MIDI score for the synthesizers you have and quantize the notes so that they line up perfectly as eighth notes, sixteenth notes, and other values. Enter any tempo changes you want in your MIDI score so that the recorder changes the rate of MIDI clocks as it plays the score.

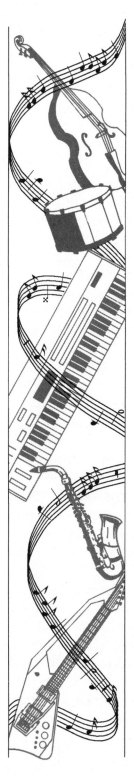

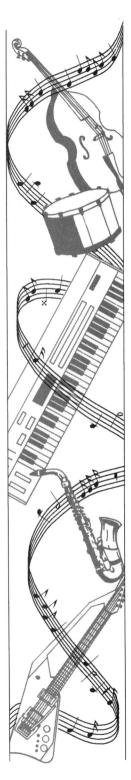

Next, connect the MIDI Out port of your MIDI recorder to the MIDI In port of the MIDI sync converter. Set up your tape deck to record the audio output of the sync converter on one tape channel, and then play the entire MIDI score as you record. The sync converter will lay down a series of MIDI clocks on tape that record the tempo changes in your MIDI score.

To record your MIDI score on tape, set the tape deck to record your synthesizers. (Be sure you don't set it to record over your MIDI clock track!) Set your MIDI recorder to run on external clocks from its MIDI In port. When you play back the tape on the tape deck from the beginning of the recorded MIDI clock track, the sync converter sends out MIDI clocks to the MIDI recorder so that it plays your score at the tempos you recorded on tape.

Once you finish recording your first MIDI score, you can record a new one, while listening to the score you already recorded. You can quantize the score and then record it on tape the same way you recorded the last MIDI score, using the pre-recorded MIDI clock track to make the MIDI recorder play at exactly the same tempos, synchronizing it exactly to the previously recorded MIDI score. As long as you don't erase the MIDI clock track, you can erase and add MIDI scores to the other tape tracks and keep them perfectly synchronized by means of pre-recorded MIDI clocks.

Of course, MIDI sync isn't a perfect solution. Once you've recorded a tempo on tape, you can't edit it the way you can a MIDI recording. Also, the different manufacturers of MIDI sync converters often use different methods to record clocks on tape. As a result, a clock track recorded by one converter frequently won't play back on another converter. This incompatibility makes it difficult to exchange tapes with a friend to add tracks. Still, MIDI sync is much less expensive than using SMPTE and opens up new creative channels if you use a multi-track tape recorder.

non-MIDI clocks into MIDI clocks. These MIDI clocks are fed into a MIDI mixer, a SynHance MIX Plus, that mixes the Linn Drum's output with the output of the KX76 keyboard (coming in through the TB-1 box) so that both signals can be sent to the Mac for recording.

In a studio, it's important to be able to connect audio equipment easily and to rearrange the connections without difficulty. To do so, Scott uses eight Fostex Model 3010 patch bays. Each patch bay has 16 audio input jacks and 16 audio output jacks, so that the combined patch bays have 128 input and 128 output jacks. Scott runs a cable from the audio output of each synthesizer, tape deck channel, mixer channel, effect box, and other audio devices to a labeled audio input jack on the patch bay. He also runs a cable from each audio input of every audio device to a labeled audio output jack in the patch bay. To connect the output of any particular audio device to the input of another audio device, Scott merely connects a cable between the output and input jacks of the two devices on the patch bay.

Working with Video   Synchronizing the VCR with the audio tape decks presents some unusual problems and requires some special equipment. When Scott records a section of a movie score, he wants that section to start at a precise moment in the action on the screen and to continue over a specified time period until another instant in the screen action. If he fast forwards or rewinds the video tape to a certain frame in the movie, he expects the audio tape to move to the corresponding point in the score. The movements of the two tapes, though independent, must be constantly coordinated.

Scott uses the Fostex 4030 synchronizer to synchronize his VCR and his audio tape decks using SMPTE. The 4030 can receive SMPTE code specifying a specific frame in a film and can then command a tape deck to move the tape to that frame. Scott's 4030 controls both his B16D audio deck and his VCR so that when one machine moves to a new location on the tape, the synchronizer moves the other tape to the corresponding point. It also keeps two tape decks running in complete synchronization once they begin to play. Scott uses a Fostex 4035 controller to let him identify a specific SMPTE location that he wants to see. The 4035 sends the location he requested to the 4030, which moves the tapes of the connected tape decks to that frame. Scott can then start playback on both decks at that precise location.

Because some of Scott's music is also recorded as a MIDI score on the Macintosh Plus using *Performer,* it's important that the MIDI score also play back in synchronization with the video and audio tapes.

The Fostex 4050 Synchronizer/Autolocator, another synchronization device, takes a SMPTE location punched in by Scott or sent by any of the tape decks, and it converts that location to a MIDI Song Position Pointer message that it sends to *Performer* on the Mac. *Performer* takes the new location sent in the Song Position Pointer message and gets ready to play its recorded MIDI score at that point. When the tape decks begin to play, the Fostex 4050 converts timing information received as SMPTE signals into MIDI timing clocks that it sends to the Mac to control the tempo of the MIDI score playback. Scott pre-programs the tempos the 4050 uses to send MIDI clocks as it follows SMPTE locations. It's a simple matter to change tempos so that a MIDI recording is stretched or shrunk to match the action on the video tape.

If all this sounds a little bit complex, you're right. It is. It's complicated enough to keep professionals such as Tom Scott constantly looking for new equipment to make it less so. To understand how Scott's equipment is tied together, take a look at the following list, and then look carefully at the diagram in Figure 10-3.

Components in Tom Scott's recording studio
___

Synthesizers
      Yamaha DX7 synthesizer
      Yamaha TX7 expansion module
      Roland Planet S expansion module
      Roland digital piano
      MIDI = Bass sampled-sound bass synthesizer
      Oberheim Expander module
      Moog Model 12 synthesizer
      Linn Drum machine

MIDI Controllers
      Yamaha KX76 master keyboard controller
      Lyricon wind driver (with MIDI retrofit, unused in this system)

Computer Equipment
      Macintosh Plus computer
      Opcode Studio Plus MIDI interface
      External floppy disk drive
      DataFrame XP Twenty 20-megabyte hard disk drive

Computer Software
      DX/TX Editor/Librarian from Opcode Systems
      Cue, a film-scoring program from Opcode Systems
      Performer, a MIDI recorder from Mark of the Unicorn
      Professional Composer, a musical notation program from Mark of the Unicorn

Audio Tape Decks
      Fostex B16D ¹/₂-inch 30 ips 16-track tape deck
      Fostex Model E2 ¹/₄-inch 15 ips 2-track tape deck
      Technics 2 Track 1500 ¹/₄-inch 15 ips 2-track tape deck
      Technics M07 stereo cassette deck

Audio equipment
  8 Fostex Model 3010 patch bays
  RAMSA WR-8816 audio mixer, 16 inputs, 4 monitor channels, 2 outputs
  2 Hafler Model P255 power amplifiers
  2 custom speakers

Effects
  Rockman Sustainer
  Kepex II sound enhancer
  Lexicon Model 200 digital reverberator
  Fostex Compressor/Limiter Model 3070

Video Equipment
  JVC BR8600U VHS video tape recorder
  Sony 13-inch video monitor

Connection and synchronization equipment
  Casio TB-1 MIDI Thru box
  Garfield Electronics Doctor Click timing device
  J. L. Cooper MIDI Sync box
  SynHance MIX Plus MIDI mixer
  Fostex 4050 SMPTE/MIDI synchronizer/autolocator
  Fostex 4035 SMPTE controller
  Fostex 4030 SMPTE synchronizer

Using the Studio   Scoring a movie or a TV show starts when Scott is asked by a director to write the music for a film or show. "The director usually sits down with me," Scott says, "and together we look at the movie on a stop-and-go machine so we can stop the movie and talk about it and then continue or go back. We decide exactly where music should go in this movie." Each section of music in the movie is called a *cue*. A cue can be as short as a few seconds or many minutes long.

Within each cue, there are events on-screen that are important to emphasize with the music in the cue. These key moments are called *hits*. A music editor identifies these significant events within each cue and supplies the information to the composer. "It's up to the composer to look at the scene and decide later what, if any, of this information is important to him."

Not all the events in a cue are important enough to be hits. Those that become hits may fall on the beat of the music the composer writes, called *hard hits,* or they may fall off the beat. It's the composer's job to try to make something special happen on each hit. If the hit occurs off the beat, the composer may have to change the tempo of the music or rewrite entirely to put the hit on the beat.

Some scenes are harder to score than others. "Difficulties come up most in television, and I suppose in the movies too, in the chase scene," Scott explains. "A long chase may go back and forth from, say, an action

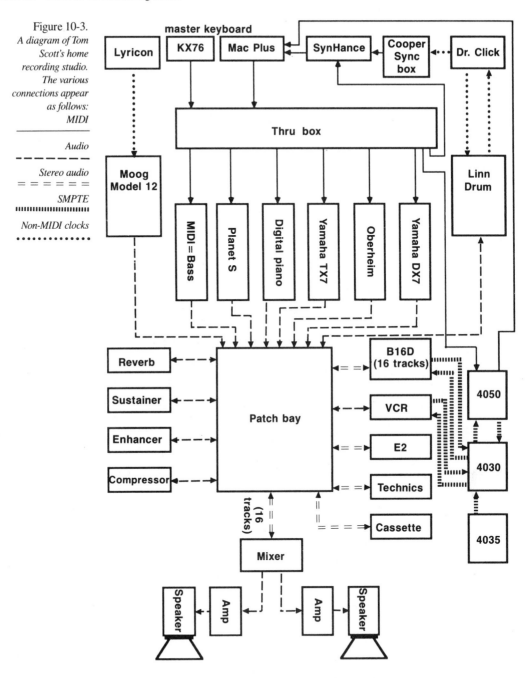

Figure 10-3.
A diagram of Tom Scott's home recording studio. The various connections appear as follows:

MIDI
————————

Audio
— — — — —

Stereo audio
= = = = = =

SMPTE
|||||||||||||||||||||||||

Non-MIDI clocks
• • • • • • • • • • • • •

chase to the inside of one of the cars where there's a conversation and they're talking and they're huddled. They're passing on critical story information or something that you've got to hear. You can't be bashing away with this chase; you've got to get out of the way for that moment but still continue the thread of the thing. You've got to know exactly where that cut to the interior is and exactly where it goes back to the chase." It's Scott's job to make these quick changes into hits and match them with the music he writes, not an easy job. "Obviously, the more hits you try to make within a cue," he says, "the more difficult it is for any one tempo to accommodate them all."

To make tempos and hits match, film composers have traditionally kept written records of their cues and hits in a cue book, an odious task that isn't necessary now that computers can do the task for them. Scott and other musicians in his studio recently bought *Cue*, a film-scoring program from Opcode Systems that they're using extensively. "We're all freaking down there!" he says. "This is the best program we've ever seen for this kind of thing. We make up the cue sheet, and then we designate any timing that we think should fall on a beat of whatever tempo we're in, and we assign that a hit. We check this box: Hit." *Cue* takes the hits that Scott enters and automatically shows him what tempos will work to catch the most hits on the beat. It saves him a lot of time and lets him concentrate on writing music instead of matching tempos and hits. "This program is worth its weight in gold to us," says Scott.

Once Scott knows what cues he needs to compose and has an idea of the tempos he can use, he can start working on the music itself. "Generally, the first thing you've got to do is look at the scene," he says, "and see if the scene that you're writing music for moves you in any particular direction. Ideally, you watch a scene and it leads you, it steers you. The emotional content of the scene generates music within you. Then it's just a question of translating what you're hearing in your head."

To do that, he tries different ideas on the keyboard and sometimes plays with different sounds and tempos on his synthesizers. "If I go into a scene," he explains, "and I know it involves an oriental kind of guitar, a koto kind of sound, I'll get that up on the synth and start screwing around with it. If it's a rhythm thing and I know it's a drum pattern at a certain tempo, I'll go over to the drum machine and set that up."

Scott currently works with two other musicians—percussionist Steve Schaeffer and keyboardist/composer Joe Conlan—in a recording trio named Rareview. The trio meets in Scott's recording studio to create video and movie scores, and each member crowds in with his own share of equipment. All three members have their own Macintosh computers with sequencing programs.

Each member of Rareview brings his own expertise to the sessions. Scott and Conlan split the work of composing. Conlan uses his Yamaha DX7 to play different tracks in the score and uses a Yamaha QX1 sequencer to record his MIDI tracks. (The QX1 is a specialized sequencer, a stand-alone unit. It doesn't run other programs as a computer does, and it doesn't have its own voices as a drum machine does.) Scott adds some tracks on keyboard and also records saxophone and other wind tracks. Schaeffer sets up and plays his own bank of drum machines to create rhythm tracks.

The wind tracks are usually among the last to be recorded for a score. Scott can play a wide variety of wind instruments—bari, tenor, alto, and soprano saxophones, alto and soprano recorders, clarinet, bass clarinet, alto flute, flute, and piccolo. He can record tracks for each of these instruments, multi-tracking to sound like many players at once. He often uses wind tracks to fatten up synthesized sounds, doubling the bass line with a bari sax or bass clarinet, doubling soprano lines with clarinet, sax, or flute. He finds they bring a richness to the sound that synthesizers can't duplicate. It takes skill and accuracy to play with a pre-recorded synthesizer score, though. "I've got to go in there and play against a track that's all pre-time-corrected, pretuned, and pre- everything else," says Scott. "I've got to be on the case."

When Scott looks to the future, he sees changes. To date, many of Scott's scores have been written for light, comedic movies. He'd like a chance to write some dramatic music as well. "In comedy," he says, "the requirements of the music for a picture usually don't call for something very memorable. I'd love to be able to break out of comedy a little bit."

He also keeps his eye on changing technology, dropping in frequently at music and computer stores to talk to the salespeople. He gets advice and information from the other members of his trio and from other members of the music studio community in Hollywood and Los Angeles. Scott has learned a considerable amount about adding computers to the studio. "I was asking a friend of mine about music synthesizers and computers," says Scott. "He said, 'Gee, you really ought to get the Atari.' And I said, 'Really? Why's that?' 'Well,' he says, 'the MIDI Ins and Outs are built in the back.' I thought to myself, you know, that's really not a great reason to choose a computer—on the basis of which one has the MIDI installed on the back! None of the hardware matters. Go find the software that fits your needs, and then buy the matching hardware."

With the right software, computers are an invaluable aid to film composition. "We just made a giant leap here in the last 15 years or so from the way I used to do things," he says. "Nowadays, the content of the music is, I think, very much affected by all the technological advancements. It's a different way of writing." And it promises to change even more as MIDI, SMPTE, and computers evolve to provide even more musical power to the individual composer working in the recording studio.

11 | MIDI IN EDUCATION

One of the last places for MIDI to make its mark is the world of music education. Traditionally trained music teachers don't always warm easily to the idea of synthesizers and computers coming into the classroom. Educators who are interested in using synthesizers and computers find that it requires a whole new area of expertise in addition to their formal music and performance training. In addition, most music department budgeteers see a MIDI system as a substantial investment for an unknown return.

These barriers to MIDI in the classroom are falling rapidly, however, as teachers learn about the immediate benefits of MIDI systems. Students are naturally drawn to synthesizers as an exciting, new vehicle for music. Schools with MIDI systems and qualified teachers can often increase their music enrollment. Teachers find that employing MIDI allows them to allocate time more productively. They can use MIDI equipment to monitor student progress in courses that require a great deal of supervised practice, courses such as ear training, sight singing, and keyboard skills. Such applications of MIDI free teachers to spend more time aiding individual students and working on their own musical projects. Computerized MIDI systems with sequencer and musical notation software are revolutionizing traditional music composition and orchestration courses. By playing student pieces as soon as they're written, MIDI systems enable students actually to hear what they write. And of course, learning to run a MIDI system often becomes a complete course in itself.

This chapter gives you a close look at the electronic music program at Mills College, a school at which the electronic music facilities are geared almost entirely to teaching composition. Because the faculty and students at Mills have been involved with computers and synthesizers since long before MIDI came to be, they have a view of MIDI that is often unorthodox and surprising. They use their electronic music systems and MIDI in ways that range from the traditional to the experimental. By reading about these experimental uses and the theories behind them, you can begin to see new directions for computer music, many of which go beyond what MIDI has to offer.

ELECTRONIC MUSIC AT MILLS COLLEGE

At first glance, Mills College doesn't seem the most likely institution to harbor a hotbed of American new music. It's a small, four-year liberal arts college for women in Oakland, California, with a few graduate programs that are open to men and women alike. Tucked away in the residential Oakland hills, the well-groomed grounds and traditional architecture of Mills College in no way resemble the avant-garde and sometimes anarchic strains of music that resound through the rooms and halls of the music building. And yet, in the last half century Mills has employed and educated some of the most innovative minds in contemporary music. In 1985, the music department issued a three-record album to mark the centennial of Mills's founding. The album showcases some of the well-known composers who worked and studied at Mills. It includes compositions by Darius Milhaud, Steve Reich, Lou Harrison, Terry Riley, Luciano Berio, Morton Subotnick, and Anthony Braxton, among others.

The Mills music department offers both undergraduate and graduate music programs. The undergraduate program offers a fairly standard curriculum, with courses in music history, music theory, performance, and chamber music, as well as some unusual courses in electronic and computer music, composition, and sound-recording techniques.

The graduate music program offers the master's degree in four areas of study: music history and literature, performance and literature, composition, and electronic music and the recording media. The programs in composition and in electronic music make the most extensive use of Mills's electronic music labs and of a unique institution in residence at Mills College: the Center for Contemporary Music.

The Center for Contemporary Music

The Center for Contemporary Music (called "the Center" around Mills) had its origins elsewhere. It was started across the bay in San Francisco in 1961 by Morton Subotnick and Ramon Sender. At its inception, the center was appropriately named the San Francisco Tape Music Center because

The music building at Mills College

electronic music composition at that time depended heavily on tape recording and editing. In 1966, the institution moved to Mills College at the urging of then faculty member Darius Milhaud, where it was renamed the Mills Tape Music Center and later, the Center for Contemporary Music.

Today's Center is in theory an independent entity, but its funding by Mills and location on campus tie it strongly to the college. Most of the Center's staff members are paid by Mills and wear two hats—they are teachers and composers at the Center, and they serve as Mills faculty members. Students at the Center are considered Mills College students.

What makes the Center more than an extension of Mills is its connection with the music scene outside of the college. Through several active programs, the Center makes its facilities available to non-profit artists who are not part of the college. To foster awareness and growth in new music, it sponsors a series of concerts during the year that feature resident and guest performers, and it holds a series of public seminars that focus on the theories and aesthetics of new music. The Center also supports short-term residencies of guest artists who work with the broader musical community, it helps organizations in the San Francisco Bay area with special music projects, and it answers questions about computer music. Larry Polansky, the assistant director of the Center, says, "One of our intentions has always been to be an information clearing house. We're able to spread ideas fast."

The Center has six staff members headed by director David Rosenboom, a computer music pioneer and composer who also chairs the Mills College music department. He is assisted by Larry Polansky and Maggi Payne, both of whom are electronic music composers. Polansky and Payne also teach graduate and undergraduate courses in the music department. Scot Gresham-Lancaster, the technical director, is in charge of keeping the Center's equipment in good running condition. His assistant is Richard Povall, who oversees the Center's recording studio and audio production facilities. In addition to these regular faculty and staff members, composer Anthony Braxton is currently serving as the visiting Milhaud Associate Professor, a position that enables the college to invite prestigious composers to work and teach at Mills for several years at a time.

The Center attracts quite a few students for an institution of its size. "We have about forty graduates in the music department, which is an enormous number," says Larry Polansky. "About thirty-five of them are composers, two-thirds of whom spend most of their time here at the Center.

The other third spend most of their time doing instrumental music or something like that. But there's a pretty free exchange of ideas between the groups." Several of these composition students work as graduate assistants, helping to maintain and run the Center's studios.

Studios at the Center

The Center for Contemporary Music is located at one end of the Mills music building, on the second floor. The Center has a series of rooms that open into a long corridor, rooms that serve as studios, labs, and staff offices. There are three main studios at the Center, referred to by letter names. Studio M is used to teach introductory electronic music courses and is so named because of the large and old (at least by electronic music standards) Moog synthesizer within. Studio R is the recording studio, which contains an impressive array of equipment—tape decks, mixing panels, and signal processors—to record electronic and acoustic music and to provide extensive tape-editing facilities. Studio H is the heart of the Center and is named after the hybrid computer-synthesizers in the studio. Most of the graduate work and faculty composition at Mills takes place here.

The Center also has two labs that support work in the studios. The electronics lab has equipment that students and staff can use to build their own electronic music equipment or to repair existing equipment. The dubbing lab is a room with tape decks on which composers can edit their audio tapes and make copies of them.

Studio H

Of the three studios, Studio H contains the most equipment and depends most heavily on MIDI to tie equipment together. The equipment in Studio H is all in a single room, but most studio users mentally divide the studio into the west end and the east end. The west end contains commercially available synthesizers and computer equipment, while the east end contains synthesizers and computers custom-built at Mills.

Much of the commercial equipment was donated to Mills by synthesizer companies and is typical of equipment found in many public and private music studios around the country. One of these donations is a Kurzweil 250 sampling keyboard synthesizer, an 88-key instrument that makes 16-bit samples and uses sampling rates as high as 60 kilohertz for excellent sound quality. It has 12 internal voices, a built-in sequencer, and powerful sample-editing features. The Kurzweil 250 is one of the favorite commercial synthesizers in the studio.

Another popular synthesizer in Studio H is the Oberheim Xpander, a six-voice, MIDI-controllable analog synthesizer. Studio users like the quality of the analog sound and the flexibility of its digital controls. It's designed to work much like the old modular synthesizers in that it allows you to feed the signal from any one component of the synthesizer to any other component. And it has another convenient feature: It receives non-MIDI control voltages and converts them to MIDI messages. This allows composers to use non-MIDI machines in the MIDI system.

The studio also has a Kawai electronic grand piano and a Linn 9000 drum machine, which is a sampling instrument with its own sound-editing facilities and a disk drive for sample storage. The Kawai is mostly used for sonic doodling, trying out musical ideas before putting them into a composition. Composers use the Linn 9000 to add percussive sounds.

A Macintosh Plus computer controls the west end of the studio. It has a 20-megabyte hard disk drive for speed and increased data storage capacity and is connected to an Apple Imagewriter II printer to print scores and other computer information. Software for the Mac includes *Professional Composer,* for entering and printing out traditional music scores; *Performer,* for recording and creating MIDI scores; and a patch librarian for storing patches from the Kurzweil synthesizer. The Mac also runs HMSL, a music program written by the Center staff.

A Garfield Masterbeat synchronizer helps the Mac control the MIDI system by setting tempos. The Masterbeat can read MIDI and SMPTE signals, as well as non-MIDI clock signals from drum machines, and can convert them to MIDI, SMPTE, or clock signals—whichever you require. (For an explanation of SMPTE, see Chapter 10.) It can send a stream of MIDI clocks at any tempo and can send SMPTE pointers to attached SMPTE-controlled tape recorders (which the Center would like to buy when they become more affordable). One very convenient feature of the Masterbeat is that you can set a tempo using pulses on an incoming audio signal. For example, if you have a microphone connected to the synchronizer, you can clap your hands twice to set a tempo. The Masterbeat will start sending MIDI clocks using your clapping tempo.

Most of the equipment in the east end of the studio was custom-built by the staff of the Center. One of the instruments in this end is the ERG machine. It's a computer built around a 68000 microprocessor, the same chip that is the heart of the Macintosh, Amiga, and Atari ST computers. It has the Forth computing language built into its ROM chips and was used to program the first version of HMSL. The ERG machine tightly controls a Buchla 400, an early digital synthesizer with eight voices, and also serves as a master controller for both ends of the studio by sending and receiving MIDI messages through its MIDI ports.

The east end also has a TOUCHE computer-assisted keyboard instrument—basically a computer with a built-in five-octave keyboard and the innards of a Buchla 400 synthesizer. Although you can use the keyboard for live performance, the TOUCHE is not a standard keyboard instrument. Rather than using the keys to play notes of different pitches, you would typically use them to control sound parameters and waveform shapes in live performance. Because the TOUCHE doesn't have MIDI ports, it's used most commonly as a stand-alone performance instrument. Designed and built by Don Buchla, a synthesizer pioneer, and David Rosenboom, the director of the Center, the TOUCHE is an uncommon machine. "They only made six of them," says Larry Polansky, "and we have three."

Tying all the equipment in Studio H together could be a very difficult task, but it's made much easier by cable networks that run throughout the room. Each MIDI device has MIDI In and MIDI Out cables running to a rack in the center of the room. The cables are connected to a J.L. Cooper 16/20 MIDI-programmable patcher, which has 16 MIDI In ports and 20 MIDI Out ports. Each MIDI device is plugged into one MIDI In port and one MIDI Out port on the patcher. Using the patcher, you can connect a device attached to any of its MIDI In ports to any device or set of devices attached to its MIDI Out ports. These connections are made on the front panel of the patcher, and once they've been made, they can be stored in the patcher's internal memory. The patcher has sufficient internal memory for eight different connection patterns, any of which can be selected by remote control using MIDI messages sent to the patcher.

The second cable network in the studio handles audio connections. A series of audio jack pairs located throughout the room make it possible to plug the audio input and output of any instrument into the audio network. The cables running to each instrument's input and output are brought together in a *patch bay* in the center of the studio. A patch bay (shown in Figure 11-1) consists of a panel with a set of jacks lined up in rows. Typically, each jack is labeled as the input from or output to an instrument somewhere in the room. Using a patch cord, you can route the audio signal from one instrument to a receiving instrument by connecting the input jack for the first instrument to the output jack of the second instrument. Working at the patch bay, you can make all your connections conveniently, using short patch cables; you don't have to run around the room trying to make connections between instruments with long, twisting cables.

Figure 11-1.
*A typical patch
bay with outgoing
signal jacks in the
top row and
incoming signal
jacks in the
bottom row.*

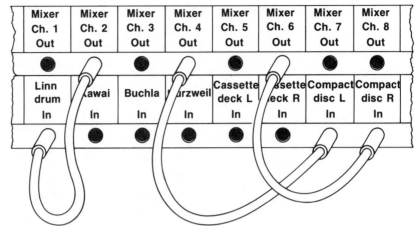

To hear instruments play, you can use the audio patch bay to feed incoming audio signals to a Ramsa WA8210 audio mixer. This mixer has ten jacks for incoming audio signals and mixes the incoming signals down to four (or optionally two) outgoing signals. The outgoing signals are fed to a Carver amplifier connected to two JBL 4430 studio monitor speakers. This audio system is powerful and clean enough to produce an optimum sound from the equipment in the studio. To aid in teaching, there are also a compact disc player, a cassette deck, and a turntable in the studio that plug into the audio system to play composition examples in class.

To understand how all the equipment in Studio H works together, read the following list of equipment, and then look at Figure 11-2 to see how it's all connected. For convenience, the equipment list is sorted into broad categories.

Equipment in Studio H

Synthesizers
> Kurzweil 250 sampling keyboard synthesizer
> Oberheim Xpander analog MIDI synthesizer
> Linn 9000 digital drum machine
> Kawai electronic grand piano
> Buchla 400 digital sound generator

Computers and Accessories
> ERG computer (custom-built)
> Macintosh Plus with a 20-megabyte hard disk drive and an external
> 3¹/₂-inch floppy disk drive
> Apple Imagewriter II dot-matrix printer
> OP-4001 MIDI interface

Software

Professional Composer (a musical notation program)
Performer (a MIDI recorder)
MIDIMac Patch Librarian (for Oberheim patches)
Kurzweil MacAttach (a librarian for Kurzweil patches)
HMSL (an algorithmic composition program, written at Mills)

Audio Equipment

The studio patch bay
Ramsa WA8210 audio mixer
Carver stereo amplifier
Two JBL 4430 studio monitors
Magnavox compact disc player
Onkyo stereo cassette deck
Dual 506 turntable
Dynaco stereo preamplifier (for the turntable)

Special Equipment

J.L. Cooper 16/20 MIDI programmable patcher
Garfield Masterbeat SMPTE-MIDI synchronizer

Figure 11-2.
A diagram of the
Mills College
Studio H electronic
music system.
The various
connections are
indicated as
follows:
MIDI
──────
Audio
─ ─ ─ ─
Stereo audio
= = = = =

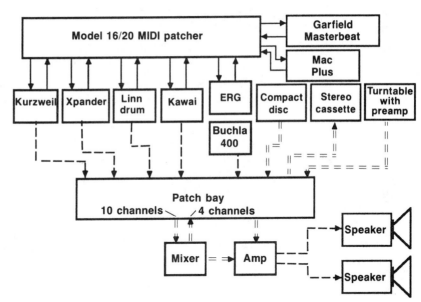

Studio R

Studio R, adjacent to Studio H, contains sophisticated recording equipment. Studio R has its own sound room for recording acoustic performances, separated from the recording room by double panes of glass for sound insulation. In the center of the recording room is a large Amek Scorpion audio mixing panel with 24 inputs and 16 outputs. The outgoing signals can be fed to an Otari MX 7800 8-track reel-to-reel tape deck, a Sony PCM digital tape deck, a Nakamichi MR-1 cassette deck, or other tape decks in the room. The recording room also has a full set of signal processors to keep audio signals clean and to add audio effects.

Studio R has audio inputs and outputs that are connected by cable to the patch bay in Studio H. It also has MIDI In and MIDI Out ports that are connected to the MIDI patcher in Studio H. The audio connections can carry signals from any instrument in Studio H directly to Studio R for recording. They can also carry an instrument's audio signal to be modified by any of the signal processors in Studio R and then sent back to Studio H.

One of the favorite signal processors in Studio R is the Lexicon PCM 70 digital effects processor. It can take an audio signal and add echo and other effects to make it sound as if it's being played in a room of any size and acoustic properties. The sound can be altered on the front panel to create an "ambience patch," the sound of a particular room. These patches can also be created by means of MIDI messages. The MIDI In and MIDI Out ports coming from Studio H allow you to control and use the Lexicon without setting foot in Studio R.

Studio M

Studio M occupies a smaller room than Studio H and has less equipment. Because it's used primarily for teaching introductory electronic music courses, the electronic music system in the studio can be relatively uncomplex. In fact, its simplicity makes it easier to use for teaching.

The most imposing piece of equipment in the studio is the Moog 3p synthesizer. Every bit the classic synthesizer of the sixties with knobs, jacks, and patch cables everywhere, the Moog is a useful teaching tool. Because it's made up of many separate analog modules—oscillators, filters, and envelope generators—you have to connect the modules with patch cords to create a new patch. Each step of creation is easily visible and gives students a concrete image that reinforces the abstract concepts of sound synthesis.

The Moog's modular construction makes it extremely flexible for creating sounds. Some composers at Mills prefer the sounds available on the Moog to the digital sounds available on other synthesizers. Consequently, Studio M has audio cables connecting it to the patch bay in Studio H so that composers can add the Moog's sound to their compositions there or can patch it into Studio R for recording. Because the Moog was created well before MIDI came to be, it isn't MIDI-compatible and can't be controlled from another synthesizer or computer. It's used strictly as a stand-alone instrument.

Studio M also has a small MIDI system available to students. At the heart of the system are four Voyetra Eight synthesizer modules. Each module has eight analog voices with digital controls on its front panel, and each module has MIDI ports for making MIDI connections. A Voyetra VPK5 five-octave master keyboard, connected to the modules with MIDI cables, controls the modules for live performance.

The computer in the Voyetra MIDI system is a PC's Limited 286, a "clone" version of the IBM PC AT computer. It has a 20-kilobyte hard disk and runs special software provided by Voyetra Technologies. One of these programs is a sequencing program; another is a voice editor and librarian.

The studio also has its own audio system with an Audio Technica AT-RMX64 audio mixer that has six inputs and four outputs, a two-track Scully reel-to-reel tape deck for recording compositions, and an amplifier with four JBL monitor speakers for playback.

The Electronics Lab   Students at the Center are encouraged to build their own equipment, and they come to the electronics lab to do it. The lab has an oscilloscope, multimeters, and a full set of tools for designing, building, testing, and maintaining electronic circuits. What makes the electronics lab successful is its open access to students and staff and the availability of help and advice from the Center's technical director.

The Dubbing Lab   The dubbing lab is used for physically editing audio tapes and making copies of them when they're finished. It has several reel-to-reel recorders, a couple of cassette decks, a mixer, and a speaker system for listening. The dubbing lab makes it possible for staff and students to work on their tapes without tying up the other studios.

Work at the Center   With the exception of the custom-built equipment in the studios, the Center's synthesizer equipment isn't much different from that found in other synthesizer studios. "The system here is not extraordinary in any way in terms of design," says Larry Polansky. "The stuff we've built ourselves is interesting, but I think most commercial studios now are using *Performer* and a Kurzweil."

What sets the Center apart from other studios is the philosophy behind the music and the way its students and faculty use the equipment. The guiding principle behind it all is a desire to be innovative with limited equipment and finances. Polansky says, "Ours has always been the small, affordable 'guerrilla technology.' That's our word for it. We can't afford ten VAXs, and we don't have a $250,000 DAC, but we do have the ability to write 6502 code," a programming language for a small and inexpensive microprocessor chip.

The inclination to guerrilla technology comes naturally to both Polansky and Rosenboom, who both got involved with computer music when it meant scrounging any available equipment and adapting it to their needs. Polansky remembers his first exposure to computer music as an undergraduate student at the University of California at Santa Cruz: "The only computer we had at that time was an Interdata Model 3 that the Army had given to us. The machine reached the ceiling and took up about as much room as my office does today." Giving computer concerts took quite a bit of effort. "I remember one day we had 10 guys lifting this Model 3 onto a truck and moving it across campus to do absolutely nothing. You could write tons of code, and it would do nothing because it was such a weak machine. It was a strange experience."

Polansky, who was a math major working in music, spent a lot of time programming the Model 3 so that it would write music. He would set parameters for the music he wanted the computer to create by writing them into the program; when he ran the program, the computer would write the music a note at a time using Polansky's aesthetic guidelines. This kind of music is called algorithmic music, a reference to the algorithms a composer uses to create the computer programs. An algorithm is a series of logical steps arranged in a proper order to get desired results. After creating an algorithm, a programmer turns it into computer code that instructs the computer to follow the steps. By creating musical algorithms, Polansky expresses a musical aesthetic, embodying it in his musical guidelines for computer composition rather than in a particular score.

A key element of algorithmic music is a random-number generator, a section of a computer program that creates a series of random numbers. Using a random-number generator in algorithmic music introduces variety into the pieces the computer creates. Polansky got a random-number generator from an unusual source. "There was an Interdata Model 3 users' group—I kid you not. They would send each other paper tapes. [At that time, paper tapes rather than floppy disks were commonly used for storing program listings.] There was this dentist in New Jersey who had written a random-number generator in octal. I was using it, but it just wasn't generating random numbers. It took me three months to find the bug."

Polansky worked on computer music with James Tenney and David Rosenboom at York University in Toronto and later went to a graduate program at the University of Illinois. When he came to Mills College to teach in 1981, his early experiences in computer music on limited equipment stood him in good stead. "The equipment—you just couldn't believe what we had to deal with. The entire computer facility up here in 1980 was a Commodore Pet. That was it. The first thing David and I did was to buy a 68000 [a powerful microprocessor that was new at that time] and build it up. It turned out not to be the most useful machine here, but at least we were working on the latest technology and the students were working on it. If we had waited three years, we would have had a more useful machine, but the amount of learning that went on with that 68000 was just phenomenal. The technology doesn't last, but the ideas last."

Since the equipment in the studios has been upgraded, the main emphasis in composition and teaching at the Center has shifted to computer languages. Polansky, together with David Rosenboom and Phil Burk, is working on HMSL (Hierarchical Music Specification Language), a computer language that lets you do a host of things, including creating your own algorithmic music and using computers in live performance. By creating HMSL, Polansky, Rosenboom, and Burk put their theories of music into practice for others to apply. "HMSL is a computer language," says Polansky, "but to me, it's also a theory of working."

HMSL was originally programmed on the ERG machine, the Center's custom-built 68000 computer, but it has now been ported over to Macintosh and Amiga computers. Polansky's preference for HMSL is the Amiga computer, which he likes for its computing power. He recently set up a live performance in San Francisco's Museum of Modern Art with four Amigas creating music under the control of audience members.

The students at Mills are using HMSL in their own compositions, running it on the Macintosh Plus in Studio H. Music created using HMSL can be played using the Mac's own sound generating capabilities, or it can be played on attached synthesizers by means of MIDI.

Students also make compositional use of another Mills facility—the frog pond adjacent to the music building. Polansky says, "In the spring, when those frogs go into heat, they produce this really unbelievable sound. It's such an incredible sound that there are basically three or four pieces each year that use it. Every graduate student at some point does his frog pond piece."

**MIDI Systems for
Standard Music
Education**

For a school that has been in the forefront of computer music for as long as
it has, Mills College uses surprisingly little synthesizer and computer
equipment in its standard music courses. Part of the problem is a (not uncommon) reticence on the part of regular music faculty to use computers
and synthesizers.

Larry Polanski observes that he and Rosenboom initially found
themselves isolated from the rest of the faculty because of their enthusiasm
for computers. This attitude is changing, however, in part because of the
widespread use of computers elsewhere on campus. "Mills signed a big
handshaking deal with Macintosh," Polansky says. "There are Macintoshes all over campus, the faculty can buy them very cheaply, and we have
a really good support system for the Mac. And there's money in the program that lets each department buy quite a bit of software."

To make computers useful to the faculty, Mills has created a computer center. "At Mills we have something called the Computer Learning
Studio, which is just like heaven," says Polansky. "It's run by a woman
named Carol Lennox, who is really the maven of the Macintosh and the
VAX system [a large computer system also used on campus]. It basically
consists of three Macintoshes and a Laserwriter and a hell of a lot of software with a hell of a lot of support. There's someone there all the time. The
faculty members get a key so we can go there anytime day or night and just
crank away. It really gets a lot of use."

Polansky would like to see the music department set up an operation
for music education similar to the Computer Learning Studio. He envisions
a lab with a bank of Macintoshes and perhaps an IBM PC and a broad sampling of educational software for the faculty to try. "Whatever program
you decide to accept as your standard is going to be obsolete the next week,
so you want to budget for keeping updated. You want somebody who does
the work of knowing what's coming out and sitting down with the new
software and playing with it for an hour or two, and who can then tell the
faculty members about it." Once faculty members find the software they
want, they could use it for teaching their courses and send their students to
the lab to run the software on the computers there.

To a limited extent, some of the software in Studio H is already used
for teaching standard music courses. "We've got a Kurzweil sitting there
running *Performer* and *Professional Composer.* It's an electronic music

MUSIC EDUCATION SOFTWARE

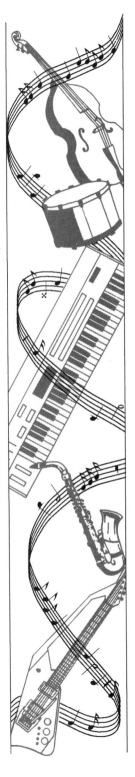

As more people realize the promise of computers and MIDI keyboards in music education, they are writing an increasing amount of educational music software. One comprehensive music education system, called *Musicom,* is available through RolandCorp US, the synthesizer company. *Musicom* is a combination of add-on hardware for a computer and a series of programs designed to teach different aspects of music theory, keyboard skills, ear training, and sight singing.

Musicom works with the IBM Personal Computer. To use the program, you need some extra hardware. In the first place, you need some special processing cards that you attach inside the computer. You also need a Roland smart MIDI interface (the MPU-401), a microphone, and a MIDI keyboard. The internal cards (circuit boards) add a pitch tracker to the computer. When a student sings into the microphone, the pitch tracker follows the succession of notes and senses rhythms. The MIDI interface enables the computer to sense what's being played on the MIDI keyboard.

The various *Musicom* programs teach different areas of music fundamentals. One program teaches ear training and sight singing, and another teaches the fundamentals of keyboard playing to help players read musical notation. Other programs teach elementary music theory, concepts in two-part composition, triad structure (to teach you to use and write chords), keyboard technique, and jazz piano skills. Although buying the necessary hardware to run these programs can be expensive, the full series of programs is well written and teaches its set of topics in depth. Each program is designed to be used with or without teacher supervision and can repeat any drills to permit self-pacing.

Electronic Courseware Systems offers a full line of music education software that works without additional hardware on the Apple II, Commodore 64, IBM PC, and Tandy 1000, 1200, and 3000 computers. If a program teaches keyboard skills, it does, of course, require an additional MIDI interface and a MIDI keyboard. More than 40 programs in the ECS catalog teach ear training, music theory, woodwind fingerings, and a variety of keyboard skills. Additional programs provide services, such as maintaining band accounts and helping to write marching band drill routines.

studio facility, but everybody in my orchestration class wants to use *Professional Composer.* They aren't on the key list, so they're clamoring for access. It's a problem. When the lines get erased between the electronic music studio and straight music, there are access problems. The solution is to get a Macintosh outside of the studio running *Professional Composer.*"

Experiences with MIDI

Although Mills College uses MIDI in its studios and may also use it in the future in music labs, the staff and students at the Center don't look to MIDI as the last word in computer music technology. They and other computer music composers were creating sophisticated music long before MIDI arrived and are used to the powerful results computers can bring to music. "That explains why a lot of people didn't jump up and down when MIDI came along," says Polansky. "They'd been doing it for a long while."

One of Polansky's major frustrations with MIDI is that it was designed to accommodate traditional music and doesn't do many of the things he needs to do in the experimental music he writes. "The basic problem is that any time you try to define a standard," he says, "you close out a lot of people's ideas. After all, one connotation of 'standard' is 'flag'—MIDI becomes a flag that people wave. I hate to see musicians adopting any standard. I think if you adopt a standard in music, you're dead. You've basically eliminated experimentation."

One of the specific MIDI concepts that Polansky finds objectionable involves the rigid definitions of the MIDI messages. "MIDI has all these words—Note On, Note Off, Aftertouch—and they're not just words," he says. "They're actually defined. They restrict information significantly." As another example, he points out that MIDI doesn't pass any information about envelopes. It assumes that each synthesizer sets its own envelopes; MIDI doesn't let you control the envelopes individually from a computer. He also points out that MIDI is locked into one type of tuning, the standard, 12-tone scale, and won't allow experimental tunings or non-standard scales with more than 12 tones in an octave. These limitations, along with a slow data transfer rate and a lack of substantial control of timbre and other musical parameters, make MIDI unsuitable for much of the music created at Mills.

Polansky does admit that MIDI is useful at times. He finds it handy to pass information between computers over MIDI cables without using MIDI messages. Computers at Mills have been programmed to transfer information between themselves without using MIDI messages; that is, they dump a series of bytes through the MIDI cable at 31,250 baud, something like the data bytes in a system exclusive message. Both the sending and receiving computers interpret the information as they've been programmed to interpret it. MIDI is also handy in traditional teaching situations. "It saves us a lot of time," he says. "It makes a lot of things a lot easier to teach."

Polansky has some feelings of resentment toward the ease with which MIDI users are able to make music. "I'm really a champion of people who still do guerrilla technology. It's harder than ever to do now because there's such a temptation to use the stuff that's so powerful. My philosophy is to recognize that the technology has become more powerful; it allows you to do ten times as much. But I maintain that you should spend the same amount of time on a piece—work just as hard and do ten times more." At Mills, the guerrilla war rages on.

12 | MIDI AT HOME

MIDI in the professional domain lives in a pampered world of expensive synthesizers, unlimited cables, powerful computers running the best software, and budgets large enough to look extensive repairs straight in the eye without flinching. In return, it's expected to produce—to turn out smash hits, to educate a host of musicians, and to make enough money to buy more MIDI equipment and support its owners in style.

MIDI at home doesn't usually have it so easy. It's kept on a low-salary diet. Its owner builds a system incrementally, piece by painful piece, and often faces the unenviable task of justifying its existence to less enthusiastic family members. Because MIDI at home usually returns nothing more than enjoyment and intense satisfaction (mixed occasionally with complete frustration), the keeper of a home MIDI system must be constantly looking for ways to cut corners without cutting quality.

In this chapter, you'll get a close look at a successful, satisfying, and low-cost MIDI system that shares a home with David Ocker. Ocker put together his home MIDI system a few years ago for less than $2,000, at a time when prices were much higher than they are today. You'll also find supplemental sections that provide some tips on adding a mixer to your home stereo system to accommodate your MIDI system, as well as information about adding self-powered speakers to your MIDI system. Another sidelight introduces a computer program that turns computers into performing instruments that anyone can use.

David Ocker

DAVID OCKER, HOME MIDIPHILE

David Ocker is a musician straddling three disciplines—a difficult task for a normal, two-legged man; he plays the clarinet, composes music, and makes his living copying music scores for orchestras and other composers around the country. He works in his own home, a modest bungalow in the Los Feliz district of Los Angeles, where he has a room devoted to his music-copying business and a growing MIDI system in his bedroom.

Ocker's interest in music developed at an early age. "I started playing clarinet in fifth grade, and I haven't stopped yet," he says. "I've been a professional-level amateur clarinetist ever since then." He first went to college in the early seventies at Carleton College in Northfield, Minnesota, where he studied clarinet and composition and turned in a one-year stint teaching a course in electronic music on the college's synthesizer.

Graduate studies took Ocker to Valencia, California, to the California Institute of the Arts, then as today a center for avant-garde music. At CalArts, he was able to study with many prominent teachers, among them clarinetists Richard Stoltzman and Michelle Zukowsky, and composers Earle Brown, Stephen Mosko, Paul Chihara, and Morton Subotnick.

When he graduated from CalArts, Ocker moved to Los Angeles and turned himself loose on the local music scene. With several other young composers, he founded the Independent Composers' Association, a group devoted to performing the new works of local Los Angeles composers. He served as its president on and off for a total of two and a half years. In June, 1977, he took a job as full-time music copyist for Frank Zappa, a job he held for seven years.

Working for Zappa brought Ocker in contact with the world of commercial music and also with Zappa's dense, complex, and innovative style of composition. Although Zappa is perhaps best known for his rock recordings, he is also a prolific composer of contemporary music for orchestra and assorted chamber music ensembles. It was Ocker's job to turn the rough music manuscript from Zappa into finished full scores and parts. "He would deny it, and he certainly wasn't trying to teach me anything," says Ocker, "but I learned more from working for Frank for seven years than I did from all my other composition teachers put together."

While working as Zappa's copyist, Ocker continued to compose and to perform on the clarinet. He gave solo clarinet recitals where, he says, "I played lots of esoteric twentieth-century literature, including my own." In January of 1983, he performed and recorded a piece with the London Symphony Orchestra, a clarinet concerto written for him by Zappa. Ocker also played in different chamber ensembles during this period, including the infamous "Echo Quartet Quartet" and ad hoc groups formed for Independent Composers' Association concerts.

Synthesizer Experience

David Ocker's experience with synthesizers is unusually extensive because he worked with them in college at a time when they were too expensive for most individuals to buy. The first synthesizer he used was an Electrocomp 100 owned by Carleton College, a relatively inexpensive modular analog synthesizer popular in the mid-seventies. He occasionally had a chance to use the Moog synthesizer system across town at St. Olaf College. He still remembers the Moog's impressive tangle of patch cords and lights, remarking that today's synthesizers simply don't have the same formidable look. "You should be able to buy devices to go into a rack-mount panel that have nothing but blinking lights on them. They could have MIDI inputs so they would respond to certain channels whenever they got a certain note on a certain channel." He laughs, "I think there'd be a market for them. They'd be cheap, too."

When he went to school at CalArts, Ocker worked with a Buchla synthesizer, a prototype that was one of the first synthesizers controlled by a computer. The computer in this case was a minicomputer the size of a filing cabinet. The Buchla didn't lack in patch cords and banks of knobs; it did lack in programming for its computer. Ocker remembers the instrument as "an amazing albatross" because no one at CalArts had enough time to program the computer properly. As a result, it was never really fully functional.

Things improved after the school year. "The year I graduated, in '76, I hung out in Newhall (a town close to CalArts) during the summer. During the school year, I'd get two or three hours a week on the synthesizer. But because I was working on music at CalArts during the summer, they gave me a key. I got to go into the synthesizer lab and set up a patch system— you know, with thousands of patch cords—that would actually produce a piece. By the end of the summer I managed to produce a piece called "Three Strokes of Twenty-Five"—it has three movements, and I finished it on my twenty-fifth birthday. At that time, it was the only piece that had been completed on that particular Buchla system."

The Buchla wasn't particularly sophisticated when it came to synchronizing the notes played by its different voices, but Ocker used this idiosyncrasy to good advantage. "There was one movement that had a pretty steady beat. I had devised this hard-wired analog system to keep four voices in sync at once. If I turned the computer off, these voices would start to phase because there'd be nothing sending out signals at the right time. They'd go out of sync for a while; then I'd turn the computer back on in the middle of the piece, and they'd sync up again. I was able to make a pretty interesting sound out of the failure of the system to keep itself in sync."

For six years after he left CalArts, Ocker had no access to a synthesizer. He was reluctant to purchase his own equipment, deterred by the expense required to set up even a marginally successful system. In 1983, Frank Zappa began to use a Synclavier, a high-quality sampling synthesizer, in his recordings, and he asked Ocker to start learning to use the Synclavier system. Ocker started designing Synclavier patches and entered Zappa's scores in the Synclavier's sequencer using its own computer. MIDI was beginning to appear on synthesizers at the time, but Ocker didn't use it in Zappa's studio. Because the Synclavier was a self-contained system, he had no need to connect it with other equipment using MIDI.

**Beginnings of a
MIDI System**

Ocker heard plenty about MIDI as it began to develop. He was intrigued by the possibilities of inexpensive synthesizers tied to an equally inexpensive computer, and one synthesizer in particular caught his attention: the Sequential Circuits 6-Trak. "It was polytimbral," Ocker says, "which excited me tremendously because I was very impressed with the polytimbral capabilities of the Synclavier." It also worked with a Commodore 64 computer: "Sequential came out with the interface and the expansion software that would actually allow you to sequence polytimbrally."

There was nothing else like the 6-Trak on the market at the time, so Ocker parted with his hard-earned money to buy one along with a Commodore 64 computer. "I would not have bought a synthesizer were it not for MIDI and were it not for the computer. It was the fact that I could use the computer and the synthesizer together that finally loosened the money out of my pocket."

The 6-Trak and its accompanying interface and software weren't everything Ocker wanted, however. The Sequential MIDI interface for the Commodore 64 computer is a smart interface with its software on a ROM chip. The software for the interface and Sequential's sequencing software for the Commodore were not easy to use. "This stuff was far ahead of its time, and let me tell you, it was marketed much too early," Ocker says. "I spent eleven to twelve hundred dollars on this synthesizer and the sequencer and the software, and I had it for almost a year before I bought new software. I didn't finish one piece during that year because the software was so inconsiderate to humans."

Since buying the 6-Trak and Commodore 64, Ocker has added slowly and carefully to his MIDI system, one piece at a time. He uses his system strictly for entering music he's written and then hearing it in a rough form. Consequently, he isn't concerned about the quality of the sound: "The philosophy is that anything I have to rationalize in terms of improving the sound is not relevant. I've got a system that lets me hear pitches and rhythms, and that's what I worry about when I write." His philosophy has helped him hold down the cost of his system.

**David Ocker's
Current MIDI
System**

Ocker divides his MIDI system into three parts: the synthesizer system, the computer system, and the audio system. The synthesizer system has two components—the 6-Trak synthesizer and a Roland TR-505 drum machine that he bought to add percussion sounds. He also has a Yamaha CP-20 electric piano that he bought before he started building his MIDI system. Because it lacks MIDI ports, it stands apart from the system as a piece of auxiliary equipment.

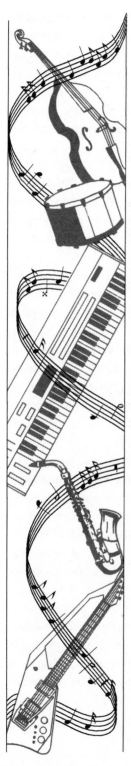

MUSIC MOUSE

If you have more musical aspirations than you do keyboard skills, you should take a look at *Music Mouse* (shown in Figure 12-1), a program for the Macintosh or the Amiga computer. *Music Mouse* turns the computer into a performing instrument easy enough to afford a beginner immediately gratifying results, yet sophisticated enough to reward accomplished users with highly expressive results.

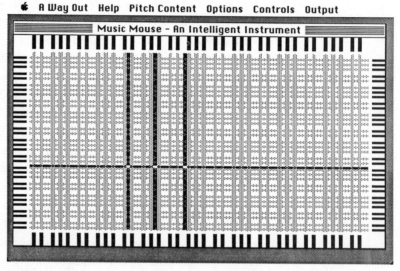

Figure 12-1. *The screen of* Music Mouse, *a music performance program for Macintosh or Amiga computers.*

Music Mouse was written by Laurie Spiegel, a New York-based composer, and is published by OpCode Systems, a music software firm in Palo Alto, California. To use it with your MIDI system, you need to connect your Macintosh or Amiga computer to a synthesizer with the help of a MIDI adaptor and a cable. Once you make the necessary connections, you can use the computer's mouse and keyboard to play notes on the synthesizer, or you can use the computer's own internal sound chips.

Music Mouse is based on a simple premise: Rolling the mouse up or down raises or lowers the pitch of a set of voices, while rolling the mouse left or right raises or lowers the pitch of a second set of voices. *Music Mouse* uses four voices, which you can assign to the mouse axes in various ways. You can assign one melody voice to vertical mouse motion and three accompanying voices to horizontal mouse motion, or you can assign two voices to vertical motion and the two other voices to

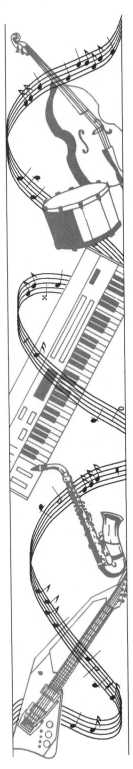

horizontal motion. You can also decide whether the voices controlled by a mouse axis move parallel (rise and fall together in pitch) or contrary (move in opposite pitch directions).

From the description, you might expect the music you produce with *Music Mouse* to sound primitive and to lack finesse. Yet Laurie Spiegel has imparted her aesthetic sensibilities to the program, laying down a sort of "aesthetic template" that limits the notes you play to pleasing and interesting harmonies and rhythms. Anyone, from child to adult, can get pleasing results from the start.

Music Mouse also accommodates the accomplished musician. Small mouse movements give you control of what would be fistfuls of notes on a music keyboard and allow you to play types of music that would be almost impossible to play on a keyboard. You can use one hand to roll the mouse and the other hand to press keys on the computer keyboard. By pressing different computer keys, you can add variety and expression to the notes you play with the mouse. The keyboard lets you pick new harmonic templates, change patches on the synthesizer, and set the overall volume up or down in a smooth *crescendo* or *diminuendo*. You can also use the keyboard to transpose the key of the performance up or down, to increase or decrease the overall tempo of the rhythms created by the mouse, to turn *portamento* on and off, to control note articulation, and to set the modulation wheel, breath controller, foot control, velocity, and aftertouch values for the synthesizer.

Music Mouse has an optional feature that plays sequences of notes automatically when you stop rolling the mouse. You can choose among ten preset sequences by using the number keys on the computer keyboard. These sequences start playing at the pitches on which you stop the mouse, so you can change the entire sound of the sequence by moving the mouse only occasionally, creating changing flights of notes with a minimum of effort.

The real test of a performance program isn't the number of features it contains, but the satisfaction it brings. Many such programs quickly become boring once you master their limited possibilities, but *Music Mouse* continues to hold your interest by revealing new worlds of possibilities as you learn more about the program. Let's hope that *Music Mouse* is only the first of many programs that will offer similarly satisfying performance experiences within the aesthetic worlds of their creators.

The computer system is somewhat more involved. Ocker has two Commodore 64s. One of them uses a Dr. T Model-T MIDI interface (a dumb interface). The other uses the Sequential Circuits smart interface that he bought with his 6-Trak synthesizer. He uses a Casio TB-1 Thru Box to send MIDI messages from both computers to the 6-Trak and the TR-505.

Although it's unusual to have two computers in a MIDI system, Ocker finds them both useful. "One of them is somewhat souped up," he explains. "It has an IEEE interface, a third-party double drive, and an 80-column card that I can't use because it's not compatible with my graphics program." He also uses this enhanced computer to create music programs using the BASIC programming language. These programs generate their own notes and send them to the attached synthesizers. Ocker uses his unmodified Commodore 64 computer to write his own music using a sequencer program.

After abandoning the Sequential Circuits sequencer, Ocker switched to *Dr. T's Keyboard Controlled Sequencer.* "I like the Dr. T sequencer because it's not based on a tape recorder metaphor," he says. "I know there are lots of good sequencers that are designed for people who play keyboards, but I'm not one of those people. I can play some things on the keyboard, but I can't play the kind of music I can write. I can conceive of music that people have a difficult time playing. If I have to enter it on a keyboard playing in real time, I'm a dead duck. *Dr. T* has a good step-entry function, and it has the ability to manipulate note lists in a sort of word-processor format that I really like."

Ocker saved a sizable amount of money on his audio system by using the stereo system he already owned. To supplement the stereo system, he bought a used Realistic stereo audio mixer (sold through Radio Shack) that has six audio inputs and one set of stereo outputs. By plugging his synthesizers into the mixer, he can adjust their relative volume levels and feed the resulting stereo audio signal directly into the receiver of his stereo system. His stereo system has a reel-to-reel tape deck and three cassette decks, so that he can easily record anything he plays on his synthesizers. He also has three pairs of speakers set up within his house. All are connected to a speaker switcher, so that he can pipe the sounds of his compositions to any speaker set. A special fourth set of speakers sits over his synthesizers to let him listen to the sound of the synthesizers closely as he works with them.

The table on the next page lists the equipment Ocker uses in his MIDI system. In Figure 12-2, the diagram that follows the table, you can see how all his equipment is connected.

Components of David Ocker's MIDI system

Synthesizer system

    A Sequential Circuits 6-Trak synthesizer
    A Roland TR-505 drum machine

Computer system

    Two Commodore 64 computers
    A Sequential Circuits MIDI interface
    A Dr. T Model-T MIDI interface
    A Casio TB-1 Thru box
    Dr. T's Keyboard Controlled Sequencer (a sequencer program)

Audio system

    A Realistic (Cat. No. 32-1210) stereo audio mixer
    A Kenwood KR-4070 stereo receiver
    A Technics 1500 two-track reel-to-reel tape deck
    Three cassette decks of different makes
    A speaker selector switch of unknown manufacture
    Three pairs of speakers of different manufacture
    A monitoring speaker, also of unexceptional origin

Additional equipment

    A Yamaha CP-20 electric piano

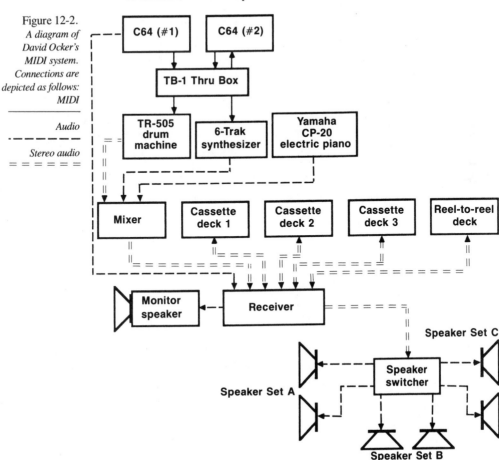

Figure 12-2.
A diagram of David Ocker's MIDI system. Connections are depicted as follows:
MIDI

Audio

Stereo audio

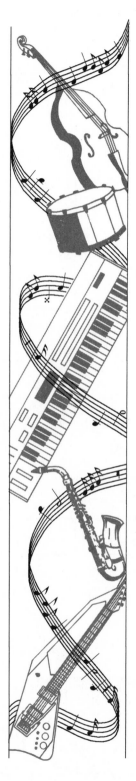

SETTING UP A MIXER FOR A HOME SYSTEM

You can probably save a substantial amount of money setting up your home MIDI system if you can use your existing stereo system as an audio system to let you hear your synthesizers play. This is a very simple matter if you have only one or two synthesizers: You can plug them into the standard inputs on your amplifier, such as the Auxiliary input or the Tape In input, one synthesizer on the left channel and the second on the right channel. When you select the appropriate input (using a knob or button on the front of the amplifier), you can hear your synthesizers play on your stereo system. The first synthesizer plays only on the left channel, and the second synthesizer only on the right channel. By selecting the monophonic playback mode on your amplifier (if it has one) you can hear both synthesizers on both speakers.

Problems arise if you have more than two synthesizers. Although your amplifier might have a sufficient number of inputs to plug in numerous synthesizers, very few amplifiers let you play the audio signals coming from more than one set of stereo inputs at a time. Consequently, you won't be able to hear more than two synthesizers playing together. Also, some synthesizers (the Yamaha FB-01 expansion module and the Roland TR-505 drum machine, for example) put out stereo signals; you can plug only one of them into each set of stereo inputs on the amplifier. The solution to these problems is to add a mixer to your stereo system.

A useful mixer can have anywhere from four to dozens of input jacks, the number of jacks usually dependent on the price of the mixer. If you're economizing by using your home stereo system as the MIDI audio system, you'll most likely get a mixer with four, six, or eight input jacks. Each input should have a switchable input level that lets you plug in either the strong audio signal of a synthesizer or the weak signal of a microphone. Each input also needs its own volume control so that you can set the balance among the audio signals coming into the mixer.

Most mixers are built to merge incoming audio signals into two outgoing signals that you can feed into an amplifier. (One outgoing signal is the left channel of a stereo pair; the other is the right channel.) You should be able to assign each incoming signal to either the left or

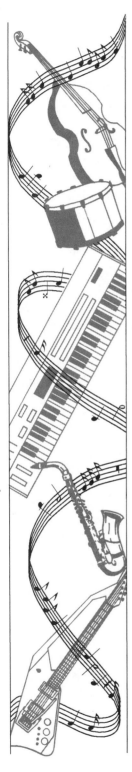

right channel or to both channels. Good mixers also let you *pan* an incoming signal between channels. The incoming signal emerges on both channels, but you can make it stronger on one channel than the other. When you hear the result played through stereo speakers, the original signal seems to come from some point between the two speakers, not strictly from the left or right speaker. By changing the panning setting of an incoming signal, you can set its apparent location between the speakers, an effect called *imaging*.

If you plan to do a great deal of recording with your MIDI system, you might consider buying a cassette deck with a built-in mixer. The deck's mixing panel lets you plug in four incoming audio signals and mix them down to two outgoing stereo signals that you can send to an amplifier. The mixing panel also lets you send all four signals separately to be recorded on four different tracks on a single cassette. (Compare this with the two tracks available on a standard stereo cassette deck.) You can play the four recorded tracks later, remixing them as you like. Most of these four-track tape decks allow sophisticated effects such as overdubbing, which lets you create a one-person recording by adding your own acoustic tracks to the synthesizer tracks from your MIDI system. Some typical four-track cassette decks are the Tascam Ministudio Porta One (shown in Figure 12-3) and the Yamaha MT1X.

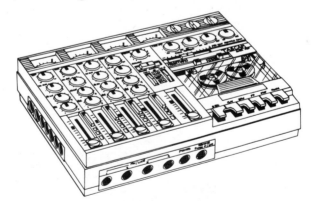

Figure 12-3. *The Tascam Ministudio Porta One tape deck with built-in mixer.*

Using His MIDI System

Ocker gets good use from his MIDI system. He uses it to compose pieces of two types: musical scores for acoustic instruments and environmental music for synthesizers driven by a computer. To create his acoustic scores, he sits down at his electric piano and tries out different musical ideas on the keyboard. If he comes up with something he likes, he enters it into the computer a note at a time, using step-time entry on his sequencer program.

At any time, Ocker can play back the score to listen to the notes he's entered. (Self-powered speakers can be handy at this point. See Figure 12-4 and the description on the next page.) "You hit the button and lie back in the chair, and you listen. From that perspective, you can relate more as a member of the audience than as a composer," he explains, "which is important if you want to get a feel for the way a piece of music works." He listens to the pitches and rhythms to see how they fit but ignores the timbres of the synthesizer patches, imagining instead the sound of the instruments that will play the piece. "By keeping my system well sub-standard," he says, "I force myself to deal with the fact that I'm really interested in the sounds of acoustic instruments, which are still much more flexible than those of any synthesizer."

Once Ocker finishes a piece, he plays it back on his MIDI system and records it on a cassette. He also copies the entire score and the separate instrumental parts in traditional musical notation, an easy feat for an accomplished music copyist such as Ocker. Although he has looked at many

Figure 12-4.
The Yamaha KS10 self-powered speaker.

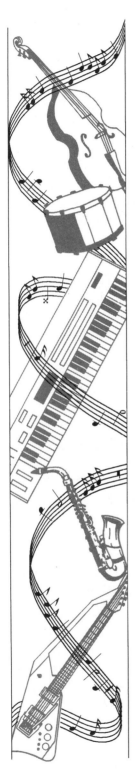

SELF-POWERED SPEAKERS

Using your home stereo system as a speaker system for your MIDI equipment is often impractical. If your stereo system is in the living room and your MIDI system is down in the basement, you'll have to run audio cables the entire distance between the two systems. If you need extra-long audio cables to make the connections, the cables are prone to pick up 60-cycle hum and other extraneous noise before they reach the amplifier. Even if you do make successful connections, you need a pair of extension speakers in the basement to let you hear what you're playing as you play it.

A simpler speaker solution is to use small and relatively inexpensive self-powered speakers. These speakers have built-in amplifiers and accept an audio signal directly from a synthesizer or from a mixer. Some self-powered speakers even run on batteries; you can use them to perform outdoors or in other places that lack a handy AC outlet.

Most synthesizer manufacturers make self-powered speakers specifically for use with synthesizers. Some examples are the Yamaha KS10 speaker (shown in Figure 12-4) and the Casio AS-20 speaker. If you decide to get a self-powered speaker for your MIDI system (or two speakers for stereo), be sure you don't confuse them with some of the small self-powered speakers sold for use with small, portable cassette players. Most of these smaller speakers are designed to amplify the audio signal coming from the headphone jack of the cassette player, a signal that has already been amplified slightly. They won't provide enough amplification to play the audio signal that comes directly from the audio Out port of a synthesizer. To be sure a speaker will work with your synthesizer system, check to see that it has a *line level* input, a jack that accepts the low-level audio signal sent by most synthesizers.

Another way to add speakers to your MIDI system might be as close as the next room, where you might have a portable cassette player with its own speaker system (often called a "boom box"). Most of these cassette players have a pair of line level inputs into which you can plug the output cables from your synthesizers or your mixer. You can then play your MIDI system on the speakers of the boom box with the added advantage that you can record your performances on the cassette recorder while you play.

different musical notation programs to help him with his scores and to increase the efficiency of his music-copying business, he still prefers to do his work with a pen and ink. He has yet to find a program for any computer that can entice him to write music with a computer and a printer. No current product combines sufficient power with the flexibility he needs in notation.

Many composers find that writing a piece of music for instrumentalists is often easier than finding the players to perform the piece. Ocker has two helpful techniques to better his chances of enlisting performers. First, he often avoids assigning the parts in the score to particular instruments, so that any combination of instrumentalists can play it; for example, a trio might be played by oboe, clarinet, and bassoon as well as by violin, viola, and cello. Second, he uses the tape he created of the MIDI performance to attract prospective performers. "I've gotten performers by giving people tapes," he says. "Instead of handing people an obtuse, rather complicated score that they may or may not have the time and ability to understand, I give them something they can just sit down and enjoy, something I know is good because I sat down and enjoyed it myself."

The second type of composition Ocker writes is environmental music, long pieces meant to be played in the background to create a musical environment. He first started by composing 45-minute pieces for solo instruments and recording them on tape. One of his first pieces was for solo viola; another was for eight clarinets. He realized that his 45-minute compositions were taxing the endurance of the performers (especially evident when he played one of them himself). As a result, he switched to recording natural sounds on a portable tape recorder, then editing and mixing the sounds to create environmental pieces lasting as long as five hours.

As his MIDI system evolved, Ocker began to think about creating environmental pieces by programming the computer to generate the notes in the piece and to send them to the synthesizers to play. For one of his current projects, he has programmed the computer to generate notes and rhythms using fractal equations, equations that adeptly describe complex and often beautiful patterns. In its current, primitive stage, this project is not one that Ocker wants to put his name on; it may, with further refinements, turn into an environmental piece.

To record the finished piece, Ocker plans to use the facilities of a professional recording studio. "I would probably take the program to a studio that has a Commodore 64—I actually know of two studios that have Commodore 64s in them—and lots of high-quality synthesizers, good tape decks, and other things. The sound my own synthesis equipment produces is simply not adequate for me to give a tape to someone and say 'Listen.'" The other possibility is to turn the piece into an "installation": Ocker would set up the computer and the necessary synthesizers in a room or gallery and run the software to create the piece—a kind of sonic sculpture.

Experiences with MIDI

After working with his system for several years, Ocker has definite ideas about the way to set up a MIDI system. He would like to add some more equipment to his system—a touch-sensitive MIDI keyboard, an expansion module for some extra voices, a new computer with more memory than the Commodore 64—but he feels that the software you use to run a MIDI system is more important than the hardware. As he puts it, "The quality of the system depends on the software. The fact that the hardware is low-end and somewhat hodge-podge is no problem for my projects. What's important to me is the flexibility of the software."

Although computers and synthesizers have been tremendously useful to him in writing music, Ocker feels that synthesizers have a long way to go to match the flexibility, spontaneity, and expressive powers of acoustic instruments: "If I hear the best programmed DX7 or Synclavier sound, it's still vastly disinteresting to me in comparison to somebody playing a good modulated note with *vibrato* and *crescendo* and *diminuendo* on a clarinet, a note which can occur in the most diverse situations. A synthesizer is very primitive compared to that." As a solution, he half-jokingly proposes "MIHI," the Musical Instrument Human Interface, designed to give more expressive capability to synthesizers and the computers controlling them.

One way that Ocker hopes to benefit more from his MIDI system is to understand MIDI as thoroughly as possible. "To really understand MIDI, I think it's important to understand how those commands are put together. I know that it's complicated mathematically, and some of them don't make all that much sense, but that's the level that I would like to know more about." He also hopes that the MIDI standard expands to set standards for the way patches and sequences are stored. "You should be able to take somebody else's file from another sequencer program," he says, "put it into your sequencer, and have it play."

Even with the current limitations in MIDI and in the quality of synthesized sound, Ocker is a confirmed MIDIphile. He says, "The mere existence of MIDI has been such a tremendously productive contribution to the world of music that it's mind-boggling. The fact that manufacturers could come up with a MIDI standard that they could all agree upon is even more mind-boggling." MIDI has certainly placed a powerful music tool in the home and in the hands of David Ocker.

AFTERWORD

MIDI is a promise—a promise from hardware manufacturers and software publishers that they will make products that work together and a promise that technology will serve the art of music. As that technology grows, so will your creative possibilities as a MIDI user. Although it's not easy to predict the ways MIDI will grow (sometimes happily so), you can expect to see changes in several areas: constantly improving MIDI hardware, innovations in MIDI software, and further refinements in the MIDI standard itself.

At the heart of MIDI hardware development, synthesizers are undergoing constant change as manufacturers strive to offer richer sounds and greater flexibility. The line between traditional synthesizers and sampling devices continues to blur as more synthesizers use sampled sounds as the initial waveforms for their patches and as more samplers give you power to drastically alter their sampled sounds. New synthesis techniques will allow synthesizers to be much more flexible when responding to controlling values such as attack velocity, release velocity, and aftertouch. While some synthesizers are designed to recreate acoustic sounds with more accuracy, others will likely move in the opposite direction to recreate the tremendous flexibility and warm sounds of the old analog synthesizers and yet to capitalize on the low cost, compactness, and stability of digital technology. Perhaps the most important change to anticipate in synthesizers is in the area of value: You can expect the new synthesizers to offer more features for lower prices as manufacturing prices drop.

Controllers should also change for the better. The greatest barrier to playing a synthesizer expressively is the relatively unresponsive nature of an electric keyboard. It doesn't have the depth of nuance and expression that a good vocalist, wind player, or string player can evoke in a long, lyrical melodic line. While today's pitch trackers can turn acoustic performances into MIDI data, they often respond slowly and fail to capture all the subtle changes in timbre, dynamics, and pitch that are present in a live performance. They are also unable to deal with more than one note at a time. As pitch trackers continue to improve, they will be able to capture more of these nuances and to handle polyphonic performances.

Manufacturers should come out with new MIDI controllers to allow those who play traditional acoustic instruments to play synthesizers as well. At this writing, saxophone controllers are coming to market. They play exactly like acoustic saxophones but convert the musician's actions directly to MIDI messages. The success of these controllers and of controllers like them depends on their ability to detect performance nuances, such as changing lip pressure, air speed, and air pressure, and to send this information to a synthesizer. It's also possible that radically new controllers not based on any traditional instruments will evolve. Although the development of such controllers is a worthwhile goal, their acceptance is a difficult and gradual process. Even if someone builds the perfect new controller today, it will take time for people to learn to play it well enough to want to buy one. Most manufacturers don't have the time, money, or patience to wait for years until a market of skilled players develops for a new controller. Most likely, new controllers will evolve slowly from simple novelty controllers.

If you use a computer in your MIDI system, you will benefit from improvements to that equipment, as well. As computers increase in power and drop in price, you'll be able to afford to run ever more powerful software on your system. Computer manufacturers should also start to build MIDI ports into their machines or to make it easier to add MIDI ports to them. Increasing numbers of manufacturers might have synthesizer-quality sound chips built into their computers, so that a computer can function in a system not only as a recorder and a sequencer and a librarian, but also as a full-blown synthesizer.

Some of MIDI's hardware advances will take place in areas where MIDI is not commonly used today. MIDI is already used to control equipment such as lighting panels, amplifiers, and mixers, and its use can easily expand to include control of other devices, as well. MIDI might be able to control digital tape recording and so to assist with the precise editing and mixing down of tracks. It's also rumored that some Japanese home audio manufacturers are including unlabeled 5-pin DIN plugs on the backs of some of their products. Possibly MIDI will be used to control and synchronize the components in home stereo and video systems.

Some of MIDI's biggest revolutions will take place in software. Large manufacturing resources are not required to create new programs; they're often written by one or two people in their spare time. New and radical ideas can make it out into the world much more easily as software than as hardware. As a result, it's harder to predict what might happen as MIDI software advances, but there are some trends to anticipate.

You can expect MIDI recorders to become easier to use and to increase in power and flexibility. Currently, most recorders are based on a tape recorder metaphor, a metaphor that is inadequate to accommodate many advanced features. New models for MIDI recorder controls should evolve that will make it easier to record, edit, and play back a piece of music.

As musical notation programs become smarter and faster, they will be able to turn live performances directly into musical notation while the music is playing. They should become increasingly adept at making the subjective decisions of musical notation—meters, note lengths, stylistic markings—based on pre-programmed experience. The music they turn out will offer at least one respectable interpretation of many possible interpretations, rather than presenting a literal music transcription that no one wants to read.

For people who have musical ideas but no formal training in notation or performance, programs that help with composition are likely to appear. Those programs will take care of the fundamental building blocks of music, such elements as harmonies or small rhythmic patterns, and will let the composer concentrate on the overall structure of the music. Other programs might start at the other end by algorithmically composing a full piece and then letting the composer alter it to get a desired result.

Music education can make some big advances. CD-I (Compact Disc Interactive) technology is an exciting new aspect of CD ROM (Compact Disc Read Only Memory) technology that makes some of these advances possible. CD-I is a method of storing vast amounts of data on a small compact disc that looks exactly like a standard audio compact disc. A computer connected to a CD-I/CD ROM player can quickly retrieve data anywhere on the disc and show it on the computer monitor as text, sound, or pictures. An intelligent music education program could retrieve music lessons from a disc containing thousands of lessons that teach keyboard skills, sight singing, music theory, or other musical disciplines. The program could test a student's skills on a MIDI controller and then address the student's weaknesses by presenting an appropriate lesson from the disc.

Software built into synthesizers, drum machines, and other MIDI devices should also improve as the microprocessors and displays for those devices improve. More powerful microprocessors and enlarged memory make it possible for synthesizers to create more elaborate patches and to store greater numbers of them. Bigger and more elaborate displays make it increasingly easy to display patch data and make it possible to equip devices with patch-editing software comparable to the patch editors used on computers today.

The MIDI standard itself will evolve to fit changing technology. Because too much change endangers a standard, MIDI won't evolve radically, but it is constantly being refined. At this writing, the MMA is working on new MIDI specifications that allow different models of sampling devices to exchange standard sampled sounds. The MMA is also expanding the MIDI specifications to include new timing messages that count time in hours, minutes, seconds, and frames, much as SMPTE does. As technology increases its demands on MIDI, the standard will evolve to meet those demands.

There will come a time, of course, when MIDI is no longer capable of keeping up with technological and aesthetic demands. Its relatively slow serial data transmission rate, its tendency to become clogged with messages, and some of its built-in aesthetic assumptions will become untenable as new synthesizers with more powerful microprocessors and internal programming have more and more data to send, and as users ask MIDI to step beyond its traditional musical bounds to work with new music, video, and other arts. At that time, a new standard will emerge, perhaps one with parallel data transmission, new data definitions, and other changes difficult now to predict. That new standard will owe its existence to MIDI— the first data transmission standard dedicated to music and musicians, a tool of unprecedented potential for musicians and artists everywhere.

A | APPENDIX: GETTING TECHNICAL

If you intend to get under MIDI's hood and get your hands dirty—to take on projects such as writing your own MIDI computer programs, using system exclusive messages effectively, or understanding exactly what your sequencer is doing—then you need to know how MIDI works at its most fundamental level: how it sends bits and bytes using electric current over a MIDI cable.

In Chapter 5, you read a basic explanation of MIDI messages. It examined their general format and identified the message groups. Within each group, you looked at the particular types of messages you can use and at the information each message conveys. This appendix continues the investigation of MIDI messages begun in Chapter 5. It analyzes the message format for each major message group and then scrutinizes the various kinds of messages within each group to see how information is encoded in specific bytes and bits.

To understand the message descriptions in this appendix, you must be familiar with binary numbers. If you aren't familiar with them, read the first section of this appendix, an introduction to bits, bytes, and the binary number system. If you're curious as to how these bits and bytes make their way over the MIDI cables, you can read the next section, which explains the basics of serial communication. If you're a seasoned computer hacker, you can skip directly to the message descriptions.

**A BINARY
ARITHMETIC
PRIMER**

To understand binary numbers, begin by thinking of the odometer (mileage indicator) in a car. Each digit of the odometer is a wheel that can show 10 different values: 0 through 9. As you drive, the rightmost digit of the odometer rotates through its values, 0 through 9, and when it reaches 9, it turns over to 0 again. When it turns over, it advances the digit immediately to its left by one count. This neighboring digit also moves through the values from 0 through 9, and with each full rotation, it advances the digit to *its* left by one count. The process is repeated up the line to the leftmost digit.

Because each digit of the odometer has 10 different values, it takes 10 full counts of the rightmost digit to advance its neighboring digit one count, 100 counts of the rightmost digit to advance the digit to the left of its neighboring digit, 1000 counts to advance the next digit, 10,000 counts for the digit after that, and so on. This means that each digit in the odometer counts the rotation of the rightmost digit in powers of 10 that increase from right to left. This counting system is called the *decimal* system because it's based on the 10 possible values for each digit. (*Decem* is Latin for "ten," hence the word *decimal*.)

Now imagine the same odometer, but instead of digit values from 0 through 9, each odometer wheel has only two values: 0 and 1. As the rightmost digit makes a full rotation, it advances the digit to its left by one count. When this neighboring digit makes a full cycle, it advances the digit to its left by one count, and so on up the line. Figure A-1 shows eight consecutive counts on this odometer, starting at 0.

*Figure A-1.
A binary odometer
counts from 0
through 7.*

0	0	0	—	0
0	0	1	—	1
0	1	0	—	2
0	1	1	—	3
1	0	0	—	4
1	0	1	—	5
1	1	0	—	6
1	1	1	—	7

Because each digit of the odometer has only two possible values, it takes only two counts for the rightmost digit to advance its neighboring digit by one count, four counts of the rightmost digit to advance the digit to the left of the neighboring digit by one count, eight counts to advance the digit after that, sixteen to advance the digit after that, and so on. In the same way that the 10 values for each digit on the decimal odometer determine that each digit represents a power of 10, the two values for each digit on the binary odometer determine that each digit represents a power of two: 2, 4, 8, 16, 32, 64, 128, 256, and so on. This counting system is called the *binary* system (after *bini,* a Latin word for "two").

Bytes and Bits

A single byte is an 8-digit binary number. Each digit is called a bit, a word that's short for *binary digit.* The bits in a byte are usually numbered from right to left starting with 0, because the rightmost digit represents the smallest power of 2, and the digits increase in value as you move to the left. For this reason, the digit on the far right is called the *least significant bit,* and the digit on the far left is called the *most significant bit.* Figure A-2 shows how the bits in a byte are numbered. In this appendix, a specific bit is identified by its bit number preceded by a D (that stands for digit). The term D5, for example, specifies bit number 5, the sixth bit from the right.

Figure A-2.
The bits in a byte are numbered from right to left.

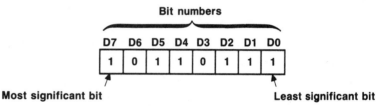

A single byte has eight bits that can represent numbers from 0 to 255. (To verify this, you can sit down with a pencil and paper and try running the imaginary binary odometer through its full range of values, writing down each count on paper. You should get 256 different counts before the odometer turns over and starts repeating again.) By adding an extra bit to the byte (to get nine bits), you double the range of possible values, so that each byte can represent numbers from 0 to 511. Subtracting a bit from the byte (to get seven bits) halves the range of possible values, so that each byte can represent only numbers from 0 to 127. Each bit you add to a binary number doubles its range; each bit you eliminate from a binary number halves its range.

Because each byte is limited to eight bits, a single byte cannot represent any value higher than 255. However, if you combine two bytes, you have a total of 16 bits with which you can represent values from 0 to 65,535. Once you create a binary number with 16 digits, you can break it in half to create two separate bytes. The left byte is called the *most significant byte,* or *MSB* for short; the right byte is called the *least significant byte,* or *LSB* for short. You can send the two bytes over a connecting cable (a MIDI cable, for example) to a receiving device that puts them back together and reads the full 16-bit value you sent.

A SERIAL TRANSMISSION PRIMER

When a MIDI device sends a MIDI message, it breaks each byte in the message into bits. The device then transmits the bits sequentially through the MIDI cable using a fluctuating electric current. When no message is being sent, a small current flows steadily through the cable from one device to the other. When a device sends a 1 bit, it stops the current for a very brief moment. When the device sends a 0 bit, it resumes the current again. This sounds quite simple, but it can get more complicated. If a device sends three 1 bits in a row, won't the receiving device interpret the break in the current as a single 1 bit? No, it won't. The sending and receiving devices both time signals to break them into discrete bits.

Baud Rate

All MIDI devices are set to both send and receive data at a rate of 31,250 baud, which is 31,250 bits per second. The sending device sends each bit as either an on or off current state that lasts $1/31250$ second. The receiving device analyzes the incoming current in $1/31250$-second segments and reads each segment as either a 1 (current off) or a 0 (current on). This timing standard allows devices to send a series of consecutive 1s or 0s without causing confusion or loss of data.

Start and Stop Bits

Setting a common baud rate for MIDI devices solves the problem of separating bits from each other, but if bits come over the MIDI cable in a constant stream, how can the receiving device separate the bytes? How can it tell when a byte begins and when it ends? And if the first bit in a message is a 0 bit (which is no different from the inactive state), how does the receiving device know that the bit was sent? MIDI uses two extra bits for each byte to mark the beginning and end of the byte. The first bit, called the *start bit,* is a 1 bit that comes at the beginning of the byte. The second bit, called the *stop bit,* is a 0 bit that comes at the end of the byte.

To see how start and stop bits work, consider this example. Two MIDI devices are connected to each other and aren't sending any messages. The receiving device looks at its MIDI In port and sees a constant current coming through from the sending device, indicating that there are no bytes being sent. The sending device then sends a byte, beginning with a 1 as a start bit, followed by the eight bits of the byte, and ending with a 0 as the stop bit. The receiving device, constantly on the lookout for changes in the current, detects a sudden break in the current when it receives the start bit. (Remember that the start bit is a 1 bit, which is signaled by a lack of current.) It discards the start bit, and counts the next eight bits, applying its 31,250-baud receiving rate. When it receives the stop bit following those eight bits, it stops receiving the bits of that byte; it then puts together the eight bits as a byte and interprets the byte as part of a MIDI message. It discards the stop bit, which, because it is a 0, has returned the current at the MIDI In port to its normal state of rest. The receiving device then keeps a constant lookout for the next start bit, which signals the beginning of a new byte.

As you can see, MIDI devices send bits back and forth at a high rate of speed and require accurate timing. If the timing is defective (a rare occurrence) or if the current is distorted for a small fraction of a second (slightly less rare, unfortunately), the result can be a change in the value of a bit or series of bits. Reversing a single bit can change the value of an entire byte, which can change the meaning of an entire MIDI message, which can change an entire performance, and so on, in ever-increasing spirals of bad luck. You can see why it's important to take care of your MIDI cables and to be sure that all connections are good.

MIDI MESSAGE FORMATS

Chapter 5 introduced you to the different kinds of MIDI messages, and you saw that these messages could represent values in a range from 0 through 255. If you look at these values as binary numbers, which is the way MIDI devices send and receive them, then the rules and limits that govern their use seem logical rather than merely abitrary.

One thing in particular becomes clear when you look at MIDI values as binary numbers: MIDI doesn't use the bytes in messages as single 8-bit binary numbers that range in value from 0 through 255. Instead, it breaks up each byte into smaller groups of bits, each group standing alone as its own number. For example, a status byte can be divided into three groups of bits, as shown in Figure A-3 on the next page. One group consists of a single bit capable of representing two values, 0 or 1; another group consists of three bits capable of representing values from 0 through 7; and a third group comprises the remaining four bits capable of representing values from 0 through 15. In this case, a single byte actually carries three different numbers, a fact that is not obvious if you look at each byte as a single decimal value from 0 through 255.

Figure A-3.
By dividing its bits into groups, you can use a single byte to represent three distinct numbers.

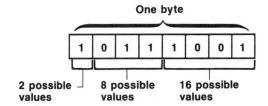

The next two sections show how the two types of MIDI bytes—status bytes and data bytes—are usually segmented to carry different values within a single byte.

Status Bytes

A status byte is always divided into three sections using this format:

1*mmmxxxx*

The most significant bit (D7) always has a value of 1. A MIDI device receiving a 1 as D7 interprets the byte as a status byte and not as a data byte. The second group of bits, D6 to D4 (shown in the format as *mmm*), specifies the kind of message this status byte transmits. Because there are three bits, they can represent eight different kinds of messages.

The third group of bits, D3 to D0 (shown in the format as *xxxx*) can represent different types of information, depending on the kind of message specified by the second group of bits. If the message is a channel message, such as Note On or Note Off, then the four bits convey the MIDI channel number, a value from 0 to 15. (Because MIDI channels are numbered 1 through 16 in everyday practice, a MIDI device usually adds 1 to the binary value when it displays a channel number.) If the message is a system common or system real-time message, the last four bits further define the kind of message it is. (Subsequent sections of this chapter describe system common and system real-time messages more fully.)

Data Bytes

Data bytes have a simpler format than status bytes. They have only two groups of bits:

0*xxxxxxx*

The first bit (D7) always has a value of 0. A MIDI device that receives a 0 as D7 always interprets the byte as a data byte and not as a status byte. The last seven bits (D6 to D0) convey a data value from 0 through 127.

Most MIDI messages convey *low-resolution* data. Each message uses a single data byte to represent a value from 0 through 127. Other types of MIDI messages require a wider range of data values than 0 through 127. To accommodate them, MIDI can combine two data bytes to convey *high-resolution* data. A device receiving two high-resolution data bytes usually interprets the first data byte it receives as the least significant byte and the second data byte as the most significant byte. (You will notice an exception to this rule in the description of the Control Change message later in this appendix.) After discarding the D7 bit from each data byte, the receiving device combines the remaining 14 bits. Altogether, they can represent a value from 0 through 16,383.

INDIVIDUAL MIDI MESSAGE FORMATS

This section provides a complete list of the MIDI messages, each with its component bytes identified in the order they're sent. Each byte is further analyzed to show its format. The format includes the values of any bits that have fixed values in a particular message. Bits that have variable values are represented by lowercase letters. Repeated letters in a message belong to the same group of bits (and do not imply an identical value for each bit). Following each message format is a brief explanation of the bit values.

The messages in this section are described in five groups:

◆ Channel voice messages

◆ Channel mode messages

◆ System common messages

◆ System real-time messages

◆ System exclusive messages

Each group of messages is introduced by an explanation of the format common to the messages in the group.

Channel Voice Messages

A channel voice message uses bits D6 through D4 in its status byte to specify exactly the kind of status message it represents. It uses bits D3 through D0 to specify the channel number it's sent on. Channel voice messages are always followed by either one or two data bytes.

Note On

The Note On message signals the beginning of a note and tells the pitch and attack velocity of the note.

Format: 1001*nnnn* 0*kkkkkkk* 0*vvvvvvv*

nnnn (0–15) specifies the channel on which the message is sent.

kkkkkk (0–127) specifies the pitch in half-steps; the higher the value, the higher the pitch. A value of 60 indicates middle C.

vvvvvv (0–127) specifies the key attack velocity; the higher the value, the higher the velocity. A value of 0 indicates no velocity at all and is equivalent to a Note Off message. For keyboards that are not pressure-sensitive, the default velocity is 64.

Note Off

The Note Off message signals the end of a note and tells the pitch and release velocity of the note.

Format: 1000*nnnn* 0*kkkkkkk* 0*vvvvvvv*

nnnn (0–15) specifies the channel on which the message is sent.

kkkkkk (0–127) specifies the pitch in half-steps; the higher the value, the higher the pitch. A value of 60 indicates middle C.

vvvvvv (0–127) specifies the key release velocity; the higher the value, the higher the velocity.

Polyphonic Key Pressure

The Polyphonic Key Pressure message reports the pressure put on an individual key of a keyboard. It is sometimes referred to as an Aftertouch message.

Format: 1010*nnnn* 0*kkkkkkk* 0*ppppppp*

nnnn (0–15) specifies the channel on which the message is sent.

kkkkkk (0–127) specifies the pitch of the key in half-steps; the higher the value, the higher the pitch. A value of 60 indicates middle C.

ppppppp (0–127) specifies the key pressure; the higher the value, the higher the pressure.

Channel Pressure

The Channel Pressure message reports the pressure put on the entire keyboard. It is sometimes referred to as an Aftertouch message.

Format 1101*nnnn* 0*ppppppp*

nnnn (0–15) specifies the channel on which the message is sent.

ppppppp (0–127) specifies the overall pressure; the higher the value, the higher the pressure.

Program Change

The Program Change message signals a patch change in a synthesizer, a rhythm change in a drum machine, or similar changes in other devices.

Format: 1100*nnnn* 0*ppppppp*

nnnn (0–15) specifies the channel on which the message is sent.

ppppppp (0–127) specifies the number of a new patch or rhythm.

Control Change   The Control Change message conveys the setting of synthesizer controls of various types.

Format: 1011*nnnn* 0*ccccccc* 0*vvvvvvv*

nnnn (0–15) specifies the channel on which the message is sent.

ccccccc (0–127) specifies the number of the controller being moved or a number indicating a particular MIDI device parameter being changed. The MIDI specifications assign different numbers to different controller and parameter types as follows:

0	Undefined
1	Modulation wheel or lever
2	Breath controller
3	Undefined
4	Foot controller
5	*Portamento* time
6	Data entry MSB
7	Main volume
8	Balance
9	Undefined
10	Pan
11	Expression controller
12–15	Undefined
16–19	General-purpose controllers (numbered 1 to 4)
20–31	Undefined
32–63	LSB for values 0 to 31
64	Damper pedal (sustain)
65	*Portamento*
66	*Sostenuto*
67	Soft pedal
68	Undefined
69	Hold 2
70–79	Undefined
80–83	General-purpose controllers (numbered 5 to 8)

(continued)

84–91	Undefined
92	*Tremolo* depth
93	Chorus depth
94	Celeste (detune) depth
95	Phaser depth
96	Data increment
97	Data decrement
98	Non-registered parameter number LSB
99	Non-registered parameter number MSB
100	Registered parameter number LSB
101	Registered parameter number MSB
102–121	Undefined
122	Reserved for channel mode messages. (For more information, read the description of channel mode messages in the next section.)

vvvvvv (0–127) specifies the value of the new control setting. In the case of a continuous controller, the value can range from 0 through 127. If the control is a switch (and has only on and off settings), then the values 0 through 63 represent off, and the values 64 through 127 represent on.

There are some functions in the data value list that need further explanation: Notice that values 32 through 63 carry the LSB for a corresponding value in the range 0 through 31. MIDI uses two Control Change messages together, one from each value range, to convey one high-resolution value. Suppose, for example, that you move the foot controller on a particular device. The first Control Change message the device sends specifies controller number 4 in the first data byte and uses the second data byte to send the most significant byte of the new setting value. In the second Control Change message, the device specifies controller number 36 (the fifth value of the LSB range of controller numbers, just as 4 is the fifth value of the MSB range) and includes the least significant data byte. The receiving MIDI device combines the LSB data byte from the second Control Change message with the MSB data byte from the first message to produce a high-resolution data value in the range from 0 through 16,383.

If a continuous controller needs only low-resolution data, then the sending device sends an MSB Control Change message and doesn't follow it with an LSB Control Change message. The receiving device then interprets the single incoming data byte as one low-resolution value from 0 through 127.

There are eight different controller values in the list that transmit new synthesizer parameters set by data controllers. These values are 6 and 38 (data entry MSB and data entry LSB), 96 and 97 (data increment and data decrement), 98 and 99 (non-registered parameter number LSB and non-registered parameter number MSB), and 100 and 101 (registered parameter number LSB and registered parameter number MSB). To send a new parameter, a device first sends a pair of non-registered or registered parameter number Control Change messages that convey the LSB and the MSB of the parameter number in the second data byte. The receiving device combines the values to create a parameter number from 0 to 16,383. This parameter number corresponds to a synthesizer parameter, such as the setting for part of a patch envelope or a sampling rate. Common parameters are assigned numbers in the MIDI specification; these parameters can be sent using registered parameter number Control Change messages. Synthesizers with parameters not assigned a value by the MIDI specification can send those parameters using non-registered parameter Control Change numbers.

Once a receiving device has received a pair of parameter number Control Change messages that specify a certain parameter, it then waits for a data increment, data decrement, or data entry Control Change message to set a new value for that parameter. If the device receives a data increment (96) or data decrement (97) message, it uses the setting value in that message to increment or decrement the current parameter setting by the specified amount. If the device receives a data entry MSB message (6), it sets the parameter to a new value from 0 to 127 carried by the setting value of the message. If a data entry LSB message (38) follows, it sets the new parameter value to a new value from 0 to 16,383.

Once a parameter number has been set by a pair of parameter number Control Change messages, any subsequent data increment, data decrement, or data entry Control Change messages affect that particular parameter until a new pair of parameter number Control Change messages identifies a new parameter number.

Pitch Bend Change The Pitch Bend Change message reports a change in the setting of the pitch bend wheel.

Format: 1110*nnnn* 0*bbbbbbb* 0*bbbbbbb*

nnnn (0–15) specifies the channel on which the message is sent.

bbbbbbb bbbbbbb (0–16,384) specifies the value of the new pitch bend setting. The two data bytes combine to convey a high-resolution value; the first byte is the LSB, and the second byte is the MSB. A value of 8192 is the center setting and specifies no pitch bend. Values below 8192 specify a drop in pitch, while values above 8192 specify a rise in pitch. The more a value differs from 8192, the greater the pitch bend.

Channel Mode Messages

There are six channel mode messages, all of which use the same status byte as a Control Change message (described earlier). The status byte of a Control Change message is followed by two data bytes. The first data byte defines the type of controller that's being moved. If that data byte specifies one of the six numbers from 122 through 127, the Control Change message becomes a channel mode message.

Because channel mode messages are actually a type of Control Change message, they have the same format as a Control Change message—one status byte followed by two data bytes. Bits D7 through D4 of the status byte specify the binary number 1011, and bits D3 through D0 specify the channel on which the message is being sent. The first data byte specifies the kind of channel mode message (a number from 122 through 127), and the second data byte carries additional information, if necessary.

Local Control

The Local Control message turns the local keyboard control of a synthesizer on and off. When local control is on, the synthesizer responds to notes played on its own keyboard and to controls manipulated on its own control panel.

Format: 1011*nnnn* 01111010 0*ccccccc*

nnnn (0–15) specifies the channel on which the message is sent.

01111010 (equivalent to decimal 122) identifies the message as a Local Control message.

ccccccc (0–127) specifies the status of local control. A value of 0 turns local control off; a value of 127 turns local control on. The intervening values 1 through 126 are ignored.

All Notes Off

The All Notes Off message asks a receiving device to turn off any notes that it's playing.

Format: 1011*nnnn* 01111011 00000000

nnnn (0–15) specifies the channel on which the message is sent.

01111011 (equivalent to decimal 123) identifies the message as an All Notes Off message.

00000000 simply fulfills the requirement that a Control Change message have two data bytes.

Omni Mode Off

The Omni Mode Off message asks a receiving device to turn off Omni receiving mode. With Omni mode turned off, the receiving device receives messages only on the channels to which it is set. The Omni Mode Off message also instructs a receiving device to turn off any notes it's playing.

> Format: 1011*nnnn* 01111100 00000000
>
> *nnnn* (0–15) specifies the channel on which the message is sent.
>
> 01111100 (equivalent to decimal 124) identifies the message as an Omni Mode Off message.
>
> 00000000 simply fulfills the requirement that a Control Change message have two data bytes.

Omni Mode On

The Omni Mode On message asks a receiving device to turn on Omni receiving mode so that the device can receive messages sent on any MIDI channel. In addition, the message asks a receiving device to turn off any notes it is playing.

> Format: 1011*nnnn* 01111101 00000000
>
> *nnnn* (0–15) specifies the channel on which the message is sent.
>
> 01111101 (equivalent to decimal 125) identifies the message as an Omni Mode On message.
>
> 00000000 simply fulfills the requirement that a Control Change message have two data bytes.

Mono Mode On

The Mono Mode On message asks a receiving device to turn on Mono receiving mode (and consequently to turn off Poly receiving mode). With Mono mode turned on, the receiving device monophonically plays notes that it receives on any single MIDI channel. The message also asks a receiving device to turn off any notes it's playing.

> Format: 1011*nnnn* 01111110 0000*mmmm*
>
> *nnnn* (0–15) specifies the channel on which the message is sent.
>
> 01111110 (equivalent to decimal 126) identifies the message as a Mono Mode On message.
>
> *mmmm* (0–15) specifies the number of MIDI channels on which a receiving device can receive messages beginning with the channel to which the device is set. If, for example, the device is set to MIDI channel 3 and the value of *mmmm* is 5, then the device receives messages on channels 3 through 7. If the value of *mmmm* is 0, the device can receive messages on all MIDI channels, from the channel on which it's set through channel 16.

Poly Mode On

The Poly Mode On message asks a receiving device to turn on Poly receiving mode (and consequently to turn off Mono receiving mode). With Poly mode turned on, the device polyphonically plays notes that it receives on any single MIDI channel. The message also asks a receiving device to turn off any notes it's playing.

> Format: 1011*nnnn* 01111111 00000000
>
> *nnnn* (0–15) specifies the channel on which the message is sent.
>
> 01111111 (equivalent to decimal 127) identifies the message as a Mono Mode Off message.
>
> 00000000 (0–127) This byte simply fulfills the requirement that a Control Change message have two data bytes.

System Common Messages

The previous two sections described channel messages, all of which use bits D6 through D4 of the status byte to specify the kind of channel message they represent and bits D3 through D0 to specify the MIDI channel on which they're sent. For all system messages—system common messages as well as the system real-time and system exclusive messages described later—bits D7 through D4 of the status byte are set to 1111. Any device receiving a status byte that starts with 1111 interprets the message as a system message and not a channel message; accordingly, it doesn't expect bits D3 through D0 to specify a MIDI channel. Instead, bits D3 through D0 specify the type of system message being sent.

System common messages have no fixed number of accompanying data bytes; they can have one or two data bytes or none at all.

Song Position Pointer

The Song Position Pointer message specifies a playback starting point within a recorded sequence.

> Format: 11110010 0*ppppppp* 0*ppppppp*
>
> *ppppppp ppppppp* (0–16,384) identifies the starting point for playback by specifying the number of beats from the beginning of a recorded sequence. Each beat is equal to 6 MIDI clocks, the equivalent of a sixteenth note. The two data bytes combine to convey a high-resolution value. The first byte is the LSB; the second is the MSB.

Song Select

The Song Select message selects a song from a bank of songs in a sequencer.

> Format: 11110011 0*sssssss*
>
> *sssssss* (0–127) specifies the number of the song you want to select.

Tune Request   The Tune Request message instructs all receiving devices to tune themselves.

Format: 11110110 (no data bytes)

EOX   The EOX (End of Exclusive) message marks the end of a system exclusive message (described later). Receiving devices that have been ignoring the system exclusive data start paying attention to all bytes again.

Format: 11110110 (no data bytes)

System Real-Time Messages   System real-time messages keep time in a MIDI system. Consequently, it is important that a controlling device be able to send them at any time. To accommodate, MIDI allows system real-time messages to be inserted between the bytes of other messages and limits them to a single status byte with no accompanying data bytes. Bits D7 through D4 are always set to 1111, and bits D3 through D0 specify the particular kind of message.

Timing Clock   A stream of timing clock messages sets the tempo for receiving sequencers.

Format: 11111000 (no data bytes)

Start   The Start message asks all receiving sequencers to start playing at the beginning of the currently loaded sequence.

Format: 11111010 (no data bytes)

Stop   The Stop message asks all receiving sequencers to stop playing the sequence they are currently playing.

Format: 11111100 (no data bytes)

Continue   The Continue message asks all receiving sequencers to start playing the currently loaded sequence at the point at which they last stopped playing.

Format: 11111011 (no data bytes)

Active Sensing   Active Sensing messages inform the receiving device that the MIDI connection is intact. They are sent at least once every 300 milliseconds.

Format: 11111110 (no data bytes)

System Reset   The System Reset message asks all receiving devices to return to their initial settings. These are the settings that apply when power is first turned on.

Format: 11111111 (no data bytes)

System Exclusive Messages

System exclusive messages are in a class by themselves and belong to no other group of messages. Each system exclusive message has a minimum of two accompanying data bytes and can have as many additional data bytes as are necessary. The end of each system exclusive message is marked by an EOX message.

Format: 11110000 0$iiiiiii$ 0$xxxxxxx$ (0$xxxxxxx$ . . .) 11110111

0$iiiiiii$ (0–127) is the identification number that corresponds to the manufacturer of the equipment to which you want to send a system exclusive message. These numbers are determined by the MIDI Manufacturers Association and can be found in the MIDI Detailed Specification. Identification numbers of some of the major manufacturers are:

1	Sequential Circuits	65	Roland
7	Kurzweil	66	Korg
15	Ensoniq	67	Yamaha
16	Oberheim	68	Casio
64	Kawai	69	Akai

0$xxxxxxx$ (0–127) can specify anything the manufacturer wants it to.

11110111 represents the EOX message that signals the conclusion of every system exclusive message.

You have now learned some fundamentals of the binary number system and of serial communication, and you have seen how MIDI works on the level of bits and bytes. If you're serious about programming with MIDI and want more detailed information, order the MIDI Detailed Specification through the International MIDI Association (listed with its address in Appendix C). In the meantime, you can begin to do your own programming using the information provided in this appendix. Once you acquire the MIDI specifications, you'll find that this appendix helps you grasp its more technical terms. Good luck in your programming!

B APPENDIX: COMPANIES MENTIONED

It's often difficult to track down manufacturers of equipment that interests you. This appendix can help you find manufacturers for the equipment mentioned in this book. Some manufacturers of classic equipment have gone out of business, however, and others have been bought by larger companies. Consequently, you won't find a manufacturer for every piece of equipment in the book, but you can find listings for most of the major devices discussed.

Apple Computer, Inc.
20525 Mariani Avenue
Cupertino, CA 95014

Products: Macintosh computer, 512K Macintosh computer, Macintosh Plus computer, Apple II computer, Imagewriter II printer

Atari Corporation
1196 Borregas Avenue
Sunnyvale, CA 94088

Products: 520ST computer, 1040ST computer, 800 computer, SC1224 color monitor, SM124 black-and-white monitor

Austin Development
227 Marin
San Rafael, CA 94901

Product: MIDIface MIDI interface

Blank Software
1034 Natoma Street
San Francisco, CA 94103

Product: *Sound Lab* Mirage patch editor

Casio, Inc.
15 Gardner Road
Fairfield, NJ 07006

Products: CZ-101 synthesizer, CZ-1000 synthesizer, CZ-3000 synthesizer, CZ-5000 synthesizer, TB-1 MIDI Thru Box, AS-20 speaker

Commodore Business Machines
Commodore-Amiga, Inc.
1200 Wilson Drive
West Chester, PA 19380

Products: Amiga computer, Commodore 64 computer

J. L. Cooper Electronics
1931 Pontius Avenue
West Los Angeles, CA 90025

Products: MIDI Sync box, 16/20 MIDI programmable patcher

Dr. T's Music Software, Inc.
220 Boylston Street, Suite 306
Chestnut Hill, MA 02167

Products: *CZ Patch* Casio CZ-101 patch editor/librarian, Model-T MIDI Interface, *Keyboard Controlled Sequencer*

Electronic Arts
1820 Gateway Drive
San Mateo, CA 94404

Product: *Deluxe Music Construction Set* musical notation program

Electronic Courseware Systems, Inc.
1210 Lancaster Drive
Champaign, IL 61821

Products: Various music education programs

E-mu Systems, Inc.
1600 Green Hills Road
Scotts Valley, CA 95066

Product: Emulator II sampling synthesizer

Ensoniq
155 Great Valley Parkway
Malvern, PA 19355

Product: Mirage sampling synthesizer

Fostex Corporation of America
15431 Blackburn Avenue
Norwalk, CA 90650

Products: B16D 16-track tape deck, E2 2-track tape deck, 3010 patch bay, 3070 compressor/limiter, 4050 SMPTE/MIDI synchronizer/autolocator, Fostex 4035 SMPTE controller, Fostex 4030 SMPTE synchronizer

Garfield Electronics
P.O. Box 1941
Burbank, CA 91507

Products: Doctor Click timing device, Masterbeat SMPTE-MIDI synchronizer

Hoshino USA, Inc.
1726 Winchester Road
P.O. Box 886
Bensalem, PA 19020

Product: Ibanez AD-230 analog reverb unit

IBM
1000 NW 51st Street
Boca Raton, FL 33432

Products: Personal Computer (PC), Music Feature expansion card

IVL Technologies, Ltd.
3318 Oak Street
Victoria, B.C.
V8X 1R2
Canada

Product: Pitchrider 4000 pitch tracker

Kawai America Corporation
2055 E. University Drive
Compton, CA 90224

Product: Electronic grand piano

Kurzweil Music Systems, Inc.
411 Waverley Oaks Road
Waltham, MA 02154

Product: 250 sampling synthesizer

Lexicon, Inc.
100 Beaver Street
Waltham, MA 02154

Product: Model 200 digital reverb unit

Mark of the Unicorn, Inc.

222 Third Street
Cambridge, MA 02142

Products: *Performer* MIDI recorder, *Professional Composer* musical notation program

Midisoft Corporation

P.O. Box 1000
Bellevue, WA 98009

Product: *Midisoft Studio* MIDI recorder

Moog Electronics

2500 Walden Avenue
Buffalo, NY 14225

Products: Memory Moog Plus synthesizer, Model 12 synthesizer

E.C.C. Oberheim

11650 West Olympic Boulevard
Los Angeles, CA 90064

Product: Xpander module

Opcode Systems

444 Ramona Street
Palo Alto, CA 94301

Products: *Sequencer 2.5* MIDI recorder, Studio Plus MIDI interface, Yamaha *DX/TX Editor/Librarian*, *Cue* film-scoring program, *Music Mouse*

Passport Designs, Inc.

625 Miramontes Street
Half Moon Bay, CA 94019

Product: *Midisoft Studio* MIDI recorder

RolandCorp US

7200 Dominion Circle
Los Angeles, CA 90040

Products: TR-505 drum machine, PAD-8 Octapad drum controller,
JX-8P synthesizer, MKS-20 digital piano, MKS-80 Super Jupiter
synthesizer, MKB-1000 keyboard controller, Axis MIDI keyboard,
MPG-80 Super Jupiter Programmer, Planet S expansion module,
SBX-80 MIDI/SMPTE synchronizer, MPU-401 MIDI interface

Sequential Circuits

3051 North First Street
San Jose, CA 95134

Products: 6-Trak synthesizer, MIDI interface

Tascam, Professional Audio Division

TEAC Corporation of America
P.O. Box 750
7733 Telegraph Road
Montebello, CA 90640

Products: Ministudio Porta One tape deck

Voyetra Technologies

426 Mt. Pleasant Avenue
Mamaroneck, NY 10543

Product: OP-4001 MIDI interface

Yamaha International Corporation

P. O. Box 6600
Buena Park, CA 90622

Products: DX7 synthesizer, FB-01 expansion module, KX-88 master
keyboard controller, SPX90 digital reverb unit, TX7 expansion module,
KX76 master keyboard controller, CP-20 electric piano, YMC10 MIDI
sync converter, MT1X tape deck, KX10 self-powered speaker

C | APPENDIX: FURTHER INFORMATION

If you're interested in reading more about the topics covered in this book, the following list of books will start you in the right direction. A list of magazines follows the book list; these publications can keep you abreast of the latest developments in the MIDI world. If you want to get technical details straight from the horse's mouth, you can write for membership information to the International MIDI Association (IMA) and the MIDI Manufacturers Association (MMA). Addresses for both groups are provided at the end of this appendix. Membership in the MMA is intended for businesses only, and the organization requires a hefty membership fee to limit participation in that way. Membership in the IMA, however, is open to anyone interested in MIDI.

BOOKS

The Acoustical Foundations of Music, by John Backus. Published by W. W. Norton and Company, 1977. An excellent introduction to the science of acoustics as it applies to music.

The Art of Electronic Music, compiled by Tom Darter, edited by Greg Armbruster. Published by GPI Publications, 1985. A collection of articles and interviews from *Keyboard* magazine that covers the history of electronic music and the people most involved with it.

Electronic Projects for Musicians, rev. ed., by Craig Anderton. Published by Guitar Player Books, 1980. A detailed book teaching the electronics used in audio effects, with a collection of build-it-yourself projects for the reader to try.

Foundations of Computer Music, edited by Curtis Roads and John Strawn. Published by MIT Press, 1985. A collection of 36 articles from scholarly journals that covers major developments in the world of computer music.

MIDI for Musicians, by Craig Anderton. Published by Amsco Publications, 1986. A clearly written guide to MIDI, geared to musicians.

Musical Applications of Microprocessors, by Hal Chamberlin. Published by Hayden Book Company, 1983. A comprehensive book that covers the theory and uses of microprocessors in music. This book is an excellent source for technological explanations and information about digital sound synthesis.

Rock Hardware: The Instruments, Equipment and Technology of Rock, edited by Tony Bacon. Published by Harmony Books, 1981. A comprehensive look at all kinds of rock hardware, with real rock musicians' setups diagrammed and explained.

Studio Recording for Musicians, by Fred Miller. Published by Amsco Publications, 1981. An introduction to the techniques of the recording studio.

MAGAZINES

Computer Music Journal. Published by MIT Press. *Computer Music Journal* is a widely respected scholarly journal. Its articles are not written for novices.

Electronic Musician. Published by Mix Publications. *Electronic Musician* covers the world of MIDI with articles, do-it-yourself projects, and equipment reviews. This is a comfortable magazine for new MIDI users.

Keyboard. Published by GPI Publications. Although *Keyboard* is aimed at keyboard players in particular (including acoustic keyboard players), it has a substantial amount of information about synthesizers, computers, and MIDI that will interest all MIDI users.

MCS: Music, Computers & Software. Published by Music, Computers and Software, Inc. *MCS* is a wide-ranging publication that explores some of the more innovative uses of MIDI and accompanying technology through articles, interviews, and reviews. Until recently, this magazine appeared as *KCS: Keyboards, Computers & Software.*

Music Technology. Published by Music Maker Publications, Inc. *Music Technology* is a general interest periodical aimed at the trade audience.

ASSOCIATIONS

The International MIDI Association
11857 Hartsook Street
North Hollywood, CA 91607
(818) 505-8964

The MIDI Manufacturers Association
c/o J. L. Cooper
1931 Pontius Avenue
West Los Angeles, CA 90025

GLOSSARY

MIDI exposes you to the technical language and the buzzwords from three overlapping fields—those of traditional music, synthesizers, and computers. It's often extremely difficult to understand what a person from another field is saying. This problem is compounded when the same term takes on different meanings in each of the fields. Take the word *program*, for example. To the computer hobbyist, it means a set of instructions used to run a computer; to a synthesizer user, a specific sound design; and to a music lover, a selection of songs or compositions in a performance.

This glossary should help. It defines words used throughout this book. You can use it as a reference if you run across an unfamiliar word while you read or when you talk to other MIDI users. If you want more detailed information than a definition can give you, refer to the index at the back of the book.

accidental. In musical notation, a symbol used to raise or lower a note above or below its written pitch. *See also* flat, sharp, and natural.

acoustic instrument. A musical instrument that vibrates to produce sound directly in the air without electronic means.

ADC. *See* analog-to-digital converter.

ADSR envelope generator. A device with four distinct stages in the envelopes it generates: attack, decay, sustain, and release. It is the most common type of envelope generator.

aftertouch. The amount of pressure applied to a key (or keys) on a music keyboard after the key has been pressed.

algorithm. In FM sound synthesis, one particular combination of a synthesizer's operators used to create a patch.

amplitude. Strength of vibration. Amplitude in sound determines the volume, or loudness, of a sound.

analog synthesis. A method of synthesizing sound using electronic components that directly create and modify an audio signal without converting it to numeric (digital) form.

analog-to-digital converter (ADC). A device in a digital synthesizer or a computer that converts an audio signal into a series of numbers (samples) that are stored in a waveform table.

application software. Computer programs designed to accomplish a specific task for a user.

attack velocity. The downward speed of a key on a music keyboard when the key is first pressed.

audio signal. An electric signal of varying voltage that becomes sound when amplified and fed to a speaker.

autolocator. A SMPTE device that can set connected SMPTE devices to start playback or recording at a synchronized location. *See also* SMPTE.

auxiliary controllers. On a synthesizer, controls used in performance to modify notes played on a keyboard.

band-pass filter. A device that eliminates both high and low frequencies from an audio signal, allowing frequencies that lie in the intermediate range to pass through.

basilar membrane. A sensitive membrane in the inner ear that converts vibrations into messages to the brain.

bass clef. *See* clef.

bass guitar synthesizer. A specialized guitar synthesizer designed to work with a bass guitar controller. *See also* guitar synthesizer.

binary numbering system. A system of counting and calculating based on only two different digit values.

bit. The smallest unit of computer data, used to represent either a 1 or a 0. It is short for binary digit. In the SMPTE timing standard, an eightieth part of a frame.

breath controller. On synthesizers, an auxiliary controller held in the mouth and governed by breath. It typically adds *vibrato* to or changes the volume of the sound produced by the synthesizer.

buffer. For a MIDI recorder, a section of computer memory used to store sections of sequences during cut and paste operations.

byte. A standard unit of computer data consisting of eight bits. A byte can represent a value from 0 through 255.

cathode ray tube (CRT). The large tube inside a television set or inside a standard computer monitor that displays text and graphics. To produce an image, an electron beam traces a pattern on phosphor particles on the face of the tube.

central processing unit (CPU). The part of a computer, usually on a single silicon chip, that performs calculations and controls the rest of the computer.

channel message. A type of MIDI message that is received only by MIDI devices in a MIDI network that are set to the same MIDI channel as the sending device.

channel mode message. In MIDI, a type of channel message that carries data about the MIDI receiving mode.

channel voice message. In MIDI, a type of channel message that carries performance data between devices.

chord. A set of pitches played together at one time. In musical notation, chords are depicted vertically, one note above the other.

chorusing. A type of audio effect that changes an audio signal to make one instrument sound like many.

clef. In musical notation, a symbol, usually at the beginning of a staff, that indicates the pitch range within which the notes on the staff fall. A bass clef indicates a low pitch range; a treble clef indicates a high pitch range.

cochlea. A spiraling cavity in the inner ear. It is filled with a liquid that transmits vibrations to the basilar membrane.

command-line operating system. Computer operating system software that lists programs and data files stored in the computer as text on the monitor. This type of operating system requires that you type commands on the computer's keyboard.

computer. A device that manipulates data according to a series of instructions called a program. Most computers used with MIDI are personal computers, small and relatively inexpensive.

continuous controller. A type of synthesizer controller, such as a slider or a knob, that offers a full range of settings.

control panel. On a synthesizer, a set of controls—buttons, switches, knobs, sliders, and so forth—and a data display that you use to regulate the operation of the synthesizer.

control voltage. In an analog synthesizer, a current used to regulate the operation of other modules such as a voltage-controlled oscillator or a voltage-controlled amplifier.

cps. Cycles per second, a unit used to measure frequency. Cps is often used in place of the unit hertz.

CPU. *See* central processing unit.

crescendo. In music, a gradual increase in volume.

crossover network. In a speaker, a system of filters designed to separate an audio signal into different frequency ranges.

CRT. *See* cathode ray tube.

cue. A section of music in a film or television score.

cursor. A flashing symbol on a computer monitor that shows you where you are typing.

cut and paste. Features in a MIDI recorder or a musical notation program that allow you to mark a section of a sequence or a score and then move it to a new location, duplicate it, or remove it from the sequence entirely.

cutoff frequency. The frequency at which a filter begins to filter out sound from an audio signal.

DAC. *See* digital-to-analog converter.

daisy chain. In MIDI, a method of connecting devices in a chain using MIDI cables, with each device passing MIDI messages along to the device following it.

data byte. A byte that follows the status byte in a MIDI message and that transmits the accompanying information for that message. Some messages have no data bytes; others have one, two, or even more data bytes.

data format. The arrangement of digital information as it is sent between devices, stored in memory, or stored on a recording medium such as a floppy disk.

de-flamming. A MIDI recorder feature that lines up notes in chords so that their attacks are simultaneous.

decibel. A unit of measurement used to measure amplitude. In sound, one decibel is the smallest change in loudness that a human ear can detect.

decimal numbering system. A system of counting and calculating based on ten different digit values.

decrescendo. In music, a gradual decrease in volume. A *decrescendo* is also called a *diminuendo*.

dedicated computer. A computer designed to perform one specific task.

default settings. The settings to which a device is set when the device is first turned on.

delay. A type of audio effect that delays a version of the incoming audio signal to create a synthetic echo or reverberation.

digital. Stored or transmitted as a numerical value.

digital synthesis. A method of synthesizing sound by creating and modifying a series of numbers in a waveform table. The series is later converted into an audio signal.

digital-to-analog converter (DAC). In a digital synthesizer or a computer, a device that converts the values in a waveform table to an audio signal.

diminuendo. In music, a gradual decrease in volume. A *diminuendo* is also called a *decrescendo*.

DIN plug. A standard type of plug used at each end of a MIDI cable.

disk drive. A computer device that magnetically stores information on and retrieves information from a disk.

distortion. A type of audio effect that alters an audio signal to add a heavy-metal sound quality.

dot-matrix printer. A printing peripheral for a computer that produces text and graphics by imprinting small dots of ink on paper.

dotted note. In musical notation, a note with a following dot. The dot indicates that the note should be played half again as long as it would be played without the dot.

downbeat. In a measured rhythm, the beat within a repeated group of beats that regularly stands out from the rest.

drum box. *See* drum machine.

drum machine. A synthesizer that specializes in producing percussion sounds. A drum machine usually includes a built-in sequencer that stores and plays back rhythms using the percussion sounds.

drum pad controller. A set of rubber pads with accompanying electronic components that is designed to work as a MIDI controller, converting drumstick strokes into MIDI messages.

dumb MIDI interface. A MIDI interface that has no microprocessor or internal software.

duration. In describing sound, the length in time of any single attribute of sound or of any combination of sound attributes.

dynamic marking. In musical notation, an expression printed in a score that indicates the volume of the music.

dynamics. A musical term that describes the volume of music.

effect. An audio signal processor that modifies the quality of an audio signal coming from a synthesizer, mixing panel, or other source.

EG. *See* envelope generator.

electronic instrument. A musical instrument that uses an audio signal, amplification, and a speaker to create sound.

enharmonic pitch spellings. Different note names that describe the same pitch. For example, B flat and A sharp describe the same pitch.

envelope. A graph of frequency, amplitude, or timbre of a sound over time.

envelope generator (EG). A module in an analog synthesizer that creates a changing control voltage. The control voltage shapes the frequency, amplitude, or timbre of each note the synthesizer plays.

expansion module. A synthesizer without a keyboard, designed to add voices to a MIDI system without adding a keyboard.

filter. A component of an analog synthesizer or of an audio system that eliminates a range of frequencies from an audio signal.

flanging. A type of audio effect that changes an audio signal to add a metallic quality to the sound.

flat. Lower in pitch than another tone. A flat is also a symbol (♭) in traditional musical notation that is used to lower a note one half-step below its written pitch.

floppy disk. A thin, flexible disk of magnetic recording material in a protective covering used in a computer disk drive to store information.

FM synthesis. A type of digital synthesis that combines the outputs of separate digital oscillators using different combinations called algorithms to create patches.

foot control. On a synthesizer, an adjustable flat pad controlled by foot that adds *vibrato*, changes volume, or adjusts other qualities of a synthesizer's sound.

foot pedal. On a synthesizer, a floor switch that lets you turn a synthesizer feature on and off. It is commonly used to add sustain.

forte (f). In traditional musical notation, a term describing loud music.

fortissimo (ff). In traditional musical notation, a term describing very loud music.

Fourier analysis. A process used to separate and analyze the component frequencies of a sound or of an audio signal.

frequency. The rate of vibration. Frequency in sound determines the pitch of a sound.

fundamental frequency. In a sound or an audio signal, the lowest frequency. The fundamental frequency determines the pitch of a sound or of an audio signal.

glissando. A run of half-step notes between a starting and an ending pitch.

grand staff. A large staff made up of two five-line staves braced together one above the other. The top staff is usually marked with a treble clef, the bottom staff with a bass clef.

guitar controller. A guitar designed to work as a MIDI controller to convert guitar performances into MIDI messages.

guitar synthesizer. A synthesizer designed to work with a guitar controller. It is usually designed so that you can place it on the floor and operate it with foot controls.

half-step. The smallest standard pitch interval in traditional music.

hammer, anvil, and stirrup. Three small bones in the middle ear that transmit vibrations from the outer ear to the inner ear.

hard disk drive. A type of computer disk drive that uses a rigid metal disk instead of a floppy disk to store information.

hard hit. A hit in a film or television cue that falls on a beat of the music. *See also* cue, hit.

hertz. A unit of measurement (abbreviated Hz) used to measure frequency. One hertz is equal to one cycle per second.

high-pass filter. A device that eliminates the low range of frequencies from an audio signal.

hit. In film and television scoring, a moment in a music cue at which the music should emphasize an action on-screen.

icon-based operating system. Computer operating system software that shows programs and data files in the computer as small pictures on the monitor instead of as text. Such a system generally allows you to choose commands and files without typing them on the keyboard.

IMA. An acronym for International MIDI Association, a non-profit organization that distributes information about the MIDI specification.

IMUG. An acronym for International MIDI Users Group, the original name for the International MIDI Association (IMA).

interface. A connection between pieces of hardware. The interface includes both the physical connection and the format requirements for interaction between hardware components.

interval. The difference in pitch between two notes.

jack. A socket into which you can insert an electrical plug to make a connection.

JMSC. An acronym for Japanese MIDI Standard Committee, an organization of music equipment manufacturers and software publishers in Japan that, along with the MIDI Manufacturers Association, helps refine and maintain the MIDI standard.

keyboard. On a synthesizer, a row of black and white keys used to play notes. On a computer, several rows of keys with characters on the key caps, used to type commands and data.

keyboard splits. A music keyboard feature that enables you to play different patches at the same time on different sections of the keyboard.

key signature. In musical notation, a set of accidentals usually placed at the beginning of a staff to indicate the key of the music that follows.

laser printer. A computer printer that uses a laser, a steel drum, and xerographic techniques to print high-quality text and graphics on paper.

LCD. *See* liquid-crystal display.

least significant bit. In a binary number, the bit that is located farthest to the right.

least significant byte (LSB). The byte in a series of combined bytes located farthest to the right.

LED display. *See* light-emitting diode display.

leger line. In musical notation, a small horizontal line above or below a staff. Leger lines are used to show pitches beyond the range of the staff.

LFO. *See* low-frequency oscillator.

light-emitting diode display. A type of display that uses glowing diodes to create text and graphics. The technology involved is commonly employed in synthesizer displays and occasionally in computer monitors.

line-level signal. A low-level audio signal transmitted by most synthesizers, tape decks, and other audio devices.

liquid-crystal display. A type of display that uses polarized liquid crystals to create text and graphics. The technology involved is commonly employed in synthesizer displays and sometimes in computer monitors.

low-frequency oscillator (LFO). In an analog synthesizer, an oscillator that sends a slowly oscillating voltage to control other synthesizer modules.

low-pass filter. A device that eliminates the high range frequencies from an audio signal.

LSB. *See* least significant byte.

master device. In MIDI, a single device that controls several other subordinate, or slave, devices.

master keyboard. A music keyboard without built-in sound generators, designed to control other MIDI devices by means of MIDI messages.

measure. In musical notation, a section of music set apart at each end by vertical bar lines.

memory. In a computer and in a synthesizer, the capacity to store information electronically on silicon chips.

message filter. A MIDI recorder feature that allows you to remove certain types of messages from incoming or outgoing MIDI data.

mezzo forte (mf). In traditional musical notation, a term describing moderately loud music.

mezzo piano (mp). In traditional musical notation, a term describing music of moderately low volume.

microprocessor. A small central processing unit built into a single silicon chip. *See also* central processing unit.

MIDI. An acronym for Musical Instrument Digital Interface. MIDI is a communications standard for exchanging data between musical instruments and associated devices.

MIDI adaptor. A device that adds MIDI ports to a computer.

MIDI cable. A cable with 5-pin plugs on each end used to carry messages between MIDI devices.

MIDI channel. A MIDI message transmission scheme that allows messages to be sent over a MIDI network to individual devices without being received by all the devices on the network.

MIDI clog. A state that exists when a MIDI device or several MIDI devices attempt to send more MIDI messages over MIDI cables than MIDI is capable of carrying.

MIDI device. Any device equipped with MIDI ports and a microprocessor that is able to either send or receive MIDI messages.

MIDI interface. A device that adds MIDI ports to a computer.

MIDI lag. A delay in passing MIDI messages from the MIDI In port of a device to a MIDI Thru port, resulting in inaccurate timing for notes sent through MIDI.

MIDI message. A piece of data sent between MIDI devices that communicates a single musical event, such as the beginning of a note or a bend in the pitch of a note.

MIDI port. A 5-pin socket built into a MIDI device, used to plug in a MIDI cable. There are three kinds of MIDI ports: MIDI In, which receives MIDI data; MIDI Out, which sends MIDI data; and MIDI Thru, which passes a copy of MIDI data received through the MIDI In port.

MIDI recorder. A type of computer software that records incoming MIDI messages, allows you to edit the messages, and plays the messages back using attached MIDI devices.

MIDI/SMPTE synchronizer. A device that can interpret both SMPTE signals and MIDI messages and can use them to synchronize MIDI and SMPTE devices.

MIDI sync. A method of recording MIDI clock messages on tape and playing them back later. MIDI sync is used to synchronize MIDI performances with pre-recorded tape tracks.

MIDI Thru box. A device that passes messages from a single MIDI In port through multiple MIDI Thru ports.

mid-range speaker cone. A speaker cone designed to produce middle-frequency sounds.

MMA. An acronym for the MIDI Manufacturers Association, an organization of music equipment manufacturers and software publishers in the United States that, along with the Japanese MIDI Standard Committee, helps refine and maintain the MIDI standard.

modulation wheel. A wheel controller on a synthesizer that adds *vibrato* or other qualities as it is turned.

monitor. The component of a computer system that displays information for you to read or look at.

monophonic aftertouch. The overall pressure applied to the keys of a music keyboard after they have been pressed.

monophonic synthesizer. A synthesizer that plays only one note at a time. A monophonic synthesizer can play only melodies with no chords.

monotimbral synthesizer. A synthesizer that can play notes using only one patch at a time.

most significant bit. In a binary number, the bit that is located farthest to the left.

most significant byte (MSB). In a series of combined bytes, the byte located farthest to the left.

mouse. A hand-held device rolled on a desktop to control a computer. Movement of the mouse usually results in corresponding movement of a pointer on the computer's monitor.

MSB. *See* most significant byte.

musical notation software. A type of computer program that allows the user to write, edit, and print music in traditional musical notation. Some musical notation software can translate a musical performance directly into notated music.

NAMM. An acronym for National Association of Music Merchants, an organization of music retailers and wholesalers.

natural. A symbol (♮) in traditional musical notation used to cancel the effect of a preceding flat or sharp symbol.

notch filter. A device that eliminates frequencies in a given range between the low and high frequencies of an audio signal.

note head. In traditional musical notation, the round portion of a note.

note off. The instant at which a key on a music keyboard is released.

note on. The instant at which a key on a music keyboard is first pressed.

note stem. In traditional musical notation, the vertical line extending from a note head.

octave. A standard pitch interval that spans thirteen consecutive keys on a music keyboard. The upper pitch in an octave is twice the frequency of the lower pitch.

operating system software. Software that runs the most fundamental functions of a computer. The operating system is essential to make the computer work.

operator. A digital oscillator used in FM sound synthesis. *See also* FM synthesis.

oscillation. A state of vibrating back and forth.

overdrive. A type of audio effect that changes an audio signal to add a heavy-metal sound quality.

overdubbing. A recording technique that allows a single performer to record one track at a time and then play back the tracks simultaneously. The recorded result sounds as if there are numerous performers playing.

overtone. In a sound or an audio signal, a frequency that is higher than the fundamental frequency.

panning. In an audio mixer, the process of moving an incoming audio signal from one side of a stereo output signal to the other side.

parallel data transmission. A method of sending computer data over a cable eight or more bits at a time.

parallel port. A connection socket on a computer, synthesizer, or other digital device. The device can transmit data through the port eight or more bits at a time.

patch. On a synthesizer, a specific sound design created using the synthesizer's controls. A synthesizer plays notes using the sounds that are defined as patches.

patch bank. A set of patches stored in the memory of a synthesizer or of a computer.

patch bay. A collection of audio jacks that allows you to make connections easily between audio devices connected to the bay.

patch buttons. On a synthesizer control panel, a set of buttons that you use to select patches.

patch cable. A cable used to make a connection between two audio jacks. In synthesizers, patch cables connect different synthesizer modules. In a patch bay, patch cables connect audio devices wired into the patch bay.

patch editor. A type of computer software that stores synthesizer patches in computer memory and on disk, allows you to edit those patches on the computer, and transfers patches between the computer and an attached synthesizer.

patch librarian. A type of computer software that stores synthesizer patches in computer memory and on disk and transfers patches between the computer and an attached synthesizer.

perilymph. The liquid that fills the cochlea (in the inner ear).

peripheral. A device connected to a computer using data-carrying cables.

pianissimo (pp). In traditional musical notation, a term describing music of very low volume.

piano (p). In traditional musical notation, a term that describes music of low volume.

pitch bend wheel. A wheel controller on a synthesizer that raises or lowers the pitch of notes as the wheel is turned.

pitch follower. A MIDI device that reads an incoming audio signal, determines the fundamental pitch of the signal, and signals changes in pitch and amplitude by sending appropriate MIDI messages.

polyphonic aftertouch. The pressure applied to each individual key of a music keyboard after the key has been pressed.

polyphonic synthesizer. A synthesizer that can play more than one note at a time. Such a synthesizer, as opposed to a monophonic synthesizer, is capable of playing chords.

polytimbral synthesizer. A synthesizer that can play more than one patch at a time.

portamento. A smooth slide in pitch between a starting note and ending note.

program. A set of instructions to a computer that directs it to accomplish a specific task; on a digital synthesizer, a specific sound design. *See also* patch.

pull-down menu. On a computer, a list of possible commands that you can display at the top of a screen. Commonly, you use the mouse to display pull-down menus.

punch in. A MIDI recorder or tape recorder feature that allows the recorder to switch from playback to record mode at a preset location in a sequence or on a reel of tape.

punch out. A MIDI recorder or tape recorder feature that allows the recorder to switch from recording to playback at a preset spot in a sequence or on a reel of tape.

quantization. A MIDI recorder feature that adjusts irregular note lengths to compensate for sloppily played rhythms.

QWERTY keyboard. A computer keyboard with keys arranged like those of a standard typewriter.

rack-mount equipment. Equipment designed to fit in a standard audio equipment rack.

radio frequency interference (RFI). Any unwanted reception of radio in an audio or video system. These disruptive signals are commonly caused by household appliances and nearby CB radios.

RAM chip. A chip that stores information in a way that allows you to erase or write over the information when you desire to do so. It is short for random access memory chip.

real-time recording. In a MIDI recorder, a recording method that records MIDI messages with the exact timing they have as they come into the computer. *See also* step-time recording.

reception mode. In MIDI, any of four different modes that determine how a device receives MIDI messages and how it, in turn, plays the notes that the messages indicate.

release velocity. The upward speed of a key on a music keyboard when the key is released.

resolution. In sampling synthesis, the quality of the sampled sound as determined by the sampling rate.

rest. In musical notation, a symbol that indicates a period of silence of a given length.

RFI. *See* radio frequency interference.

rhythm track. A sequence of notes stored in a drum machine or in another type of sequencer and used to play back percussion sounds.

ring network. In a MIDI system, a method of connecting the MIDI devices in a loop so that any one device can exchange messages with any other device in the network.

ROM chip. A chip that stores information permanently so that the information can't be erased. It is short for read only memory chip.

running status. A MIDI message transmission scheme that allows a stream of messages of the same type to be sent without repeating the status byte for each message.

sampled sound. A digitally recorded sound.

sampling. The process of turning an audio signal into a digitally stored waveform table.

sampling synthesis. A method of digital sound synthesis that plays back waveform tables created by digitally recording audio signals.

score. A musical composition stored in a sequencer or in a computer. A score is also a printed version of a musical composition, written on paper using traditional musical notation.

SCSI port. An acronym for Small Computer System Interface port, a computer port often used to connect a peripheral such as a hard disk drive to computers.

sequence. A series of notes stored in memory for later playback.

sequencer. A device that stores a series of musical notes that it can send to other musical devices.

serial data transmission. A method of sending computer data through a cable one bit at a time.

serial port. A connection socket on a computer, synthesizer, or other digital device through which the device can send data one bit at a time.

sharp. Higher in pitch than another tone. Also, a symbol (♯) in traditional musical notation used to raise a note one half-step above its written pitch.

shielded, twisted-pair cable. A grounded cable with two internal conducting wires. Cables of this type are commonly used in MIDI cables.

sight reading. Playing or singing a piece of music when you are exposed to the written music for the first time.

slave device. In MIDI, a device that is under the control of a master device.

smart MIDI interface. A MIDI interface that includes its own microprocessor and internal software.

SMPTE. An acronym for Society of Motion Picture and Television Engineers. The term (pronounced simp′ ty) is also used to describe the timing standard that SMPTE adopted to synchronize video playback devices, tape decks, and other equipment used in creating movies or video productions.

SMPTE generator. A device that generates SMPTE timing code.

SMPTE synchronizer. A device that reads SMPTE timing signals coming from several different SMPTE devices and adjusts the playback rate of the devices so they are synchronized with each other.

software. Programs used to run a computer. *See also* program.

song. In MIDI, a fully linked set of note sequences, stored in memory and ready for performance.

sound chip. A chip in a computer that generates an audio signal.

sound generator. The circuitry inside a synthesizer that electronically creates a voice of music in the outgoing audio signal.

speaker cone. A conical piece of stiff paper or plastic mounted within a loudspeaker. A speaker cone vibrates to create sound.

staff. A set of five equally spaced horizontal lines that you use to locate notes in traditional musical notation.

star network. In MIDI, a method of connecting many MIDI devices through one central device.

start bit. In serial data transmission, a bit that signals the beginning of a subsequent byte.

status byte. The first byte of any MIDI message. The status byte identifies the type of MIDI message.

step-time recording. In a MIDI recorder, a method that records MIDI messages without regard to the performance time between the messages that comprise the recording. When you use this method, you assign the time between messages.

stop bit. In serial data transmission, a bit that signals the end of the preceding byte.

sustain. On synthesizers and pianos, an effect that allows notes you are playing to continue to sound even after you release the keys that you pressed to start them.

switch. On synthesizers, a type of controller that offers either an on or an off setting without intermediate settings.

synthesizer. An electronic instrument capable of making music and sounds by creating and modifying its own waveforms and then sending them out as an audio signal to a loudspeaker.

system common message. In MIDI, a type of system message that helps coordinate song selection and tuning among devices.

system exclusive message. In MIDI, a type of system message that enables devices to send specialized data only to other connected devices that can use that data.

system message. In MIDI, a type of message that is received by all MIDI devices in a MIDI network, regardless of the MIDI channel the devices are set to receive.

system real-time message. In MIDI, a type of system message that synchronizes performance timing among devices.

tempo. The performance speed of a musical composition.

tie. In musical notation, an arc drawn between two notes of the same pitch indicating that the two notes are to be played together as one longer note.

timbre. The tone color of a sound. Timbre is determined by the combinations of frequencies within a single sound.

time signature. In musical notation, two numerals on a staff that indicate both the length of the measures that follow and the type of note that is equal to a single beat in those measures.

track. In a MIDI recorder, a separate section of the computer's memory used to store one sequence of notes separate from other sequences. In a tape recorder, a separate lengthwise region of a tape used to record an audio signal and to distinguish it from other recorded signals.

transposition. Raising or lowering a musical composition to a new key.

treble clef. *See* clef.

triplets. A set of three equal notes that are played in the same amount of time that two of those notes would usually require.

tutti. An Italian music term meaning "all together."

tweeter. A speaker cone designed to produce high-frequency sounds.

upwardly compatible. A feature of computers and synthesizers that allows software and patches written for earlier versions of the computer or synthesizer to run on the later versions of the machines.

user interface. The system a computer program provides to communicate with you as a user.

USI. An acronym for Universal Synthesizer Interface, the original name for the interface that evolved to become MIDI.

VCA. *See* voltage-controlled amplifier.

VCO. *See* voltage-controlled oscillator.

velocity-sensitive keyboard. A music keyboard that can sense the speed of its keys when they are pressed or released.

voltage-controlled amplifier (VCA). A component of an analog synthesizer that changes the amplitude of an audio signal in response to the control voltage it receives.

voltage-controlled oscillator (VCO). A component of an analog synthesizer that creates an audio signal using a simple waveform. A control voltage fed into the VCO changes the frequency of the outgoing audio signal.

waveform. For a sound, the graphical display of air pressure over time. For an audio signal, the graphical display of voltage over time.

waveform table. A series of numbers used in digital synthesis to describe a waveform.

whole step. An interval of pitch equal to two half-steps.

woofer. A speaker cone designed to produce low-frequency sounds.

INDEX

MICHAEL BOOM

Michael Boom received his Master of Fine Arts degree from the California Institute of the Arts, where he studied with Martin Subotnick and Mel Powell. A classical oboist by training, Boom became involved with microcomputers in 1980 when he purchased an Atari 800. He is the author of **THE AMIGA**, published in 1986 by Microsoft Press. He has also written for *Compute!* magazine. For the past four years, Boom has worked as a consultant in the microcomputer field, including a year as the music consultant for Commodore-Amiga. Michael Boom currently lives in Oakland, California.

The manuscript for this book was prepared and submitted to Microsoft Press in electronic form. Text files were processed and formatted using Microsoft Word.

Cover design by Becker Design Associates
Interior text design by the staff of Microsoft Press
Musical notation by David Ocker
Airbrush illustrations by Chuck Solway
Technical illustrations by Rick Bourgoin

Principal typographer: Lisa G. Iversen
Principal production artist: Becky Geisler-Johnson

Text composition by Microsoft Press in Times Roman with display in Bauer Bodoni Bold, using the Magna composition system and the Mergenthaler Linotron 202 digital phototypesetter.